Economics of European Crises and Emerging Markets

Peter Havlik • Ichiro Iwasaki
Editors

Economics of European Crises and Emerging Markets

palgrave
macmillan

Editors
Peter Havlik
Vienna Institute for International Economic Studies
Vienna, Austria

Ichiro Iwasaki
Institute of Economic Research
Hitotsubashi University
Tokyo, Japan

ISBN 978-981-10-5232-3   ISBN 978-981-10-5233-0 (eBook)
DOI 10.1007/978-981-10-5233-0

Library of Congress Control Number: 2017945347

Printed on acid-free paper

This Palgrave imprint is published by Springer Nature
The registered company is Springer Nature Singapore Pte Ltd.
The registered company address is: 152 Beach Road, #21-01/04 Gateway East, Singapore 189721, Singapore

The project underlying this book is hosted by the Institute of Economic Research, Hitotsubashi University, Tokyo, Japan, and the Vienna Institute for International Economic Studies (wiiw), Vienna, Austria, with principal sponsorship by the Suntory Foundation, Osaka, Japan.

Acknowledgments

This volume contains the main research outcomes from the international project entitled "Economics of European Crises and Emerging Markets" launched in autumn 2014. The authors are grateful to the Institute of Economic Research of Hitotsubashi University and the Vienna Institute for International Economic Studies (wiiw)—the project's host organizations—for their considerable support.

The authors also appreciate the Suntory Foundation's principal sponsorship, which provided financing for workshops and conference presentations conducted within the project's framework. Additional financial support from the director of the Institute of Economic Research of Hitotsubashi University was useful for carrying out the editorial work and English proofreading of the book. Other financial and organizational support that authors received individually are acknowledged in their chapters.

The editors thank all contributors to this volume for their great efforts and kind collaborations. The editors are also thankful to Veronika Janyrova and Aki Yoshino for their administration of the project and to Tammy Bicket, Akira Ishida, and Mai Shibata for their assistance in preparing the manuscripts. The authors also thank their colleagues and participants in the aforementioned workshops and conferences for their valuable comments and suggestions on the research work published in this book. Those from Vasily Astrov, Mahdi Ghodsi, Doris Hanzl-Weiss, Gabor Hunya, Sandor Richter, and Hermine Vidovic are particularly acknowledged and greatly appreciated. Their involvement in the peer-review process was very effective in improving the research quality and accuracy of the text contained in this book.

Last but not least, the authors would all like to express thanks to Jacob Dreyer and Jazmine Robles of the editorial staff at Palgrave Macmillan for their kind support and careful coordination, along with production staff Sudha Soundarrajan, Vinoth Kuppan, and Rachel Crawford.

Contents

Contributors

Natalia Akindinova is Director at the Development Center of National Research University—Higher School of Economics, Moscow.

Andrey Chernyavskiy is Senior Research Fellow at the Development Center of National Research University—Higher School of Economics, Moscow.

Jan Hagemejer is Assistant Professor at the Faculty of Economic Science of University of Warsaw, Warsaw.

Jan Hanousek is Professor at CERGE-EI, a joint workplace of the Charles University and the Economics Institute of the Czech Academy of Sciences, Prague.

Peter Havlik is Economist at the Vienna Institute for International Economic Studies, Vienna.

Mario Holzner is Deputy Director at the Vienna Institute for International Economic Studies, Vienna.

Ichiro Iwasaki is Professor at the Institute of Economic Research of Hitotsubashi University, Tokyo.

Evžen Kočenda is Professor at the Institute of Economic Studies of Charles University in Prague, Prague.

Nikolay Kondrashov is Research Associate at the Development Center of National Research University—Higher School of Economics, Moscow.

Mathilde Maurel is Researcher at Centre d'économie de la Sorbonne of University of Paris 1 and Fondation pour les Etudes et Recherches sur le Développement International, Paris.

Daniel Münich is Professor at CERGE-EI, a joint workplace of the Charles University and the Economics Institute of the Czech Academy of Sciences, Prague.

Taku Suzuki is Associate Professor at the Faculty of Economics of Teikyo University, Tokyo.

Klára Svitáková is Ph.D. Candidate at CERGE-EI, a joint workplace of the Charles University and the Economics Institute of the Czech Academy of Sciences, Prague.

Andrea Szalavetz is Senior Research Fellow at the Institute of World Economics, Centre for Economic and Regional Studies of the Hungarian Academy of Sciences, Budapest.

Miklós Szanyi is Director at the Institute of World Economics, Centre for Economic and Regional Studies of the Hungarian Academy of Sciences, Budapest.

Joanna Tyrowicz is Assistant Professor at University of Warsaw, Warsaw and Director at FAME|GRAPE, Warsaw.

Andrei Yakovlev is Director at the Institute for Industrial and Market Studies of National Research University—Higher School of Economics, Moscow.

List of Abbreviations

AIG	American International Group
ASI	Agency for Strategic Initiatives
BAL	Baltic states
BIS	Bank for International Settlements
CDE	Constant difference of elasticities
CEE	Central and Eastern Europe
CEO	Chief executive officer
CES	Constant elasticity of substitution
CESEE	Central, Eastern and Southeastern Europe
CGE	Computable general equilibrium
CIS	Commonwealth of Independent States
CSO	Czech Statistical Office
DCFTA	Deep and Comprehensive Free Trade Area
DIPP	Department of Industrial Policy and Promotion
EACES	European Association for Comparative Economic Studies
EAEU	Eurasian Economic Union
EBRD	European Bank for Reconstruction and Development
EC	European Commission
ECB	European Central Bank
ECFIN	Economic and Financial Affairs of the European Commission
EFSF	European Financial Stability Facility
EMU	European Monetary Union
EU	European Union
EUR	Euro
FDI	Foreign direct investment

FIPB	Foreign Investment Promotion Board
FRB	Federal Reserve Bank
FRS	Federal Reserve System
FSU	Former Soviet Union
FX	Foreign currency exchange
G7	Group of seven
GC	Global company
GDP	Gross domestic product
GFC	Global financial crisis
GMM	Generalized method of moments
GNI	Gross national income
GRP	Gross regional products
GTAP	Global Trade Analysis Project
GVC	Global value chain
HHI	Herfindahl-Hirschman index
HQ	Headquarter
HS	Harmonized system
HUF	Hungarian forint
IER	Institute of Economic Research of Hitotsubashi University
IMF	International Monetary Fund
IT	Information technology
LAO	Limited access order
LFS	Labour force survey
MBS	Mortgage-backed securities
MENA	Middle East and North Africa
MNE	Multinational enterprise
NACE	Statistical classification of economic activities in the EU
ND	New Democratic Partly
NEI	National Entrepreneurial Initiative
NFC	Non-financial corporation
NGO	Non-governmental organization
NMS	New Member States (of the EU)
NPL	Non-performing loan
OAO	Open access order
OECD	Organisation for Economic Co-operation and Development
OLS	Ordinary least squares
PASOK	Panhellenic Socialist Movement
PPP	Purchasing power parity
R&D	Research and development

RIA	Regulatory Impact Assessment
RO	Real options
ROSSTAT	Russian Federal State Statistics Service
RTS	Russian Trade System (Moscow exchange)
SEE	Southeastern Europe
SFA	Stochastic frontier analysis
SOE	State owned enterprise
SSC	Shared services center
SWIID	Standard World Income Inequality Database
UNCTAD	United Nations Conference on Trade and Development
US/USA	The United States (of America)
USD	US dollars
USSR	Union of Soviet Socialist Republics
V4	Visegrad four countries
VA	Value added
VAR	Vector autoregressive (model)
WDI	World Development Indicator
wiiw	Vienna Institute for International Economic Studies
WIOD	World Input-Output Database
WTO	World Trade Organization

List of Figures

List of Tables

CHAPTER 1

Introduction: European Crises and Emerging Markets

Peter Havlik and Ichiro Iwasaki

International society today is trapped in the dark shadow of the global credit crunch. The collapse of private credit markets in the United States as manifest in the subprime mortgage crisis and the elevated European sovereign credit risk originating from creative accounting practices by the Greek government generated a profound economic shock throughout the world, which has left open wounds that have yet to heal. Even now, almost a decade after the eruption of the crisis, the possible resurgence of an European sovereign debt crisis cannot be entirely dismissed, which means that various countries and regions in the world could once again be facing serious financial turmoil. The five BRICS countries (Brazil, Russia, India, China, and South Africa) which had long been seen as the world's growth engine until the credit crunch hit, as well as other emerging market economies, could also feel the repercussions from the European sovereign debt crisis.

The contributors to this volume, as well as other researchers in the field, have been paying a great deal of attention to the economic impact of

P. Havlik (✉)
Vienna Institute for International Economic Studies, Vienna, Austria

I. Iwasaki
Institute of Economic Research, Hitotsubashi University, Tokyo, Japan

P. Havlik, I. Iwasaki (eds.), *Economics of European Crises and Emerging Markets*, DOI 10.1007/978-981-10-5233-0_1

the global credit crunch on emerging markets—based on the conviction that this crisis also represents an extremely valuable research opportunity in the field of contemporary economics. This chapter, which serves as an introduction to the topic addressed in this volume, focuses on the theory underlying our research.

First, let us briefly look back on what triggered the global credit crunch in 2008 and the chain of events that followed.

As economic history tells us, depressions and crises are always preceded by a period of prosperity. This is also the case with the global credit crunch discussed here, which, most experts agree, was triggered by the bursting of the information technology (IT) bubble that had driven the economic boom of the late 1990s and preceded the "millennium bug" in the United States.

The technology-heavy NASDAQ Composite Index peaked at 5048 in March 2000 and then started to fall and kept falling until the third quarter of 2002. To address concerns about the possible downturn of the country's economy resulting from this, the Federal Reserve System (FRS), which is the central bank of the United States, launched swift and drastic monetary easing measures. This led to substantially lower interest rates, which, in turn, encouraged a large number of individuals to take out mortgage loans, causing real estate prices to skyrocket.

The booming housing market encouraged financial institutions to extend housing loans not only to prime borrowers with a strong credit history but also to low-income borrowers who were likely to have greater difficulty in paying off a mortgage. This type of lending is called a subprime loan.

The lending frenzy, however, did not last forever. When the housing prices in the United States started to decline in earnest in 2007, countless borrowers who had increasing difficulty in keeping up with their mortgage payments defaulted and faced foreclosures on their loans, and the crisis in the mortgage market suddenly became evident. The financial markets were hard hit by this crisis. Two hedge funds under Bear Sterns, a major US investment bank that managed large amounts of funds by using mortgage-backed securities (MBS) connected with subprime mortgages, failed in June that year. In August 2007, a large French bank BNP Paribas halted withdrawals from its three subsidiary funds because it could no longer fairly value its subprime-related assets. This was referred to as the "Paribas shock". The bubble burst in the US real estate market thus triggered a credit crunch on a worldwide scale.

Financial institutions in the United States and Europe were shaken by the realization that the market value of the MBS they held had been grossly overestimated. In the meantime, the two US government-sponsored housing loan institutions whose share prices plummeted during the subprime crisis were placed under the direct supervision of the government on September 7, 2008. On September 15, Lehman Brothers filed for bankruptcy (under the Federal Rules of Bankruptcy Procedure) after suffering large losses from subprime loans and being unable to find any effective solution to its severe financial difficulties. The next day (September 16), the Federal Reserve Bank (FRB) offered an 85 billion USD emergency loan to stave off the bankruptcy of insurance giant American International Group (AIG).

These events that took place in the United States during a period of less than a month, which are generally referred to as the "Lehman shock", spread the turmoil to financial institutions in Europe as well, causing a number of major banks in the Netherlands, Ireland, the United Kingdom, and France to go bankrupt, to receive an injection of public capital, or to be placed under government control. To make up for the shortfall in savings in the United States, these European financial institutions had raised funds from around the world, mainly from oil-exporting countries, and then invested them in MBS to support the booming housing market in the United States. The destabilization of European financial markets soon affected real economic activity, triggering a global recession. This is how the economic turbulence spread from the United States to the rest of the world.

In October 2009, when the world economy was still trembling in the aftermath of the Lehman shock that started in the United States (dubbed a "once-in-a-century" crisis), the Panhellenic Socialist Movement (PASOK) led by Andreas Papandreou seized political power from the New Democratic (ND) party, accusing the former government of trying to cover up the extent of its massive budget deficit, and revised the estimate of the government budget deficit for 2009 from 3.7% of gross domestic product (GDP) to 12.7% of GDP. An error of nearly 10 percentage points in the national budget projections is unacceptable by any standards regardless of the level of development of a country, and it seriously undermined the credibility of the Greek government. This so-called "European Sovereign Crisis" sparked the second wave of the global credit crunch.

Although the Greek credit crisis and the previous US Lehman shock may seem unrelated at a first glance, they were, in fact, closely related in that the former had been ignited by the latter. The Greek credit crisis was, in fact, triggered by the government bailout of the domestic financial institutions that faced potential failure and severe balance sheet deterioration following the Lehman shock. On top of this, there was also massive spending on public investment projects in an effort to forestall the economic slowdown. Because similar trends were evident in many of the other European Union (EU) nations, this credit crisis that erupted in Greece, a small country in Southeastern Europe, spread throughout EU, particularly to Eurozone nations.

Beginning in November 2009, the yields on Greek government bonds rose sharply due to the plausible rumours circulating that Greece may default on its sovereign debt, which caused a steep drop in government bond prices. Similarly, yields on government bonds spiked in Ireland and Portugal, which were suffering from increasing budget deficits and severe external debt problems that were similar to, or even worse than, those observed in Greece. The crisis spread to Spain and Italy, which were also facing major fiscal difficulties, as well. This chain of events shows that markets were quickly losing faith in the countries affected by the financial crisis. The biggest headache for the EU was the fact that even the European countries with relatively low sovereign risk were vulnerable to the crisis because many of their major financial institutions held large amounts of Greek government bonds for funding purposes. If Greece and other European countries affected by the credit crisis had actually defaulted on their debts, the effects of the crisis could have instantly spread throughout the entire EU. It is therefore not surprising that the euro depreciated sharply against other major currencies during this period.

As the financial crisis became evident not only in Greece but also in Ireland and Portugal, major EU countries, the European Commission (EC) collaborated with the International Monetary Fund (IMF) to introduce various measures to tackle the crisis. These measures include the decision to provide financial assistance to Greece and Portugal in 2010, the establishment of the European Financial Stability Facility (EFSF) to provide up to 440 billion euros in emergency assistance in the form of loans to euro area countries in the event of financial difficulties, and a basic agreement reached on the establishment of the Fiscal Stability Union during the EU summit meeting held in December 2011. Furthermore, a series of non-conventional financial measures implemented by the European Central Bank (ECB) to counter the financial crisis under the supervision of Mario Draghi (who was appointed president of the ECB in November 2011) also proved to be effective to some extent.

Luckily, the serious efforts made by the EU, the IMF, and the ECB to forestall complete economic collapse prevented the financial crisis that hit Greece and several other countries from spreading throughout the whole of Europe. It is probably safe to say that the European economy is currently in a temporary lull. However, many experts agree that until the troubled countries restore financial health and unless the institutional problems underlying the lack of fiscal integration under a unified currency are resolved, we cannot deny the possibility of a recurrence of the European sovereign debt crisis. In other words, international society is still not completely out of the global credit crunch.

So far, we have reflected on how the IT bubble burst in the United States ignited the global credit crunch that still affects us today. The BRICS, the Central and Eastern Europe (CEE), former Soviet Union (FSU) countries, and other emerging market economies had no role to play in creating or resolving this tragedy. All they could do was hide behind the curtain and watch as the tragedy unfolded.

Some actually believed that these emerging market economies would remain immune to the credit crunch that hit the United States and part of Europe. There was once a heated debate over the so-called "decoupling theory", which held that BRICS and other emerging markets were becoming less reliant on the developed economies of the United States and Europe, and that they had the potential to lead the world economy and maintain rapid growth despite economic slowdown in the developed economies. Even when the financial markets in the United States were in the midst of a period of heightened financial turbulence, many people actually believed that BRICS and other emerging economies would act like a breakwater and prevent the economic crisis from spreading throughout the world.

No one knows for sure where this theory originated from and how it spread. We, as well as other researchers who specialize in the economies of Russia and other CEE and FSU countries, were extremely doubtful about the validity of this theory, at least where the emerging markets in the CEE and FSU regions were concerned, because of the high reliance of these countries on external financing from United States and West European economies, their immature economic systems, and the limited feasibility of the domestic, demand-based, growth model due to the rapid progression of a birth rate decline and ageing population.

The reality, in fact, turned out to be far from what the optimists who advocated the decoupling theory had expected. When the first wave of the global credit crunch reached its peak in 2008, the G7 economies were immediately caught in a sharp economic downturn, with simple average growth rates across G7 economies dropping to −0.3%. The growth rates of emerging economies, which continued to accelerate until 2007, also began to drop. By 2009, all major economies, except India, were facing further economic slowdown. In particular, economic growth in Russia and other CEE and FSU countries dropped to −7.8% and −3.8%, respectively, which were comparable to or much worse than the average growth rate of −4.2% recorded across the G7 countries. South Africa and Brazil also experienced a negative growth. Although all of these countries and regions returned to positive growth after 2010, the impact of the second wave of the global credit crunch has slowed down the pace of economic recovery, and it is obvious that the world economy has lost the momentum it had during the period preceding the financial crisis that erupted in 2007.

Thus, the emerging economies are extremely vulnerable to economic fluctuations in the United States and Europe, often even more so than other developing nations. The two economic shocks that hit the United States and Europe had a far greater impact on the emerging markets than the advocators of the decoupling theory had anticipated.

Empirical analysis carried out in the field of economics is usually aimed at verifying a theoretical hypothesis on the cause and effect relationship between economic phenomena by analysing real-life data by a using statistical/econometric approach. Incidentally, the problem of endogeneity or simultaneity has often given many researchers a "headache". This problem arises when an explanatory variable is statistically significantly correlated with the error term in an econometric model. To put it in simpler terms, it refers to a situation where, while there are two economic phenomena of interest, it is not clear which one is the cause and which one is the effect. A researcher is faced with the problem of endogeneity or simultaneity when he wants to verify how phenomenon A causes phenomenon B, but instead finds that phenomenon B could be influencing phenomenon A, or that these two phenomena are simultaneously causing each other.

A typical example of this would be the relationship between economic development and educational standard. One can say, for example, that people in rich countries spend a large part of their income on education, which, in turn, improves the standards of education in that country. If that is the case, you can assume that economic development is the determinant of educational standard. One can also infer, however, that the better educated people are, the more likely they are to contribute to economic development by applying the knowledge and skills they have learned. In this case, educational standard can be regarded as the determinant of economic development. In this way, a real-world setting is linked with economic phenomena in which the direction of causation is not entirely clear. We, as economists, use various analytical approaches to avert endogeneity (simultaneity) problems. The easiest solution would be to pick a case where it is reasonable to assume, from both a theoretical and an empirical perspective, that phenomenon A causes phenomenon B (in other words, a case where phenomenon A is obviously exogenous to phenomenon B).

Let us now look at the relationship between the global credit crunch and emerging economies. As described above, there are two root causes to this global credit crunch: unwise investments in MBS by financial institutions in the United States and loose financial regulation in some European nations. Although we cannot say for sure that emerging economies played no part in creating this crisis, it is highly unlikely that they had anything to do with it. Even as the financial crises that erupted in the United States and Europe evolved into a global credit crunch, emerging markets could do almost nothing but watch. In a sense, the unprecedented macroeconomic shock that spread from the United States and Europe to all over the world could be considered an incident that was purely exogenous to the emerging economies.

More importantly, as described above, this global credit crunch is a rare historical event that sent a severe shock through emerging economies. The opportunity to gain highly valuable academic insights from such a rare economic phenomenon is more than any economist could hope for. Although the global credit crunch is a regrettable event that caused so much suffering to so many people, we must embrace the opportunity to scrutinize this defining moment in the history of world economy to learn from it and discover many valuable facts that are of great significance to contemporary economics and the international community. And that is exactly why we have launched the international research project that is summarized in this volume.

There are several academic literature sources that address a topic similar to the one discussed here, including those published by Batten and Szilagyi (2011), Claessens et al. (2014), Wise et al. (2015), Brada and Wachtel (2016), and Ulgen (2016). Our research, which explored the economic impact of the global credit crunch on emerging markets in the CEE and FSU regions, provides valuable findings (summarized below) that are unique in that they shed new light upon many of the aspects which previous studies have failed to adequately address. Furthermore, the present study distinguishes itself from other published studies in that it also explores how the Russian economy was affected by the economic sanctions imposed by the United States, the EU, and other developed nations as a protest against the Russian annexation of Crimea and the incursion into Eastern Ukraine in 2014.

The structure of this book and an overview of each chapter are provided below. This volume consists of five parts and 13 chapters. Part I deals with a large-scale study that encompasses a wide range of emerging economies in the CEE and FSU regions, unfolding the entire picture of the macroeconomic shock of the global credit crunch that hit CEE and FSU countries. Part II to Part V present the findings of the country studies targeting the major countries in the CEE and FSU region, including the Czech Republic, Hungary, Poland, and the Russian Federation.

The topics covered in each chapter can be summarized as follows:[1]

The introductory Chap. 2, by Peter Havlik, analyses the impacts of the 2008–2009 global crisis on emerging economies in Central, Eastern and Southeastern Europe (CESEE: Bulgaria, the Czech Republic, Hungary, Estonia, Latvia, Lithuania, Poland, Romania, Slovakia, and Slovenia) at both the macroeconomic and sectoral levels. The author focuses on growth and economic convergence patterns in the region, briefly discusses the structural effects of the crisis, and dwells on future growth and convergence prospects in view of existing economic policies. Relying on extensive comparative studies and empirical analysis conducted regularly at the Vienna Institute for International Economic Studies (wiiw), the author underlines the diverging growth experiences and responses to the crisis of individual CESEE economies. Finally, the chapter attempts to outline some key features of the post-crisis "new growth model", which could be more sustainable and more resilient to external shocks. The author points out that the effects of the crisis have been economic, social, and political; and external (both economic and political) factors have been playing a crucial role in responses to the crisis in the CESEE region, owing to its high degree of integration with Western Europe. The latest economic developments in the CESEE region are, on the whole, encouraging. Driven by robust domestic demand, in particular by household consumption and investments, GDP growth in 2016 averaged 3% in the CEE region, and the outlook is fairly positive—despite increased geopolitical uncertainties and tensions. Accordingly, the CESEE pace of economic convergence will be maintained, albeit at a speed somewhat reduced from that prior to the crisis.

In Chap. 3, Mario Holzner describes the evolution of financialization in CESEE countries, the effects of the deleveraging period after the outbreak of the global financial crisis, the interaction of financial market conditions with income distribution, the savings propensity, and the current account and economic development of CESEE before and after the outbreak of the global financial crisis. Financialization was particularly strong in the three small Baltic states, followed by the countries from CEE and, following at a certain distance, by the economies of Southeastern Europe (SEE) and the Commonwealth of Independent States (CIS). An important distinction can be made with regard to the structure of inward foreign direct investment (FDI) stocks in the region. CEE economies and, to a certain extent and with a lag, also SEE economies were able to attract highly productive and export-oriented manufacturing FDI, while in the Baltics and in the CIS, import activities were supported by a much stronger focus on domestically oriented finance and retail trade services FDI. A major problem characterizing the deleveraging process after the outbreak of the global financial crisis has been the reversal of behaviour by the main economic agents in CESEE. In particular, the peripheral economies with large income inequality have experienced foreign-financed booms with households, corporations, and the government being net borrowers in the aggregate. However, after the outbreak of the global financial crisis, the corporate sector became a net lender. Investments have been postponed and, hence, domestic demand dampened. As a consequence, earlier unsustainably high current account deficits often turned into surpluses. CEE economies that, during transition, received a larger chunk of export-oriented manufacturing FDI, have lower levels of income inequality, and experienced less dissaving in the boom phase were partly able to avoid more extreme real adjustments due to their stronger export bases and more stable current account positions.

In Chap. 4, Taku Suzuki examines the impact of crises on FDI inflow into Eastern European countries. Despite several suggestive preceding studies, some tasks for further study remain in this study subject; i.e., an examination of the differences in the size and timing of the impact by areas or countries, distinctions of each economic shock, and efforts to measure the magnitude of crises themselves. Accordingly, his aim in Chap. 4 is to identify the pattern of the size and timing of the impact of crises by areas or countries corresponding to the task of distinctions and precise measurement of shocks. To this end, he employs interactive terms to take into account differences by areas in the patterns of the size and timing of the impact of crises and also the "shock variables" calculated by the fall in stock prices to measure the magnitude of the crises themselves. Before empirical testing, he constructs two hypotheses in accordance with the outlook of the changes in the per capita FDI inflow to specify the interactive terms and to deepen the analysis in accordance with the aim of this study. The first hypothesis is that shocks have a greater impact in countries that are more embedded in the EU than in those that are less embedded, and the second is that FDI inflow may be reduced more by lagged than by contemporaneous shock impacts. Thereafter, Suzuki conducts empirical tests employing a panel data model, a multilevel model, and a dynamic panel model based on EU and non-EU member Eastern European countries data. As a result of empirical analysis using variables and methods discussed in Chap. 4, the author confirms that global economic shocks in recent years tend to affect FDI inflow with time lag and are larger in "embedded" countries (i.e., EU members) than in others. In other words, the more deeply embedded in the global economy a country is, the greater the lagged shock from the global economy becomes in these areas. In addition, in the same way as in previous studies, he suggests that business environment, economic openness, and standard of living are important factors for attracting FDI.

The Czech Republic represents a small open market economy with large stakes in international trade in the middle of the EU. It employs an extra-large share of a relatively well-educated workforce in manufacturing industries equipped—with some exceptions—with average or outdated technologies. In Chap. 5, Daniel Münich and Klára Svitáková provide detailed analysis of longer-term trends in employment in the Czech economy from the pre-crisis period of the late economic transition, through the years of the world economic crisis, until 2015, when signs of economic recovery became evident. In particular, they investigate trends in total hours worked along with their structure and components. While overall employment has been relatively stable in the long term, more detailed insights reveal notable changes experienced by particular demographic groups. Irrespective of the crisis, many steady changes regarding the extensive margin (work participation) were experienced by the youngest (15–24) and the oldest (55–64) population groups. Having opposite signs but being of similar size, these two effects more or less compensated for each other. While developments on the lower side of the age distribution were driven by the steadily increasing average duration of initial schooling, developments on the upper side were driven by steadily improving health conditions of the older population, growing work opportunities due to a changing occupational mix, and rising statutory retirement ages. On top of changes in the mean hours of work per person due to the changing demographic structure of the population, there were also negative shifts on the extensive margin (work participation) as well as positive shifts on the intensive margin (hours worked by those who work). Although the latter component of change was smaller, it helped accommodate the adverse impact of the economic crisis that showed itself first in late 2008 and unfolded fully during 2009. The impact of the crisis seemed to be bigger due to the overheated economy and the Czech labour market, which was on the verge of the world economic crisis. The adverse impact had been partly accommodated by retirements and the extended duration of initial schooling of young generations. The most adversely affected, with the consequence of unemployment, were men's occupations requiring middle- and low-level skills in manufacturing and construction. The crisis had a lasting impact by lowering the average hours of those who work and reshuffling employment between some occupations.

In Chap. 6, Jan Hanousek and Evžen Kočenda analyse how the efficiency of firms in the Czech Republic is affected by their size, age, competition, capital structure, ownership type, and the recent global financial crisis. The authors employ a stochastic frontier approach, using a large and detailed dataset, and cover the time span 2001–2012. They show that, in general, larger firms are not associated with better efficiency. The effect of their age has only a negligible impact. The impact of capital structure is shown to be strong in large and more leveraged firms. Higher competition is not contributive to efficiency, either on the individual or the aggregate level. While the effects of firm characteristics are small, the effects of ownership are economically substantial. The authors also show that majority owners contribute most to a firm's efficiency when compared with the other categories they analyse. Minority owners with legally grounded power are able to impose significant efficiency improvements. The effect of foreign ownership is strongest when foreign owners control firms with less than a majority of voting power. Minority owners sharing control do not seem to contribute to efficiency. The impact of the crisis is not balanced but can be regarded as mildly positive in general. Firms' characteristics change only a little. In contrast, a worsening impact of the crisis is evidenced for controlling ownership categories. Finally, minority owners exhibit a limited disciplining effect to improve efficiency after the crisis.

Chapter 7 by Miklós Szanyi elaborates on the increasing economic intervention of the state in the post-crisis CEE region. Designs of the transition process relied heavily on neoliberal concepts to produce an efficient institutional framework for multinational business—the "competition state". The 2008/2009 economic crisis undermined trust in the general applicability of these concepts to economic policy. Local elites started querying the usefulness of some policies, and they also found support in the practice of crisis management in many developed market economies. Some governments began openly criticizing valid EU regulations, making massive efforts to distort the effects of policies from the rules of the competition state and favour local entrepreneurs. Preference for local firms over international competitors is not a new idea, and many developed market economies also apply such policies within the framework of the competition state. In the literature, this is called economic patriotism. However, these covert protectionist policies do not deny the beneficial effects of competition; rather, they aim to strengthen local firms to create more competition in the future. Moreover, they are neutral and based on territorial principles. What we see in CEE is the application of selective advantage and disadvantage measures, the main aim of which is to provide a competition-free environment for the businesses of political clients. This is made possible whenever polity has a strong position and does not much need the support of business (it is strong enough to capture sufficient moral and material support on its own). Another condition is a relatively weak business interest representation that makes selective bargaining possible. The Polish and Hungarian governments introduced a large number of selective advantage and disadvantage measures to reinforce business capture. This cannot be regarded as economic patriotism but rather as a shift from a competition state to patronage.

In Chap. 8, Andrea Szalavetz applies real options (RO) logic to the analysis of global companies' crisis-driven organizational reconfiguration actions. Options that companies evaluated and selected from, or applied in combination, were (1) commitment (increase of investments); (2) withdrawal; or (3) deferral. Szalavetz relies on interviews with manufacturing subsidiaries in Hungary to analyse the micromechanisms of global companies' RO implementation—as perceived by the subsidiaries. Her specific research questions concern: (1) the factors that determined the timing of global companies' investments and divestments; (2) the role of organizational experimentation in preserving flexibility; and (3) the impact of organizational restructuring and resource reallocation on the Hungarian subsidiaries. It often proved difficult to establish an unambiguous direct association between the crisis and global companies' organizational restructuring actions. Global companies considered flexibility of utmost importance when deciding on organizational reconfiguration. Flexibility was ensured mainly through deliberate organizational experimentation; consequently, parent companies' decisions often proved reversible. Szalavetz argues that, on balance, the surveyed Hungarian subsidiaries have benefited from their owners' cost-cutting and restructuring actions. The most frequent outcome of RO implementation was increased local commitment from global companies. Commitment increase was manifested in: (1) capacity expansion and product upgrading at subsidiaries; (2) tangible and intangible investments in process upgrading and efficiency increase; and/or (3) subsidiaries' functional upgrading driven by headquarters' delegation of additional tasks and responsibilities. Contrasting the empirical evidence with the findings of the received literature, she finds that evidence supports the importance of (1) host country attributes (wage level), (2) the structure of owners' existing portfolios of subsidiaries, and (3) interdependencies among activities for subsidiary survival. As for the role of path dependence in influencing subsidiary fate, the findings are ambiguous. Prior commitment was often regarded as an important explanatory factor of subsequent investments during and after the crisis. However, global companies' quests for flexibility and their systematic organizational experimentation have sometimes gone against path dependence. Some of subsidiaries' previously gained mandates were lost because of their owners' new strategic directions.

Recent military conflict in the Ukraine, directly and indirectly, is detrimental to Poland's trade flow with both countries, its major extra-EU trade partners. The effects of the conflict are difficult to track, as the period under consideration is also a period of falling prices of resources, including coal, gas, and oil, a major source of Russian GDP, which has an obvious negative effect on Russia's imports from the EU. In Chap. 9, Jan Hagemejer employs a GTAP (Global Trade Analysis Project) computable equilibrium model with the accompanying GTAP database to model the trade collapse by increasing the non-tariff barrier to a prohibitive level on non-oil imports. Given the fact that some computable general equilibrium (CGE)-based analyses of the effects of the crisis on Russian-EU economic relations are available, the author takes the opportunity to provide some more stylized results. He does not intend to perform a detailed analysis of the effects of the Russian trade ban and the EU embargo. Rather he is interested in the types of trade-related mechanisms that take place in the event of a sudden, substantial, trade collapse. He analyses two contrasting simulation scenarios, one in which one trading partner introduces a ban on a selected sector—in this case the food sector—and the other in which he compares the reactions of the Polish economy and others with a much more profound trade ban where countries cease trade on a much larger scale, encompassing all non-resource sectors. He shows that even in that drastic simulation scenario, the effects on EU economies, and Poland in particular, are very small compared to those in Russia where the trade collapse triggers a substantial drop of GDP and welfare. The contrasting results for Poland and Russia partially stem from very different trade and production structures within the EU: both Polish exports and imports are very diversified, while the trade pattern of Russia shows a clear specialization in resource-related exports.

The emergence of global value chains leads to fragmentation of the production processes and reallocation of those processes across countries. With an increasing number of production stages, the manufacturing process is located increasingly further away from the consumer. The literature suggests that the fragmentation of production increases the international transmission of shocks. The global financial crisis is believed to lead to the consolidation and shortening of global value chains and the amplification of demand shocks along the global value chains, the so-called bullwhip effect. In periods of economic crises, typically associated with structural reallocation, impulses from global trading patterns combined with local adverse shocks to productivity and demand may asymmetrically affect industries, depending on their positions in global value chains. The bullwhip effect is also believed to be more pronounced in global value chains that are not integrated with foreign ownership. In Chap. 10, Jan Hagemejer and Joanna Tyrowicz study the effects of the recent global financial crisis on employment, focusing specifically on the role of distance from the final demand (upstreamness) in this adjustment. The authors find that upstreamness matters for both labour demand and adjustment in employment during a period of crisis; however, this relationship is heterogeneous across countries. While the reaction to a crisis is indeed amplified further away from the final demand, contrary to our expectations, it is manifested more through lower job creation rates than by faster job destruction. Moreover, the authors also point out that the adverse effects of a crisis are lower in foreign firms; this difference does not depend on the distance from the final demand.

In Chap. 11, Natalia Akindinova, Andrey Cherniavskiy, Nikolay Kondrashov, and Andrei Yakovlev will argue how Russia has politically reacted to the crisis. As compared to other CEE transition economies, Russia experienced an extremely steep decline of its GDP (about 8% in 2009) during the global financial crisis but managed to maintain and even increase living standards. However, unlike CEE countries, in 2013, Russia already faced a new economic slowdown and entered recession in 2014–2016 after the acceleration of geopolitical tensions with the West within the context of the Ukrainian crisis. In this chapter the authors show the reasons for the economic slowdown in 2013, including key features of the Russian model of economic development in the 2000s, its crash during the 2008–2009 global financial crisis, and the failed attempts to change the model in 2009–2011. Their analysis is based on the limited access order (LAO) framework formulated by North et al. (2009, 2013). They attempt to explain the instability of Russian economic growth as the unpreparedness of dominant groups within the ruling elite to restrain their own ambitions and take into account the interests of other players. They also analyse the role of key elite groups (the oligarchs, federal bureaucracy, and *siloviki*) during every stage of development as well as the role of new elite groups that have also evolved within that system, including the regional bureaucracy, successful medium-sized businesses, and public sector elites. In their opinion, incentives for political survival had clearly started predominating economic efficiency arguments in policy-making in 2012 as a response to the Arab Spring and the mass protests in Moscow in December 2011. This shift in the national leadership's priorities, as well as the lack of a vision for the future, had an extremely negative influence on the incentives and behaviour of economic agents (including capital flight and declining investment). Taking into account these political constraints, the authors argue the key drivers and main risks of economic development in Russia. Finally, they discuss conditions for transition to a new model of economic development.

Lastly, in Chap. 12, Ichiro Iwasaki and Mathilde Maurel investigate the relationship between the European crisis and firm entry and turnover in Russia. In this country, after the 2008 global financial shock, there was a sharp downward shift in the firm creation rate measured by the number of newly established firms per 1000 organizations and a continuous fall in the firm regeneration rate defined as the excess of newly established firms over liquidated firms per 1000 organizations. Paying special attention to the heavy dependence of the Russian economy on the oil sector, they argue that the shock of the external crisis may strongly affect the decision-making of Russian entrepreneurs who are considering starting up new businesses, and the survivability of existing firms during great depreciation in the world oil price and the sharp increase in its volatility. To empirically examine the possible impact of the crisis on firm creation and regeneration in Russia, Iwasaki and Maurel employ regional-level panel data for the period from 2008 to 2015 and estimate a regression equation that takes the annual average and the coefficient of variation of world oil price as independent variables while controlling for other potentially explanatory factors of firm entry and turnover. They also utilize the exchange rate of the Russian ruble to the US dollar as the independent variable in addition to the world oil price as an alternative proxy for the crisis shock. Based on the empirical results, the authors report that the decline of the price of oil and the appreciation of the exchange rate during the crisis period have strongly hampered the creation and regeneration of Russian firms. They also maintain that the violent fluctuations in crude oil prices and the exchange rate have increased uncertainty in business startups and operations and, accordingly, have greatly depressed the number of Russian entrepreneurs thinking of establishing new businesses and forced a lot of companies to dissolve. Their empirical findings are robust, even if possible endogeneity between the crisis variables and dependent variables and heterogeneity among Russian regions are taken into consideration.

This chapter and the next 11 are followed by a conclusion reached by the authors (see Chap. 13) and a brief discussion of future research directions.

It is our sincere hope that this book will help readers gain a greater understanding of the global credit crunch and how it has affected emerging economies in Europe.

Notes

1. Chapter outlines have been prepared by their individual authors.

References

Batten, J. A., & Szilagyi, P. G. (Eds.). (2011). *The impact of the global financial crisis on emerging financial markets.* Bingley: Emerald.

Brada, J. C., & Wachtel, P. (Eds.). (2016). *Global banking crises and emerging markets.* New York: Palgrave Macmillan.

Claessens, S., Kose, M. A., Laeven, L., & Valencia, F. (Eds.). (2014). *Financial crises: Causes, consequences, and policy responses.* Washington, DC: IMF.

North, D., Wallis, J., & Weingast, B. (2009). *Violence and social orders: A conceptual framework for interpreting recorded human history.* New York: Cambridge University Press.

North, D., Wallis, J. J., Webb, S., & Weingast, B. R. (Eds.). (2013). *In the shadow of violence: The problem of development in limited access societies.* New York: Cambridge University Press.

Ulgen, F. (Ed.). (2016). *Financial development, economic crises and emerging market economies.* Abington/New York: Routledge.

Wise, C., Armijo, L. E., & Katada, S. N. (Eds.). (2015). *Unexpected outcomes: How emerging markets survived the global financial crisis.* New York: Brookings Institute Press.

PART I

International Comparison

CHAPTER 2

Macroeconomic Impacts of the Crisis on European Emerging Markets

Peter Havlik

2.1 Introduction

This chapter analyses the impacts of the 2008–2009 global crisis on emerging economies in Central, Eastern and Southeastern Europe (CESEE: Bulgaria, the Czech Republic, Hungary, Estonia, Latvia, Lithuania, Poland, Romania, Slovakia, and Slovenia) at both the macroeconomic and sectoral levels. It focuses on growth and economic convergence patterns in the region, discusses briefly some broader structural effects of the crisis, and dwells on future growth and convergence prospects in view of existing economic policies. Relying on extensive comparative studies and empirical analysis conducted regularly at the Vienna Institute for International Economic Studies (wiiw), the author underlines the diverging growth experiences and responses to the crisis by individual CESEE economies. Finally, the chapter attempts to outline some key features of the post-crisis "new growth model" which could be more sustainable and more resilient to external shocks.

Several additional remarks seem appropriate at the outset: the chapter focuses on the most recent crisis—sometimes dubbed the global or financial crisis of 2008–2009 (although many parts of the world, in particular China,

P. Havlik (✉)
Vienna Institute for International Economic Studies, Vienna, Austria

P. Havlik, I. Iwasaki (eds.), *Economics of European Crises and Emerging Markets*, DOI 10.1007/978-981-10-5233-0_2

were not affected by this crisis). CESEE emerging markets were severely hit, yet this particular crisis was already the third to hit the region during the previous 25 years. As compared to the transitional recession of the early 1990s, which hit the whole CESEE region, and the financial crisis in 1998, which mainly affected Russia, the crisis of 2008–2009 was more serious, with tremors from the crisis still being felt. At that time, only Poland and Albania in Europe were spared by the recession. In addition, there was also a "double-dip" recession in 2011–2012 in Western Europe that also affected CESEE. The recently established Eurasian Economic Union (EAEU, comprised of Belarus, Kazakhstan, Russia, Armenia, and Kyrgyzstan) and Ukraine were hit by the new crisis in 2014–2016, largely due to the collapse of oil prices at the beginning of 2014 and repercussions from geopolitical conflicts.

It is also important to note that the crisis has had economic, social, and political impacts (this chapter focuses mainly on the economic aspects, but it will mention the others briefly).[1] In addition, external (again both economic and political) factors are still playing a crucial role in the response to the crisis in the CESEE region, due to its high degree of integration with Western Europe. Among the main factors affecting CESEE post-crisis economic developments are the growth slowdown (stagnation) in the Eurozone—the main export market for the region—which hampers export-led growth; the East-West geopolitical conflict with Russia and Ukraine; economic sanctions and their spillovers via export losses; and rising overall uncertainty, which impairs investment. In addition, the Brexit vote in the UK referendum in June 2016 and the 2015 migration crisis (among others) currently pose serious threats to the sustainability of the whole EU and its institutions with serious repercussions on the CESEE.

Finally, there is a new competing amalgamation East of the EU (EAEU: Eurasian Economic Union), and the EU's Eastern Neighbourhood has been contested. Georgia, Moldova, and Ukraine signed Association Agreements (AA) with the EU in 2014 (including the Deep and Comprehensive Free Trade Area—DCFTA); this has fuelled geopolitical conflict with Russia (Havlik 2014b; Adarov and Havlik 2016). Partly as a consequence of this conflict, not only have the three AA/DCFTA countries been torn apart politically to struggle with "frozen conflicts", but also the Russian-dominated EAEU and many CESEE are divided and politically unstable. Finally, China is entering the European stage as well, via its Silk Road and 16+1 initiatives, while Russia has been trying to change its pivot from the EU to the East.

These global developments and the related turmoil affect the European emerging markets (CESEE, but also the Western Balkans, EAEU and DCFTA countries). Needless to say, the ongoing instability in the Middle East and North Africa (MENA), the migration flows and uncertainties related to Brexit, and the new US presidency add to the existing geopolitical and economic risks.[2]

2.2 CESEE Growth Performance After the Crisis

The slowdown in global economic growth has been the main characteristic of the crisis. Figure 2.1 provides a growth overview of the major economies in Europe. Steep growth before the 2008–2009 crisis was followed by a deep recession in 2009 (strongest in Russia), whereas the recovery afterwards has been rather weak in Western Europe (EU-15), the CESEE (EU new member states: NMS and Southeastern Europe: SEE), and Turkey. A double-dip recession that hit Western Europe in 2013–2014 resulted in another growth deceleration in CESEE. Post-crisis growth everywhere

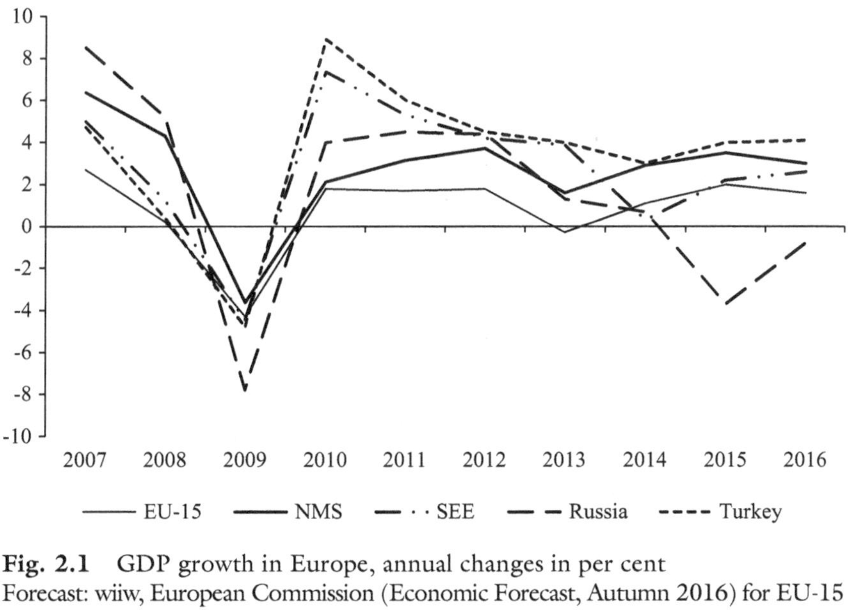

Fig. 2.1 GDP growth in Europe, annual changes in per cent
Forecast: wiiw, European Commission (Economic Forecast, Autumn 2016) for EU-15
Source: wiiw (Astrov et al. 2016), Eurostat

has generally been slower than before the crisis, and there are questions as to whether this growth slowdown now represents a new normal or whether it has just been temporary. We shall return to this issue later.

Russia slipped into a new recession in 2014–2016 (it had already been stuck in transition before—see EBRD 2013; Havlik 2015), mainly due to the oil price collapse of early 2014, the subsequent ruble devaluation, and geopolitical conflict with the West. Western European (EU-15) growth performance has been lackluster since the crisis, as there has been no real recovery after 2009. Low GDP growth, persistent high unemployment (especially of youth cohorts), a fragile banking sector that has not been sufficiently cleansed in the EU, and the European Central Bank (ECB) policy of quantitative easing so far have not been very successful in either stimulating investment or lifting inflation closer to the ECB target (close yet below 2%). The emerging consensus is that a lasting fiscal austerity represents the Achilles' heel of sluggish growth (OECD 2016). However, proposals by the European Commission to ease restrictive fiscal policies and boost economic recovery have not been accepted by the Eurogroup finance ministers, with Germany being the main advocate of lasting austerity.[3]

Currently (as of early 2017), and even for the medium-term (during 2017–2019), the wiiw economic analyses and forecasts from November 2016 (Astrov et al. 2016) and March 2017 (Holzner et al. 2017) anticipate economic growth will stabilize at an average of approximately 3% per year in CESEE NMS (this is about 1 percentage point (pp) more than in the EU-15), again with a large dispersion of growth performance across the region: Hungary, Poland, Romania, and Slovakia are performing better than the rest. At the same time, Russia, Belarus, Kazakhstan, and Ukraine will either stagnate or further disappoint with meagre growth (Belarus also will stay in recession in 2017). Diverging growth performance and current prospects of individual CESEE countries are discussed in more detail below.

Let us now turn to the growth performance of CESEE. A growth slowdown in Europe, particularly in CESEE, has been a general phenomenon observed after the 2008 global crisis. The previous rate of economic convergence of CESEE to the EU-15—about 2 pp per year observed during the early 2000s—was reduced by about half, to some 1+ pp in the post-crisis period. The average CESEE speed of convergence may have accelerated recently, closer to the pattern observed before the crisis (Dobrinsky and Havlik 2014; Holzner et al. 2017).

Different convergence paths of individual CESEE economies remain one of the key features of both early transition and post-crisis developments (Fig. 2.2). Several observations are worth mentioning in this context: most CESEE experienced an accelerated catch-up since 2000 (note that their economic growth had already been faster prior to their EU accession in 2004, respectively in 2007). This catching-up process followed a stagnation (in some cases crisis) in the second half of the 1990s (dubbed a secondary transition recession owing to banking and balance of payments crises), for example, in the Czech Republic, Romania, and Bulgaria. Subsequently, after 2005, there has been a rapid catching-up, especially in the Baltic States, but also in Poland and Slovakia in the immediate pre- and post-accession periods. A deep recession followed in 2009, and the catching-up process was

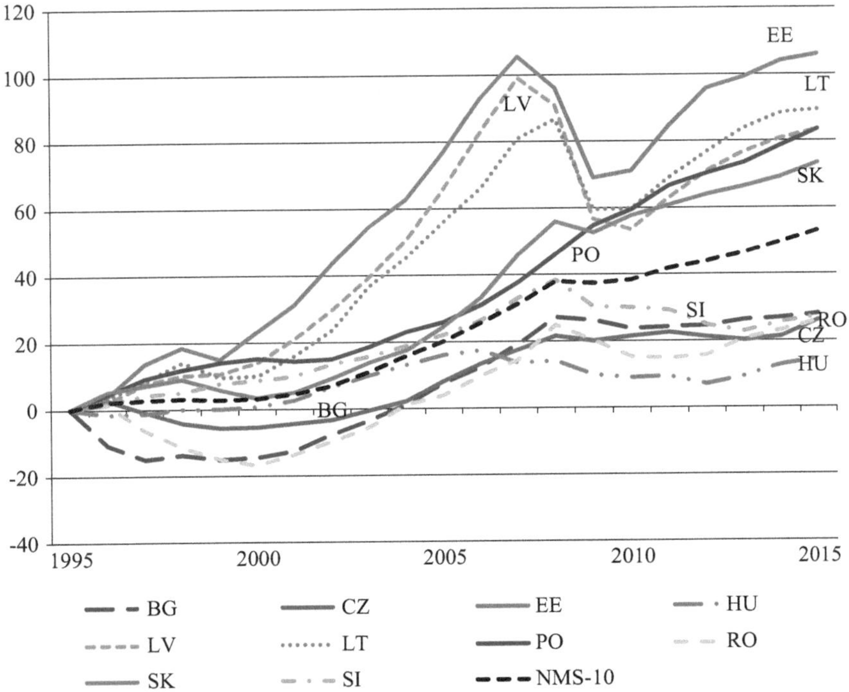

Fig. 2.2 GDP growth convergence, index 1995=100, differences from EU average in percentage points
Source: The author's calculations based on the wiiw database

interrupted, since the CESEE were hit hard by the crisis (especially in the Baltics), but not in Poland—the latter being the only country in Europe (bar Albania) that was able to avoid a recession in 2009, thanks largely to its flexible exchange rate and sizeable fiscal stimulus. Finally, a rather disappointing growth performance over the whole period in Hungary—the country which initially was the champion with respect to reforms and transition progress among the CESEE—is striking: in Hungary, hardly any catching-up (or just 10 pp) over two decades occurred between 1995 and 2015.

Nevertheless, the overall CESEE catching-up/convergence progress has been quite impressive: on average, the region gained more than 50 pp in terms of GDP growth on the EU average over the period 1995–2015. The diversity of growth performance within the CESEE region is remarkable and persistent: it ranges from about a 10 pp reduction of the GDP growth gap in Hungary to more than 100 pp in Estonia (here, the development gap was reduced by half—see below). The average CESEE speed of convergence may recently have returned closer to the pattern observed before the crisis (Dobrinsky and Havlik 2014) and as estimated earlier for a larger sample of countries (Barro and Sala-i-Martin 1995). Diverging growth performance is related to several factors, such as countries' starting development levels and past legacies, economic policies they pursued during transition, their integration in European and global markets, and their political stability.

Another perspective of convergence patterns provides the estimates of real per capita GDPs (at current purchasing power parities—PPPs) in relation to the EU average. Figure 2.3 illustrates the closing of the development gap over the longer period since 1991 and after the 2008–2009 crisis, in particular. In the immediate crisis period, development levels (measured by real per capita GDP) fell sharply in Croatia, Estonia, Latvia, Lithuania, and Slovenia. Yet Poland (and partly also Romania) managed to narrow the development gap even during that period. However, in the post-crisis period, the previously mentioned slowdown in convergence generally was visible again. Importantly, Slovenia lost its position as the most advanced CESEE (in terms of real per capita GDP) to the Czech Republic between 2008 and 2010; Slovakia had already surpassed Hungary in per capita development before the crisis. Thus, a substantial diversity in CESEE convergence patterns is visible again.

The above comparison has one important caveat that is frequently ignored: in per capita terms, convergence patterns are affected by demography. This is highly relevant for CESEE, since the majority of countries have been suffering from a substantial long-term population decline, due to the combination of low birth rates (a phenomenon common in most

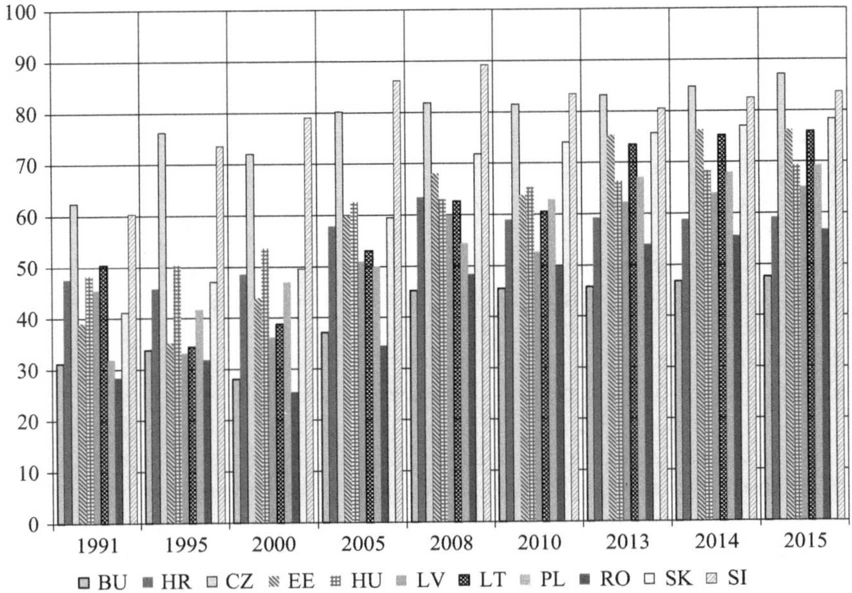

Fig. 2.3 Long-term income convergence in the CESEE: real per capita GDP levels, EU-28 average = 100, at current PPPs
Source: wiiw estimates based on Eurostat

of Europe) and, especially, substantial outward migration. Migration has been particularly pronounced in the Baltic States, Romania, and Bulgaria—especially after their EU accession. These countries have lost more than 10% of their population during the past decade or so; their process of economic convergence in GDP per capita terms would have been much slower without these demographic developments.[4]

2.3 Diverse Drivers of Growth in CESEE

We first investigate the key growth drivers in the post-crisis period, and then turn to a discussion of issues related to structural changes in the aftermath of the crisis and growth sustainability. The various factors that could possibly explain both the depth of the crisis and the speed of the subsequent recovery (such as the shares of industry and exports in GDP, various characteristics of the banking system, FDI penetration, and institutional factors)—all of which have been explored in the literature—were not very conclusive, due to statistical and other measurement problems (see, for example, World Bank 2012).

The exchange rate policy, movements of the exchange rate, and the exchange rate regime seem to have played more prominent explanatory roles in both the depth of the CESEE slump and its post-crisis recovery. Figure 2.4 indicates that transition countries with flexible exchange rate regimes (indicated by black bars) tended to master the crisis better than those with a more rigid exchange rate regime, be it countries with a peg or currency board or those, such as Slovenia and Slovakia, that were already using the euro at that time (indicated by white striped bars). As a corollary, exports played a major role in CESEE countries' recovery from the crisis; in that sense, they did indeed prevail over austerity. Indeed, in countries such as Hungary, Poland, and Romania, exports to the Eurozone were stimulated by exchange rate depreciation (see Box 1 by R. Stöllinger in Havlik et al. 2011). In addition, the depth of the recession also played a role in the scale of the growth reversal between 2009 and 2010. A recent analysis of factors underlying the weak economic growth in Europe is provided by Rzońca and Łaszek (2016). In contrast to a majority of other sources, the authors argue that the main causes of sluggish post-crisis growth in the EU (particularly in contrast to the United States) are supply-side factors. In contrast, a recent IMF paper found

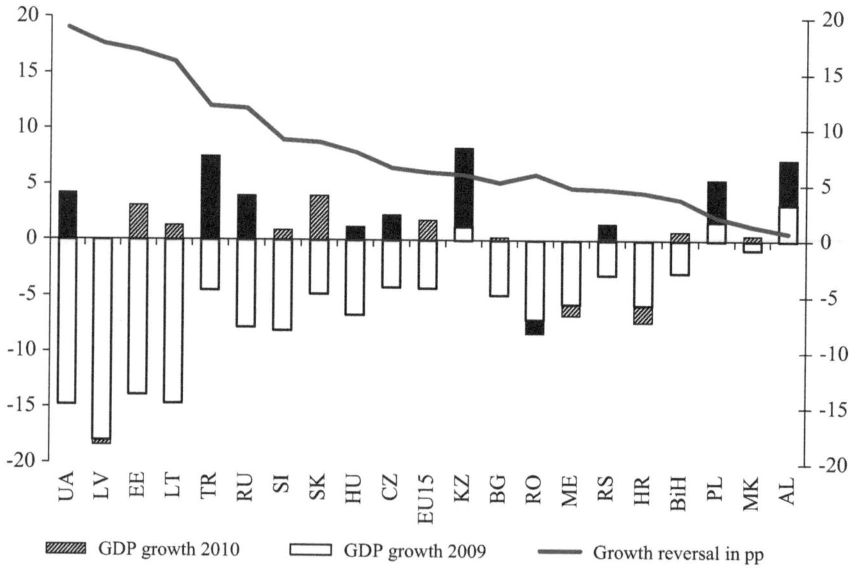

Fig. 2.4 Post-crisis growth reversal 2009–2010: up to +20 pp: effects of fixed (*white striped bars*) and flexible (*black bars*) exchange rate regimes
Source: Adapted from Havlik et al. (2011)

that "the slowdown in potential growth has been associated with common external factors" such as lower potential growth of trading partners and the evolution of global supply chains (Podpiera et al. 2017). For some countries, negative demographic developments have played a role as well.

Export-led growth has been an important characteristic of post-crisis developments in the majority of CESEE countries that are members of the EU. In contrast, the Western Balkan countries, as well as the "old" EU members in Southeast Europe (Greece, Portugal, and Spain), have been less open to exports, especially to the export of goods. The lack of export—for which there are many structural and institutional reasons, such as lower FDI inflows to the manufacturing industry, labour market deficiencies, and a poor investment climate—represents a serious bottleneck to sustainable growth. Bruegel and wiiw (2010) analysed this phenomenon in more detail in the immediate aftermath of the crisis. More recently, Landesmann and Hanzl-Weiss (2016) investigated factors behind correcting structural external imbalances and identified, apart from the role played by the tradeable sector, the role of exchange rate developments, foreign direct investments, and industrial policy instruments. They concluded that the problem of structural external imbalances has not been resolved and that the heterogeneity among various groups of countries is large. Whereas the majority of CESEE economies have been recording trade and current account surpluses, or at least recently improving their external balances, other countries in the Southern EU periphery still face serious structural imbalances and associated export weaknesses. These were manifested in run-away deficits in Western Balkan countries in the pre-crisis period with large trade imbalances and sizeable capital inflows, the latter frequently of a short-term, volatile, and speculative character. On average, current account deficits in the Western Balkans still amounted to 6–7% of GDP in 2015–2016 (compared to a roughly balanced position in the CESEE EU member states—see Astrov et al. 2016).

The Central European manufacturing core, established around Germany and including Austria, the Czech Republic, Hungary, Poland, Slovakia, and Slovenia, has been specializing in competitive export-oriented automotive, electrical, and chemical industries. This cluster of industries has been highly successful, thanks to FDI-led modernization and restructuring. It has been characterized by high productivity (especially of medium-skilled workers) and exploits outsourcing opportunities related to existing labour cost advantages in the CESEE (Stöllinger et al. 2013). The question is whether other countries in the region, especially the Western Balkan countries or Moldova and Ukraine, can follow this example and, if so, whether they should implement economic (industrial, structural) policies in order to foster a reorientation toward manufacturing (e.g., via targeted FDI policies supporting specific sectors).

2.4 The Crisis and Structural Change

Even before the crisis, essentially since the beginning of transition, CESEE countries have experienced a process of economic restructuring away from industry and agriculture and toward services (Havlik 2014a; Landesmann and Leitner 2015). In the more advanced CESEE economies, however, the restructuring pattern has been partly reversed, and manufacturing industry shares of both GDP and employment have recently (between 2010 and 2015) stabilized or even increased (e.g., in the Czech Republic and Slovakia, manufacturing employment shares reached about 25% in 2015—an unprecedented high level in the European context—see Figs. 2.5 and 2.6).

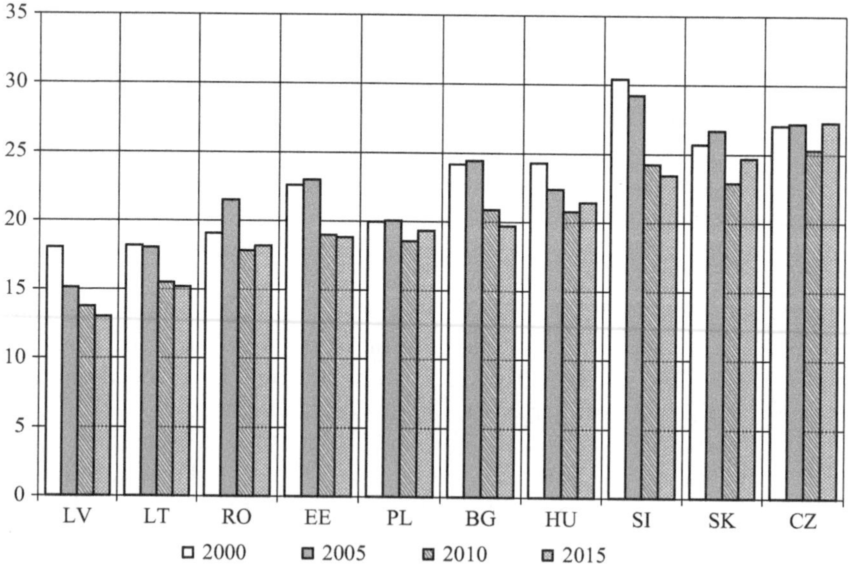

Fig. 2.5 Manufacturing employment (LFS) in CESEE as a percentage of total employment
Note: Sorted by the relative size of manufacturing in 2015
Source: The author's own calculations based on the wiiw database and Eurostat

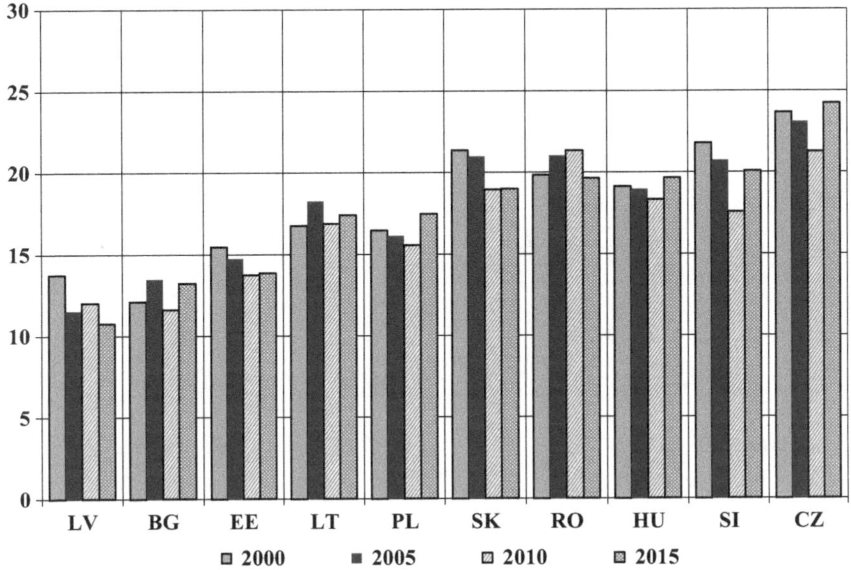

Fig. 2.6 Manufacturing value added as a percentage of GDP
Note: Sorted by the relative size of manufacturing in 2015
Source: The author's own calculations based on the wiiw database and Eurostat

This tendency toward reindustrialization has been associated with the CEE-German manufacturing cluster mentioned above. A closer look at more detailed patterns of structural change during and after the crisis reveals a rather differentiated picture.

Figures 2.7 and 2.8 illustrate the diverse responses to the crisis using the examples of four CESEE countries that all belong to the CEE manufacturing core: the Czech Republic, Hungary, Poland, and Slovakia. Panel A shows structural changes in GDP in the period from 2008 to 2011. During that period, the shares of manufacturing value added in GDP dropped in the Czech Republic and Slovakia, whereas the same shares increased in Hungary and stayed constant in Poland. The crisis hit construction hard in Hungary and Slovakia, yet not in Poland (the latter suffered a financial services bust—in contrast to the Czech Republic, Hungary, and Slovakia). In terms of employment (Panel B), manufacturing suffered everywhere, yet the reactions in other sectors were much more diverse.[5] Looking at relative changes in shares of manufacturing value added and employment, we can see some evidence that labour productivity in manufacturing (C) increased during the crisis: in

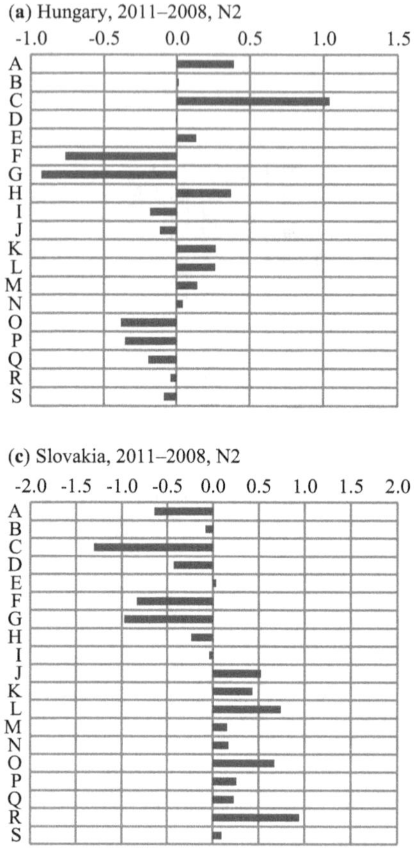

Fig. 2.7 Structural change during the crisis—sectoral VA shares in GDP (in pp). (**a**) Hungary, 2011–2008, N2. (**b**) Poland, 2011–2008, N2. (**c**) Slovakia, 2011–2008, N2. (**d**) Czech Republic, 2011–2008, N2
Source: wiiw calculations based on Eurostat

both Hungary and Poland, the shares of value added increased, while those of employment dropped between 2008 and 2011; in the Czech Republic and Slovakia, manufacturing employment shares dropped more than those of value added. As far as other economic sectors (and other CESEE countries) are concerned, the patterns of structural change during the crisis were much less clear, and the impact on productivity diverged significantly. As a rule, in the aftermath of the crisis, service employment increased (including financial services K), whereas employment in agriculture, manufacturing, and construction decreased.

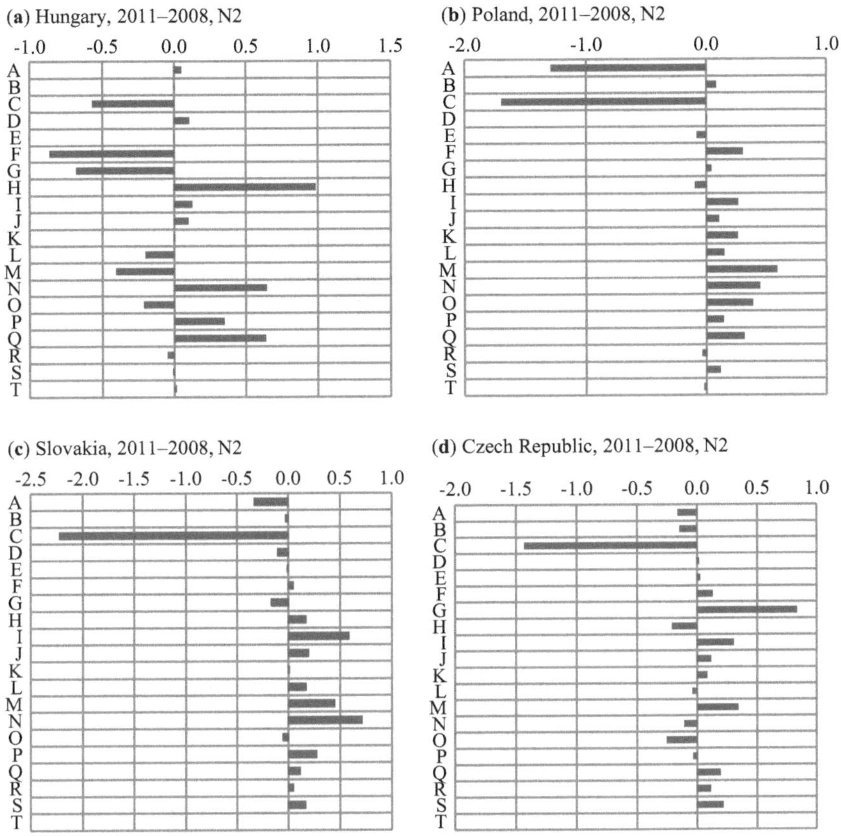

Fig. 2.8 Structural change during the crisis—sectoral shares in employment (in pp). (**a**) Hungary, 2011–2008, N2. (**b**) Poland, 2011–2008, N2. (**c**) Slovakia, 2011–2008, N2. (**d**) Czech Republic, 2011–2008, N2
Source: wiiw calculations based on Eurostat

2.5 Post-crisis Convergence Slowdown: A New or an Adjusted Growth Model?

Section 2.2 above illustrated longer-term convergence patterns and the post-crisis convergence slowdown. In the meantime, the growth slowdown has been empirically established as fact by the IMF, EBRD, World Bank, and others; it has already lasted for nearly a decade.[6] With respect to CESEE, it has also been acknowledged that the previous convergence model—based on belief in the power of institutional convergence within the Washington Consensus or EU *acquis communautaire*, free capital flows and the democracy agenda—had failed or was at least insufficient, as clearly evidenced by the crisis and post-crisis developments (Bruegel and wiiw 2010; Dobrinsky and Havlik 2014; EBRD 2013; Podkaminer 2013, etc.). Importantly, implications from the failure of the previous model extend beyond a purely economic agenda in terms of output losses, rising unemployment, and income inequality. These have also led to rising populism, a backlash in political stability, and eroding reform support coupled with declining support for the European integration project, which have brought to the fore weaknesses of EU-level governance structures that have been aggravated by the migration crisis and rising protectionist tendencies. All these disturbing tendencies have become evident in the post-crisis period everywhere, not just in the CESEE region.

The elements of the new growth model or post-transition agenda (a more detailed description of individual features is beyond the scope of the present chapter) may include the following general policy areas:[7]

- More emphasis on the development of export-oriented sectors;
- Targeted FDI policies, focusing on the tradeable sector;
- Employing elements of industrial policy;
- Focusing on skills developments, especially in younger-aged cohorts;
- Preventing the emergence of excessive income and social disparities.

Obviously, due to the high diversity of individual CESEE countries, it is extremely difficult to devise a one-size-fits-all policy for the region. For example, it is questionable whether the above-mentioned successful German-CEE supply chain cluster in automotive, electrical, and chemical industries can be copied elsewhere in Southeast Europe, due to geographic, cultural, demographic, and other reasons. The evidence is again mixed: Romania—a transition latecomer that has been characterized for many years by stop-and-go economic policies—may have recently embarked on an FDI- and export-driven reindustrialization path that resembles the earlier experience of Hungary and Slovakia (even Moldova shows some early signs of becoming integrated in global value chains—see Adarov and Havlik 2016).[8] However, elsewhere in Southeast Europe, particularly in Bosnia and Herzegovina, Serbia, Albania, and Kosovo, as well as in Ukraine, the challenges are much bigger—despite recent signs of economic stabilization or even recovery.

Turning now to the more recent period and growth prospects, wiiw analyses and forecasts from November 2016 and March 2017 suggest that household consumption has been the main driver of growth in CESEE. The average GDP growth was close to 4% in 2015 in the CEE manufacturing core (Czech Republic, Hungary, Poland, and Slovakia); the Baltic States and Slovenia lagged slightly behind. The analysis identifies a virtuous circle of rising wages and consumption, accompanied by declining unemployment, triggered by emerging labour shortages. An additional recent growth driver has been investment, partly that financed by transfers from the EU, which has been particularly important for Hungary, Poland, Romania, and Slovakia, where it accounted for up to 3% of GDP in 2012–2014 (latest available Eurostat data).

The above-mentioned phenomenon of wage cum consumption-driven GDP growth is new for the CESEE (it was analysed in more detail by Astrov et al. 2016). In this respect, and apart from the generally higher GDP growth, CESEE also differs from Belarus, Kazakhstan, and Russia

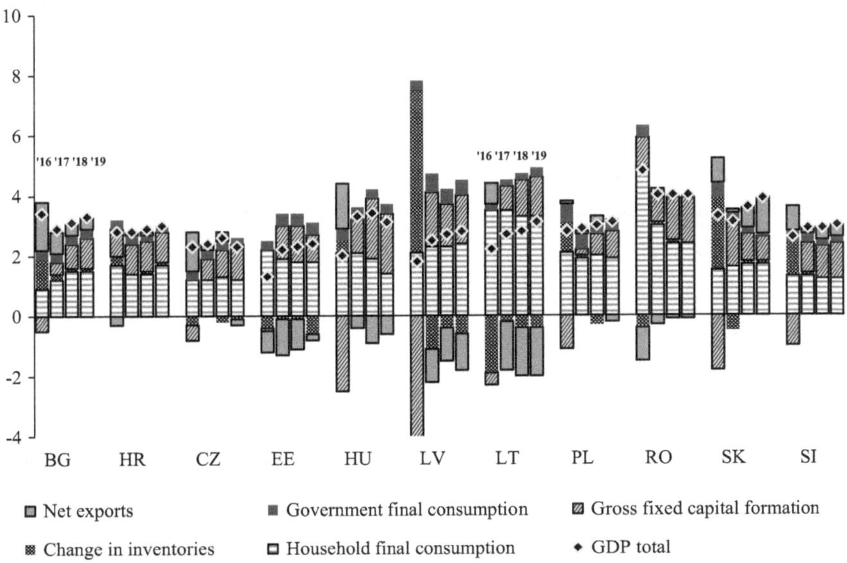

Fig. 2.9 GDP growth from 2016 to 2019 (in %) and contributions of individual demand components, in pp
Source: Adapted from Holzner et al. (2017), wiiw Forecast Report, Spring 2017

(which, together with Armenia and Kyrgyzstan, form the Eurasian Economic Union—EAEU) and Ukraine, which all had been plagued by recession from 2014 to 2015 and do not have particularly bright growth prospects, due to lasting structural and institutional deficiencies (Havlik 2015; Dobrinsky et al. 2016; Astrov et al. 2016).

The latest economic developments in the CESEE region are, on the whole, encouraging: driven by robust domestic demand, especially by household consumption and investments, GDP growth in 2016 averaged 3% in the CEE region, and the outlook is fairly positive—despite increased geopolitical uncertainties and tensions after the migration crisis, Brexit, the US presidential elections, and the Greek crisis. The latest wiiw forecast for 2017–2019 predicts a continuation of fairly robust GDP growth in the CESEE region (about 3% per year; see Fig. 2.9)—about the same growth pace as in the Western Balkans—whereas a weaker and more gradual recovery is forecast in Belarus, Russia, Kazakhstan, and Ukraine (Holzner et al. 2017). Given that the latest European Commission forecasts for the Eurozone expect GDP growth of less than 2% in 2016–2018, the CESEE pace of economic convergence will be maintained, albeit at a somewhat reduced speed from that prior to the crisis.

Acknowledgments The author would like to thank Vasily Astrov, Jan Hagemejer, Ichiro Iwasaki, and Miklos Szanyi, as well as all participants of the IER-wiiw Joint International Research Project Workshop in Vienna on December 1 and 2, 2016, for their valuable comments and suggestions for improving the quality of the chapter. Tammy Bicket helped improve the author's English.

Notes

1. Chapter 3 in this volume deals with financial aspects of the crisis.
2. It is too early to say what impact Brexit and the Trump presidency will have on the EU, and the CESEE in particular; however, the expectation of more uncertainty and more protectionist policies is probably a safe bet (see Holzner et al. (2017) for some reflections on uncertainty regarding impacts on CESEE).
3. See the website at: http://www.euractiv.com/section/euro-finance/news/eurogroup-ignores-commissions-expansionary-fiscal-target/
4. Dobrinsky and Havlik (2014) discussed various convergence measures. Previously, Barro and Sala-i-Martin (1995) discussed convergence for different countries. A critical view on CESEE convergence can be found in Podkaminer (2013).

5. The Baltic States—Estonia, Latvia, and Lithuania—were hit harder by the crisis and experienced greater structural turbulence. Comparable data for Bulgaria and Romania were not available. A more detailed discussion, covering other CESEE and selected West European countries, can be found in Havlik (2014b): "Structural Change in Europe During the Crisis." FIW Policy Brief Number 22, BMWFJ, January 2014 (http://www.fiw.ac.at/index.php?id=462#c12556)
6. The recent ECFIN economic forecast report provides the latest empirical evidence for the post-crisis growth slowdown dubbed as "new modesty" (see ECFIN 2017, Box I.2).
7. Issues related to the banking sector and financial developments are discussed in Chap. 3 of this book.
8. At the same time, the outbreak of anti-government protests against controversial amnesty and lukewarm anti-corruption policies from early 2017 signal the fragility of the political situation.

References

Adarov, A., & Havlik, P. (2016). *Benefits and costs of DCFTA: Evaluation of the impact on Georgia, Moldova and Ukraine* (Joint Working Paper of wiiw and Bertelsmann Stiftung). Vienna: Vienna Institute for International Economic Studies (wiiw).

Astrov, V., et al. (2016). *Labour shortages driving economic growth?* (Autumn Forecast Report). Vienna: wiiw.

Barro, R. J., & Sala-i-Martin, X. (1995). *Economic growth.* New York/Tokyo: McGraw-Hill.

Bruegel and wiiw. (2010). *Wither growth in Central and Eastern Europe? Policy lessons for and integrated Europe.* Brussels: Bruegel Blueprint Series.

Dobrinsky, R., & Havlik, P. (2014). *Economic convergence and structural change: The role of transition and EU accession* (Research Report No. 395). Vienna: wiiw.

Dobrinsky, R., et al. (2016). *The Belarus economy: The challenges of stalled reforms* (Research Report No. 413). Vienna: wiiw.

EBRD (European Bank for Reconstruction and Development). (2013). *Transition report: Stuck in transition?* London: EBRD.

ECFIN (Economic and Financial Affairs of the European Commission). (2017). *European economic forecast: Winter 2017* (Institutional Paper No. 048). Brussels: European Commission.

Havlik, P. (2014a). *Patterns of structural change in the new EU member states* (Research Report No. 394). Vienna: wiiw.

Havlik, P. (2014b). *Economic consequences of the Ukraine conflict* (Policy Notes and Reports No. 14). Vienna: wiiw.

Havlik, P. (2015). *Russian Federation 2015: From stagnation to recession and back* (Research Reports No. 406). Vienna: wiiw.

Havlik, P., et al. (2011). *Recovery—in low gear across tough terrain* (Current Analysis and Forecast No. 7). Vienna: wiiw.

Holzner, M., et al. (2017). *Cautious upturn in CESEE: Haunted by the spectre of uncertainty* (Spring Forecast Report). Vienna: wiiw.

Landesmann, M., & Hanzl-Weiss, D. (2016). Correcting external imbalances in the European economy. In M. Belka, E. Nowotny, P. Samecki, & D. Ritzberger-Grünwald (Eds.), *Boosting European competitiveness: The role of CESEE countries* (pp. 14–36). Cheltenham: Edward Elgar.

Landesmann, M., & Leitner, S. (2015). *Competitiveness of the European economy* (Research Report No. 401). Vienna: wiiw.

OECD (Organization for Economic Co-operation and Development). (2016). *Escaping the low-growth trap? Effective fiscal initiatives avoiding trade pitfall* (Economic Outlook No). 100. Paris: OECD.

Podkaminer, L. (2013). *Development pattern of Central and Eastern European countries (in the course of transition and following EU membership)* (Research Report No. 388). Vienna: wiiw.

Podpiera, J., Raei, F., & Stepanyan, A. (2017). *A fresh look at potential output in Central, Eastern, and Southeastern European countries* (Working Paper No. WP/17/37). Washington, DC: IMF.

Rzońca, A., & Łaszek, A. (2016). *On economic growth in Europe, or, the uncertain growth prospects of western countries* (mBank—CASE Seminar Proceedings No. 144/2016). Warsaw: Center for Social and Economic Research.

Stöllinger, R., Foster-MsGregor, N., Holzner, M., Landesmann, M., Pöschl, J., & Stehrer, R. (2013). *A 'manufacturing imperative' in the EU: Europe's position in global manufacturing and the role of industrial policy* (Research Report No. 391). Vienna: wiiw.

World Bank. (2012). *Drivers of convergence in EU11* (Special Topic in EU11 Regular Economic Report). Washington, DC: World Bank.

CHAPTER 3

The Financial Effects of the Crisis in European Emerging Markets

Mario Holzner

3.1 Introduction

Financialization reached the Eastern periphery of Europe relatively late, but all the more fundamentally. From the very beginning of the transition from central planning to a capitalist market economy at the beginning of the 1990s, the International Monetary Fund (IMF) and national central banks were the prime advocates of a comprehensive financialization of the economy, widely disregarding the productive sector (Gabor 2012). For a number of countries, the Europe Agreements with the European Union (EU) and cooperation and accession to the Organisation for Economic Co-operation and Development (OECD) also played a role. There, as compared to other emerging markets, financial deregulation has been more pronounced, with lower levels but strong increases in household debt (Karwowski and Stockhammer 2017), as they literally started from scratch. However, countries in the Western semi-periphery of Central, East, and Southeast Europe (CESEE) also received foreign direct investment (FDI) in the manufacturing sector, while the more peripheral countries further to the Northeast, East, and Southeast were predominantly attracting FDI in the financial and retail services sectors. The different

M. Holzner (✉)
Vienna Institute for International Economic Studies, Vienna, Austria

P. Havlik, I. Iwasaki (eds.), *Economics of European Crises and Emerging Markets*, DOI 10.1007/978-981-10-5233-0_3

transition paths are, *inter alia*, also reflected in differences in the distribution of household income and subsequent propensities to save as well as current account positions and, thus, vulnerability to financial and macroeconomic shocks.

The global financial crisis has affected the financial sector of CESEE countries quite strongly (although probably less than some of the Southern EU countries, largely due to the relatively less-developed financial markets). However, not all CESEE economies suffered from the following deleveraging process in the same way. This chapter describes the development of financialization in CESEE across country groups and over time according to six dimensions relevant to interpreting financialization in emerging economies as defined recently by Karwowski and Stockhammer (2017), which follows the pattern of relevant financialization literature dealing mainly with emerging markets: (1) financial deregulation, (2) foreign financial inflows, (3) asset price volatility, (4) the shift from bank-based to market-based finance, (5) business debt, and (6) household indebtedness. The different developments, before and after the outbreak of the global financial crisis, are of particular interest. Moreover, special emphasis is placed on different types of foreign financial inflows—inflows creating external debt vs. FDI—and on different types of FDI (export-oriented manufacturing vs. domestic market-oriented services).

The second section of the chapter specifically examines the post-crisis deleveraging period. Here we analyse the subsequent development of new loans, the dynamics of foreign currency (FX) loans, the evolution of non-performing loans (NPLs), and the change of households' and corporations' net lending or borrowing positions from sectoral national accounts. This is analysed in order to evaluate the impact of the different deleveraging processes on the real economy.

In the third section, the link between financialization, household income inequality, and the propensity to save (as well as current account imbalances) is identified following the recent research on this issue by Bofinger and Scheuermeyer (2016), and is applied to CESEE countries. In their empirical analysis of a set of advanced economies, Bofinger and Scheuermeyer (2016) show that different (countervailing) effects on savings rates (and the current account) dominate at different levels of inequality and financialization. A Keynesian effect prevails where inequality is low and credit financing is scarce. There, it appears (as suggested by Keynes 1936, 1939) that individual propensity to save increases with personal income, which implies that on the aggregate level, the distribution of income is key; thus, the savings rate increases with rising inequality. An effect based on the relative income hypothesis (Duesenberry 1949) or the expenditure cascades model (Frank et al. 2014) (where the increasing consumption of higher income groups encourages additional consumption by poorer households) can be found in the opposite case, when inequality is high and credit financing is abundant. There, savings rates decrease with rising inequality. In the research by Bofinger and Scheuermeyer (2016), the effect, however, vanished for the post-crisis subperiod. It is revealing to replicate their analysis for the CESEE economies. This allows us to link the two different country groups to their financial and real economy performances in the post-crisis period while also distinguishing within the two groups those economies that experienced rising inequality and financialization (and *vice versa*) before the outbreak of the global financial crisis.

Overall, the chapter attempts to describe the evolution of financialization, the effects of the deleveraging period after the outbreak of the global financial crisis, the interactions of the financial market conditions with income distributions, the savings propensity, the current account, and economic development for CESEE before and after the outbreak of the global financial crisis—and relate the individual findings to each other along the lines described above and summarized in Fig. 3.1 in a schematic way.

As Karwowski and Stockhammer (2017) indicated, financialization in CESEE is comparatively underresearched. Thus, this chapter adds to the rather scarce comparative empirical literature on financialization in CESEE (e.g., Becker et al. 2016, or Nowotny et al. 2014) that often only covers EU member states from Central and Eastern Europe (e.g., Gabor 2010) but neglects the Western Balkans and the Commonwealth of Independent States, for which data is more difficult to obtain. We close this gap by also collecting data from national sources in less-analysed countries of the region, which are typically unavailable in international databases. However, we do not look at individual countries but compare country groups. This provides us with a bird's-eye analysis that is still comparative in essence but that avoids the idiosyncrasies of a single economy's case.

3.2 The Process of Financialization in CESEE

This section follows the above-cited six dimensions of financialization as defined and theoretically justified by Karwowski and Stockhammer (2017) in analysing the development of financialization in CESEE. However, different variables and data sources are used, as our goal is to compare the

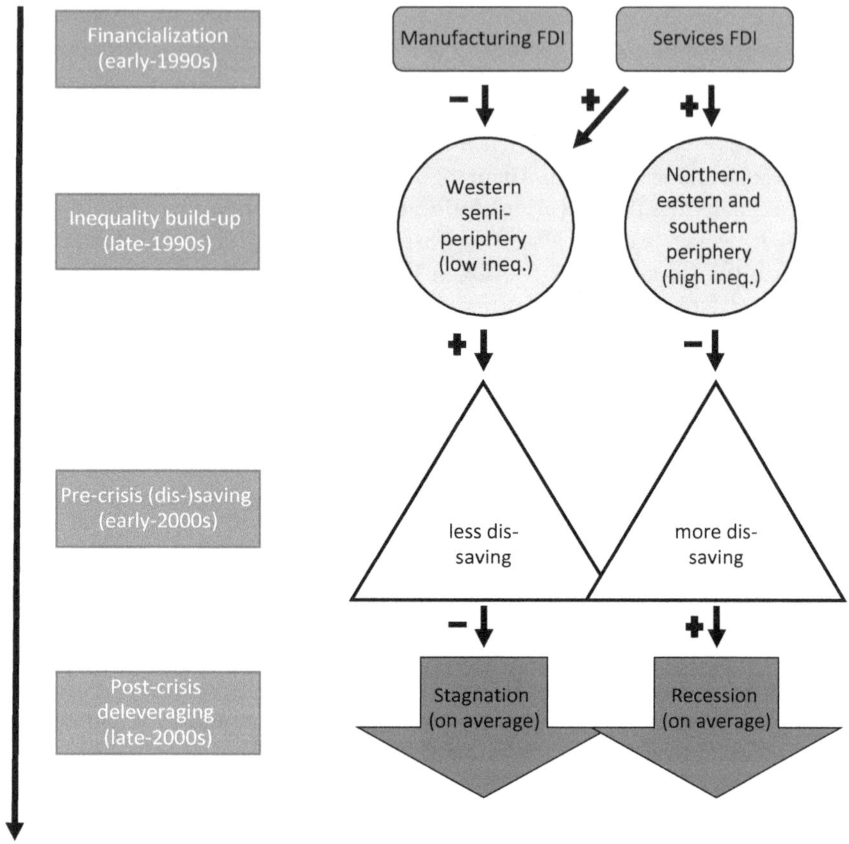

Fig. 3.1 Schematic overview of the financialization process in CESEE and its effects
Source: The author

most recent data for as many CESEE countries as possible, while the previously mentioned authors' aim was to compare selected countries from the region with other emerging economies all over the world. The term *financialization* in its broadest sense characterizes the increasing role of finance in the economy, thus allowing for many different interpretations and angles of analysis.

Our country groups consist of Europe's semi-periphery in Central and Eastern Europe (CEE), comprised of Poland, the Czech Republic,

Slovakia, Hungary, and Slovenia; the Northwestern peripheral Baltic states (BAL), Estonia, Latvia, and Lithuania; the Southeastern periphery on the Balkan peninsula—i.e., Southeastern Europe (SEE)—Croatia, Bosnia and Herzegovina, Serbia, Montenegro, Kosovo, Albania, Macedonia, Turkey, Bulgaria, and Romania; and the Eastern periphery of Europe associated with the so-called Commonwealth of Independent States (CIS), including Russia, Belarus, Moldova, Ukraine, and Kazakhstan. Figures for the country groups are simple averages across countries and time periods according to data availability.

Our first indicator of financialization is related to financial deregulation or liberalization. Specifically, we look at Chinn and Ito's (2006) index of financial openness that contains information on regulatory restrictions on cross-border financial transactions. Capital account liberalization was an important first step toward the financialization of the former communist economies and was actively supported by the international financial organizations, such as the International Monetary Fund (IMF) or the World Bank. It was hoped that deregulation would improve the efficiency of local financial markets, thereby improving the allocation of resources and generating economic growth. The potential risks of increased financial openness to macroeconomic stability were widely ignored. As can be seen from Fig. 3.2, financial deregulation was, from the very beginning, strongest in the Baltics, where it was mostly driven by the ideological agenda of the countries' authorities (Árvai 2005). By 1997, the year of the outbreak of the Asian financial crisis, these countries had almost completely liberalized their capital accounts. Countries of the other CESEE subgroups were more cautious, having achieved by that time only a low level of financial openness. Nevertheless, this was a period characterized by a series of banking crises throughout the region, interrelated with the collapse of the corporate sector. As a result of the Asian financial crisis, *inter alia*, the price of oil also plummeted, triggering the 1998 Russian financial crisis and causing strong global repercussions. It is interesting to note that from that point onward, the CIS economies did not open their capital accounts further; however, after a certain pause, the SEE and, especially, the CEE economies again started to increase deregulation efforts, mainly due to the EU accession process. They reached levels of capital account liberalization closer to that of the Baltics just before the outbreak of the global financial crisis in 2008. Since then, liberalization has again paused.

Notwithstanding, deregulation has laid the groundwork for a strong foreign capital influx into CESEE. This is reflected in the buildup of both

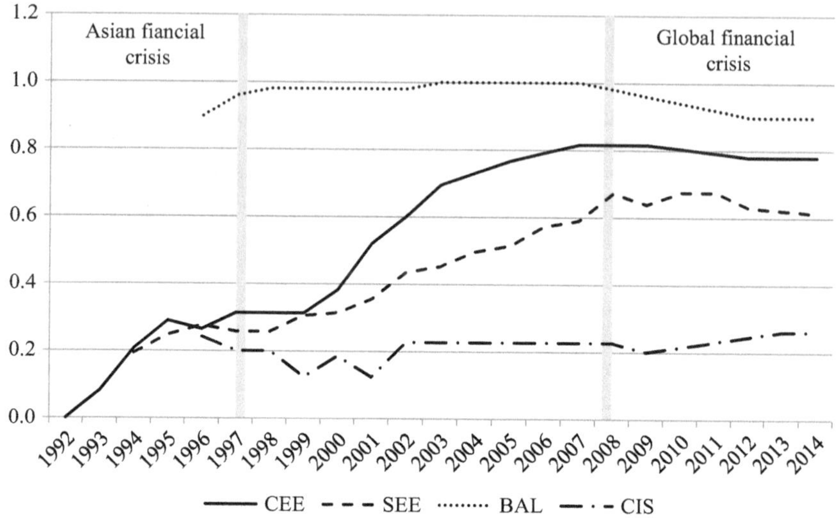

Fig. 3.2 Financial deregulation in CESEE, Chinn-Ito financial openness index, 1992–2014
Note: The index is normalized with the highest degree of financial openness captured by the value of one and the lowest by the value of zero
Sources: Chinn and Ito (2006), 2014 update, the author's own calculations

gross external debt and FDI stocks as a share of GDP (see Panels (a) and (b) of Fig. 3.3). External debt has started to surge, especially in the boom years since about 2003, particularly in the Baltics and, to a lesser extent, also in CEE. In SEE and the CIS, the development has been fairly flat. In the aftermath of the global financial crisis, the dynamics in the Baltics and CEE dampened or even reversed slightly. Meanwhile, countries from SEE and, especially, the CIS have increased their share of foreign debt for a number of reasons. The most recent range of CESEE economies is somewhere around 70–100% of GDP.

FDI inflows have developed more linearly throughout the region, with a smaller slowdown after both the Asian financial crisis and the global financial crisis. Although the Baltics and the CEE countries had led in this statistic for a long time, SEE and CIS economies have caught up, and the range of the inward FDI stock in the economies of CESEE is now somewhere around 50–60% of GDP. More importantly, there has been a substantial differentiation in the type of FDI invested in the countries

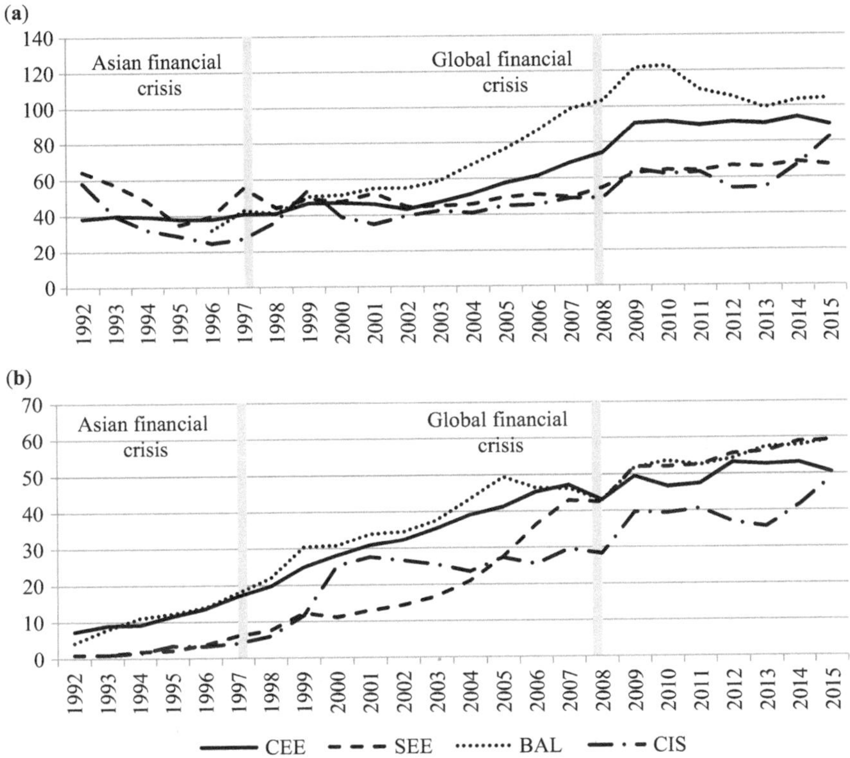

Fig. 3.3 Foreign financial inflows to CESEE—external debt and FDI stock in percentage of GDP, 1992–2015. (**a**) Gross external debt as a percentage of GDP. (**b**) FDI inward stock as a percentage of GDP
Sources: wiiw Annual Database, wiiw FDI Database, the author's own calculations

of the region. Panel (a) of Fig. 3.4 presents the FDI stock accumulated in the manufacturing sector. Clearly, the CEE countries were prime targets for manufacturing FDI early on in the process, with approximately twice the share, as compared to other, more peripheral country groups. However, more recently, CEE's share has declined slightly, and, especially, the Balkan economies are increasingly the targets of more sophisticated and export-oriented FDI in the manufacturing sector. By 2015, the average CEE country attracted manufacturing FDI stock in the order of about 14% of GDP, the average SEE economy received some 12%, and shares in

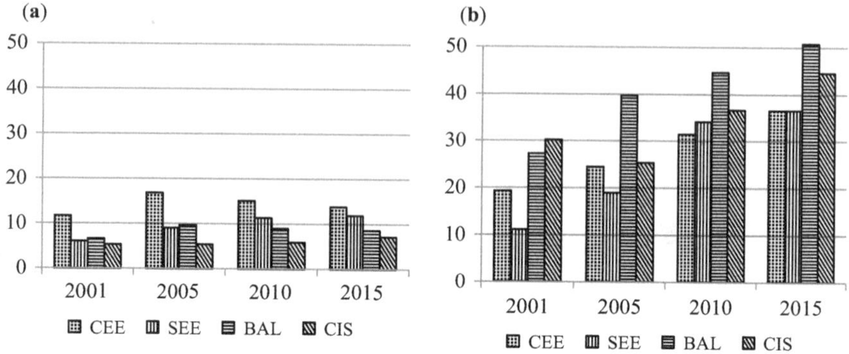

Fig. 3.4 FDI stock as a percentage of GDP in manufacturing and other sectors of CESEE, 2001, 2005, 2010, 2015. (**a**) FDI inward stock as a percentage of GDP in the manufacturing sector. (**b**) FDI inward stock as a percentage of GDP in other sectors of the economy

Note: The data is a combination of NACE Rev.1 and Rev.2 statistics, with a break around 2008—2009 in most of the countries

Sources: wiiw FDI database, the author's own calculations

the Baltics and the CIS are around 9% and 7%, respectively. Conversely, countries from the last two groups were leading the FDI stock statistics in the remaining sectors (see Panel (b) of Fig. 3.4), with 45–50% of GDP in 2015. In CEE and SEE, this is about 35% of GDP. Most of the FDI in other sectors is foreign direct investment in banking, insurance, and retail trade services oriented toward the local market, contributing to more imports than exports.

In particular, foreign capital inflows targeting the financial sector in CESEE might have triggered, among others, Minsky-type asset price inflation and volatility (where, according to Minsky (1992), the buildup of speculative asset price bubbles typically leads to system instability). Indeed, as can be seen from Panel (a) of Fig. 3.5, house price volatility was stronger in the run-up to the global financial crisis as compared to the later period, and it was also stronger in Russia (comparable data for other CIS economies were unavailable) and the Baltics as compared to the SEE and CEE economies. There was also a boom in the stock markets, especially in Russia, Turkey, the Czech Republic, and Hungary, in the years before the outbreak of the global financial crisis. Until 2007, this pushed up the respective country group averages of the ratio of stocks traded to domestic

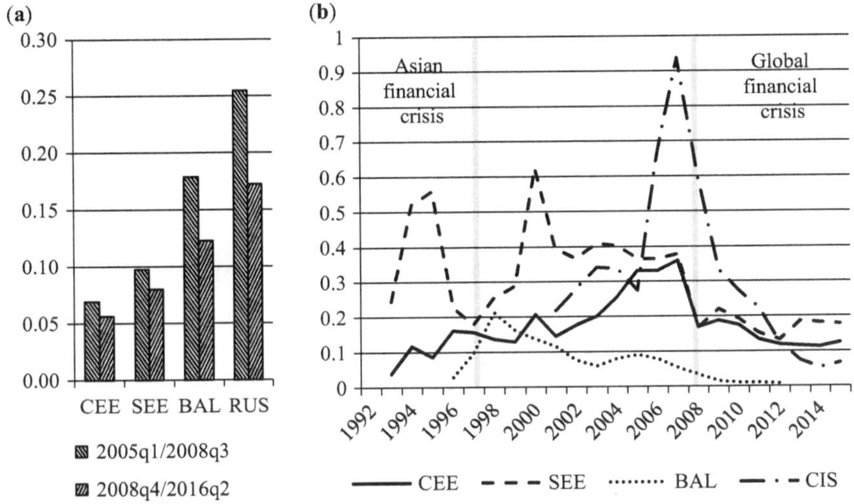

Fig. 3.5 Asset price volatility and the shift from bank-based to market-based finance in CESEE. (**a**) Quarterly real house price index coefficient of variation. (**b**) Ratio of stocks traded to domestic credit to the private sector by banks (1992–2015)
Sources: Eurostat, BIS, WDI, FRED, the author's own calculations

credit to the private sector by banks (see Panel (b) of Fig. 3.5). However, after 2008, this ratio degenerated to insignificance almost everywhere in the region. For the moment, it appears that the shift from bank-based to market-based finance has failed in CESEE.

Typically, rising levels of non-financial corporation (NFC) indebtedness have been seen as a sign of financialization, which can imply growing financial vulnerability, as ever-larger volumes of cash flow are required to meet future debt servicing commitments. Panel (a) of Fig. 3.6 shows that it was especially the Baltics and, to a lesser extent, NFCs in CEE, SEE, and CIS that hiked their indebtedness as a percentage of GDP during the boom years to unsustainable levels. In the years after the outbreak of the global financial crisis, debt ratios had to be reduced quite significantly in the Baltics and also in the countries of CEE. Elsewhere, debt levels stagnated.

Rising household indebtedness is a particularly worrisome indicator of financialization, as household debt is not typically invested in productive

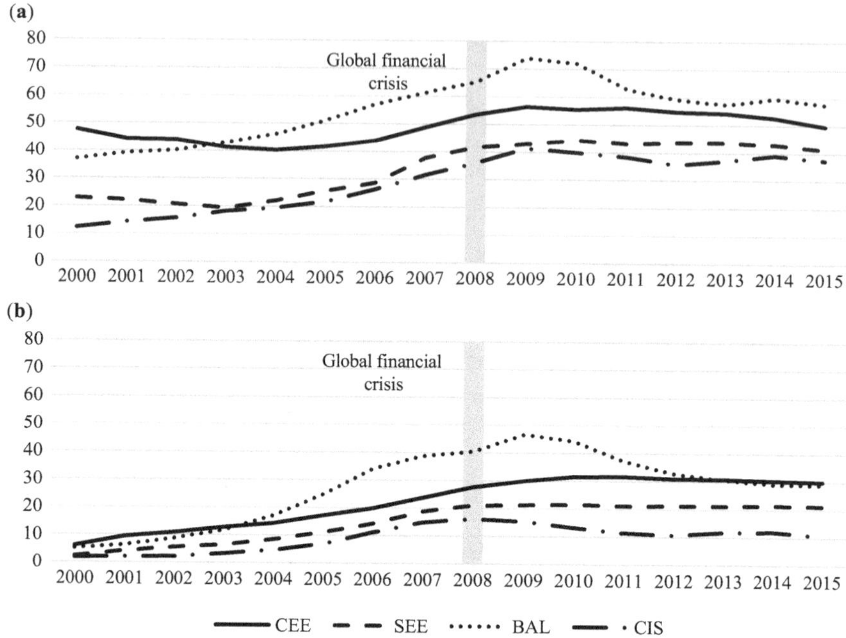

Fig. 3.6 Private debt of firms and households in CESEE as a percentage of GDP, 2000–2015. (**a**) Debt of non-financial corporations (loans and debt securities) as a percentage of GDP. (**b**) Debt of households and NPISHs (loans and debt securities) as a percentage of GDP

Note: For EU countries and Ukraine, based on consolidated balance sheets for financial accounts; for other countries, based on various banking statistics reports. For Albania, Belarus, Kazakhstan, and Russia claims. For Belarus—wiiw estimates until 2005. For Kosovo, Montenegro, Serbia, and Turkey corporate loans only

Sources: Eurostat and National Banks, the author's own calculations

activities that have the potential to generate cash flow for debt servicing. As can be seen from Panel (b) of Fig. 3.6, household debt to GDP has developed with a similar pattern to that of NFC indebtedness, but at a less dramatic pace. The Baltics also led in this statistic, followed by CEE, SEE, and the CIS. The boom stopped around 2009; since then, for example, Baltic households had to reduce their debt levels by almost 20 percentage points of GDP.

3.3 The Effects of the Global Financial Crisis in CESEE

With the outbreak of the global financial crisis, international capital flows were drying up, and interest rates increased in the region. The growth of new loans to the private sector in CESEE experienced a sudden halt (see Fig. 3.7) and went negative for about two years in most of the countries. In Lithuania (new loan data for the other Baltic countries does not exist), with the exception of a few months, the development remained negative until more recently.

A lack of new loans made it difficult to refinance old loans. The logical consequence was a substantial increase in non-performing loans, especially in the peripheral parts of the region (see Panel (a) of Fig. 3.8). Despite

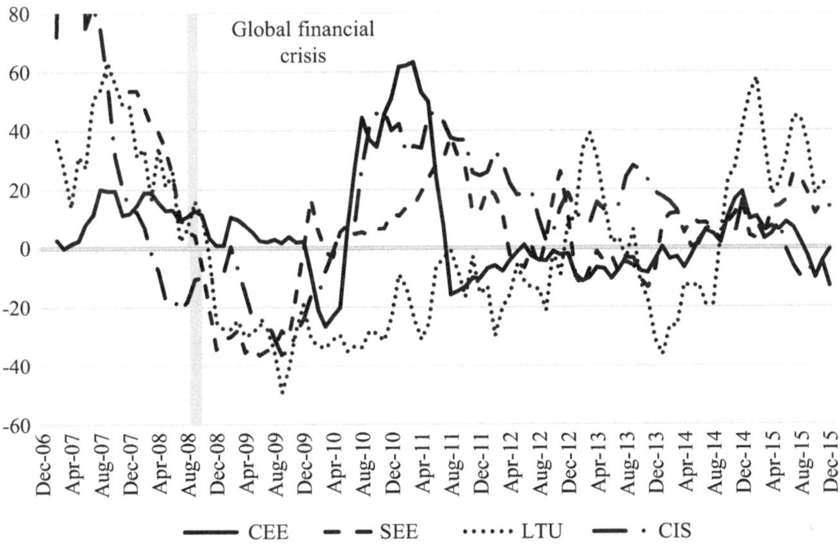

Fig. 3.7 Development of new bank loans to the non-financial private sector in CESEE, three-month moving average of year-on-year growth rates as a percentage, December 2006–2015

Note: Data on new loans is scarce; therefore, the averages of regional groups are made of a few countries only. For instance, the CIS average consists only of Kazakh and Ukrainian data

Sources: National Banks, the author's own calculations

extreme levels of NPLs by the end of 2010, the Baltics were able to tackle the NPL problem most efficiently and, more recently, have managed to reduce the problem to a fairly normal level. Especially in SEE and the CIS, NPLs are still a major obstacle to sustainable financial recovery.

The crisis and the subsequent deleveraging process brought very high levels of foreign currency denominated and indexed loans (mostly in euros) to light, which were perceived as riskier due to increased exchange rate volatility but were preferable because of lower interest rates. The shares of FX loans were particularly high in the Baltics and the Balkans, ranging around 60–80% (see Panel (b) of Fig. 3.8). Some countries—such as Slovakia and the Baltic states—seemingly solved the problem by joining

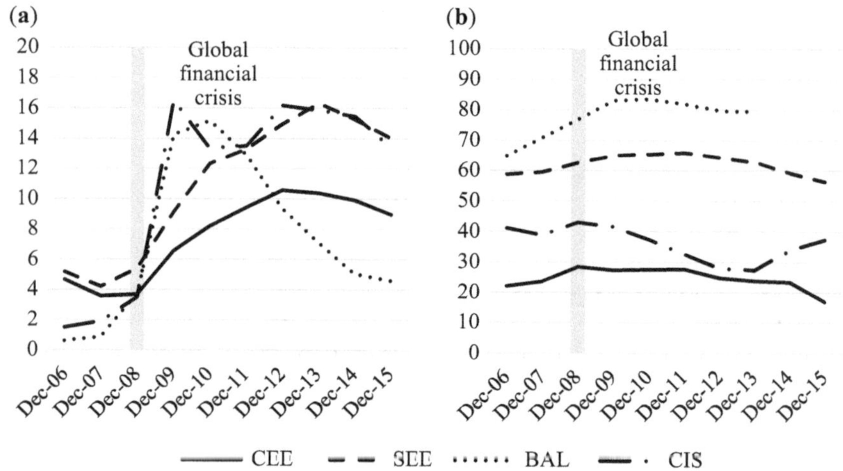

Fig. 3.8 NPLs and FX loans in CESEE, December 2006–2015. (**a**) Share of non-performing loans as a percentage of total loans, end of period, eop. (**b**) Share of foreign currency in total non-financial private sector loans as a percentage, eop
Note: The definition of non-performing loans is loans (principal and/or interest) that are more than 90 days overdue (also classified as substandard (C), doubtful (D), and loss (E).) In several cases, monthly data had to be extrapolated for a few months. In FX loans, euro area data for Latvia and Lithuania were excluded. Also, the time series for Slovakia and Estonia were excluded, due to the euro area-related break in the series. Information for Bosnia and Herzegovina was excluded as well, due to distorting, missing, indexed loan data
Sources: National Banks, the author's own calculations

the euro. Others legislated currency conversions. Overall, the share of FX loans has diminished only slightly in recent years.

Most importantly, deleveraging brought about a fundamental change in the behaviour of firms. In the late 1990s and early 2000s, a certain "economic normality" among the economic agents in CESEE was observed. CEE and SEE households were saving, and the corporate sector as well as the government were investing these funds and a certain amount of foreign funds in new productive capacities and infrastructure for example (see Fig. 3.9). The Baltics were already different at that time, as the net lending position of households was balanced; thus, all funds invested by firms and the state had to come from outside. Comparable data for longer time periods for CIS economies do not exist.

In the boom phase of the mid-2000s, households became net borrowers (except for a tiny net lending position in the average CEE country), and all funds for investment and consumption in the household, corporate, and state sectors had to come from abroad. In that period, current account deficits grew in an unsustainable way. In the period after the outbreak of the global financial crisis, the behaviour of enterprises completely reversed. Now, the corporate sector no longer invests in the aggregate but saves. The net lending positions of firms range from around 4% to 7% of GDP. This amount is currently not being absorbed by the household and government sectors but is invested abroad. Apart from sitting on cash, many corporations in the region still have to repay pre-crisis debts to foreign creditors, and part of the net lending position is also related to profit repatriation. All of this results in depressed domestic demand via a lack of investment and, hence, current accounts in surplus in many countries of the region.

Especially in the peripheral economies of the Baltics and the Balkans, where current account deficits to GDP were in the double-digit percentage range during the boom years, deficits could not be financed after the outbreak of the global financial crisis, and real income had to be deflated to reduce imports. Also, mass unemployment and mass migration brought adjustment in real terms, as changes in relative prices are typically less of an adjustment mechanism. By contrast, CEE countries in the semi-periphery that have received considerable amounts of export-oriented manufacturing FDI in the boom period already had much lower current account deficits and, hence, did not need to dramatically adjust in real terms after the outbreak of the global financial crisis.

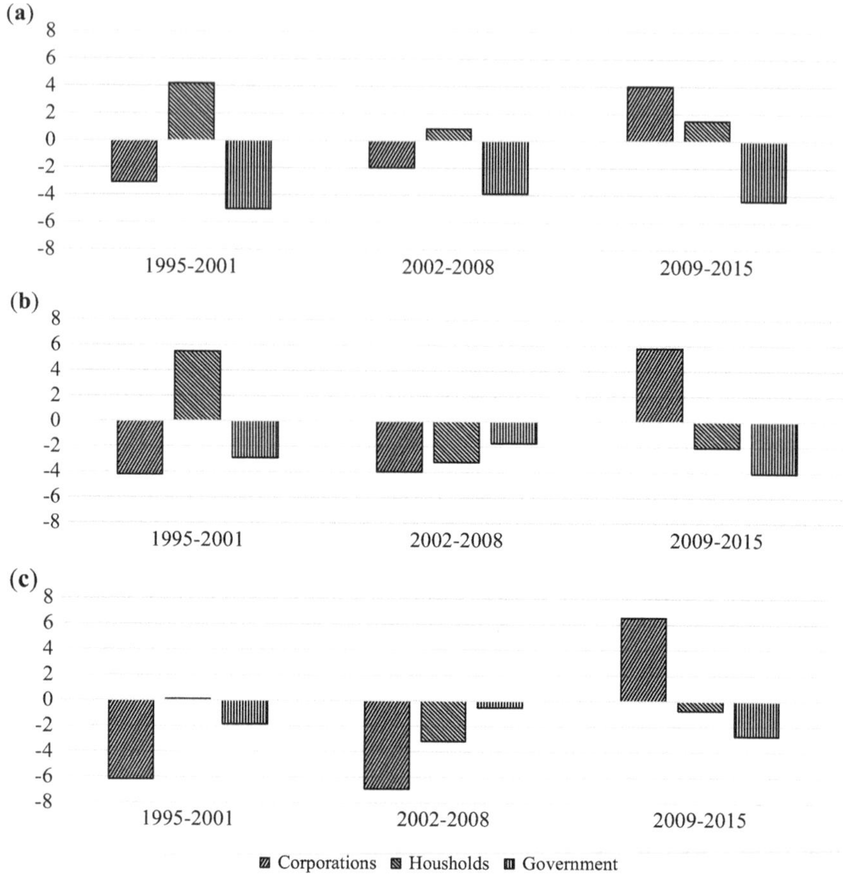

Fig. 3.9 Net lending (+) or net borrowing (−) of corporations, households, and governments in CESEE as a percentage of GDP, 1995–2001, 2002–2008, 2009–2015. (**a**) CEE. (**b**) SEE. (**c**) BAL
Note: Comparable data only from EU member states included
Sources: AMECO, the author's own calculations

3.4 Financialization, Inequality, and the Propensity to Save in CESEE

Finally, we want to shed light on the link between financialization, household income inequality, and the propensity to save (as well as the related current account imbalances) and apply to CESEE countries the recent research by Bofinger and Scheuermeyer (2016) on advanced economies. Our starting point is their baseline equation:

$$\text{saving}_{it} = \alpha + \beta_1 \text{gini}_{it} + \beta_2 \text{gini}^2_{it} + \beta' X_{it} + \alpha_i + \varepsilon_{it}, \tag{3.1}$$

where saving_{it} represents either the aggregate savings rate of the households (net or gross) or of the total economy (again net or gross), or the current account balance in country i and year t. The main explanatory variables of interest are the Gini index of inequality, gini as well as its squared term, which is included in order to check for the assumed quadratic relationship that was found by Bofinger and Scheuermeyer (2016) for high-income OECD countries. Following the methods of the same authors, control variables X are comprised of the old-age dependency ratio, the growth rate of real gross wages (as a proxy for the disposable household income variable, which is not available for CESEE), the real interest rate, and the budget balance as a percent of GDP. The baseline equation also includes country fixed effects, α_i, and an error term, ε_{it}. The subsequent fixed-effects panel regressions for 23 CESEE countries over a maximum period of 1990–2015 (due to the lack of data, regressions are based on 10–19 countries and mostly shorter time periods) use cluster-robust standard errors. Further specifications include additional control variables of the credit share of GDP, the change in real house prices (time series on stock price changes were unavailable for most CESEE economies), the log of GDP per capita at purchasing power parities, as well as consumer price inflation.

Data for the net household savings rate as a percentage of GDP stems from the AMECO database for EU member countries only. From the same source, we also obtained data for the gross household savings rate, which is augmented by national data for a few CIS countries. Data for national net savings in gross national income (GNI) and gross savings in GDP stems from the World Bank's World Development Indicator database (WDI). The current account balance in GDP was obtained from the wiiw Annual Database. As in Bofinger and Scheuermeyer (2016), the net Gini coefficient (post-tax, post-transfer) was taken from the Standard World Income Inequality Database (SWIID). The figures for domestic credit to the private sector as a percentage of GDP, the old-age dependency ratio as a percentage of the working-age population, and the real interest rate came from the WDI. From the wiiw Annual Database, we acquired data on consumer price inflation, GDP per capita, real gross wage growth, and the budget balance as a percentage of GDP. Real house price growth data was obtained from Eurostat for EU member states and augmented by Bank for International Settlements (BIS) data for Macedonia, Turkey, and Russia.

Table 3.1 presents the statistically significant results of the most important specifications comparable to those in Tables 2 and 8 of Bofinger and Scheuermeyer (2016). Due to a lack of data and, in some cases, low-quality data, the results for CESEE are not very robust. In the first linear specification [1], the coefficient for the Gini index is negative and only slightly significant in the estimation of the current account balance. This is a weak indication of an overall expenditure cascades effect, where the increasing consumption of higher income groups encourages additional consumption by poorer households and the subsequent deterioration of the external macroeconomic balances. Baseline specification [2], as described in Eq. (3.1), shows a result similar to Bofinger and Scheuermeyer's (2016). However, only for the national net savings rate did we find a weakly significant result for the coefficient of the Gini index and its squared term.

The first one was positive and the second one negative. Hence, up to a turning point of a Gini of around 31 (according to the Lind and Mehlum test), a Keynesian effect prevails; after that, the expenditure cascades effect seems to dominate. With the Keynesian effect, higher income inequality is related to aggregate higher savings rates due to the higher individual propensity for rich households to save. The hump-shaped marginal effect of income inequality on net national savings (see Panel (b) of Fig. 3.10) seems to be driven mainly by some of the oil (re)exporting CIS economies (see Panel (a) of Fig. 3.10), while for most of the other CESEE countries, a U-shaped relationship seems to hold.

Including all of the control variables as well as time-fixed effects in specification [3] yields significant results only in the case of the household net savings rate, which, however, exists only for EU member states (and more recent years), thus excluding the CIS and most SEE countries. Consequently, we find a highly significant U-shaped quadratic relationship between inequality and aggregate savings. The results are driven by low inequality and higher savings rates (1–10%) in CEE, average inequality and massive dissaving (−3% to −27%) in some SEE countries (especially Bulgaria and Romania), and high inequality and both negative and positive savings rates (−17–7%) in the Baltics, depending on the position in the economic cycle in the respective year of observation.

Table 3.1 Current account, national and household savings rate estimations

Specification no.	*[1]*	*[2]*	*[3]*	*[4]*	*[5]*	*[6]*
Dependent variable	*Current account balance in GDP*	*National net savings in GNI*	*Household net savings rate*	*National net savings in GNI*	*Household gross savings rate*	*Household net savings rate*
Net Gini index	−0.3122	2.6958	−17.6699	0.7495	2.7018	−17.8245
	(2.09)*	(1.94)*	(5.46)***	(1.29)	(0.38)	(4.69)***
Net Gini index^2		−0.0441	0.2863		−0.0217	0.2880
		(2.09)*	(5.45)***		(0.19)	(4.80)***
Credit in % of GDP			0.1818	0.1664		0.1738
			(5.07)***	(2.09)*		(3.63)***
Gini and credit interaction				−0.0059		
				(2.05)*		
High credit to GDP dummy					235.1927	
					(2.36)**	
Gini and high credit interact.					−15.7165	
					(2.33)**	
Gini^2 and high credit interact.					0.2542	
					(2.30)**	
Post-crisis dummy						−11.3047
						(0.11)
Gini and post-crisis interact.						2.5313
						(0.42)
Gini^2 and post-crisis interact.						−0.0378
						(0.37)
Old-age dependency ratio	0.5325	0.8703	−6.3751	0.6025	−1.4947	−5.7617
	(3.42)***	(2.59)**	(5.20)***	(0.60)	(1.66)	(2.71)**
Growth of real gross wages	−0.0938	0.1110	−0.0666	0.0424	0.0366	−0.0048
	(1.42)	(2.20)**	(0.56)	(0.45)	(0.38)	(0.02)

(*continued*)

Table 3.1 (continued)

Specification no.	*[1]*	*[2]*	*[3]*	*[4]*	*[5]*	*[6]*
Dependent variable	*Current account balance in GDP*	*National net savings in GNI*	*Household net savings rate*	*National net savings in GNI*	*Household gross savings rate*	*Household net savings rate*
Real interest rate	0.0060	−0.0556	0.3403	−0.0907	0.2039	0.2665
	(0.17)	(1.60)	(0.94)	(0.81)	(1.93)*	(0.75)
Budget balance in GDP	−0.1392	0.1699	0.2052	0.1793	0.3487	0.2972
	(0.88)	(0.92)	(0.55)	(0.84)	(1.28)	(0.83)
Real house price change			−0.0786	−0.0365	−0.1171	−0.0781
			(2.32)**	(1.55)	(4.31)***	(2.35)**
Log of GDP % at PPP			3.8529	15.6265	7.1369	−4.2548
			(0.48)	(2.16)*	(0.78)	(0.34)
Consumer price inflation			0.5669	−0.2495	0.0347	0.5138
			(0.96)	(1.02)	(0.15)	(0.85)
Constant	−6.9172	−52.9211	362.4547	−167.571	−87.7780	427.4885
	(1.66)	(2.09)*	(4.01)***	(1.87)*	(0.62)	(2.32)**
Country fixed effects	YES	YES	YES	YES	YES	YES
Time fixed effects	NO	NO	YES	YES	YES	YES
R^2	0.08	0.22	0.44	0.31	0.50	0.44
Countries	19	19	10	12	11	10
N	299	288	83	105	98	83

Note: *t* statistics in parenthesis. ***, **, and * denote statistical significance at the 1%, 5%, and 10% levels, respectively

Source: The author's estimations

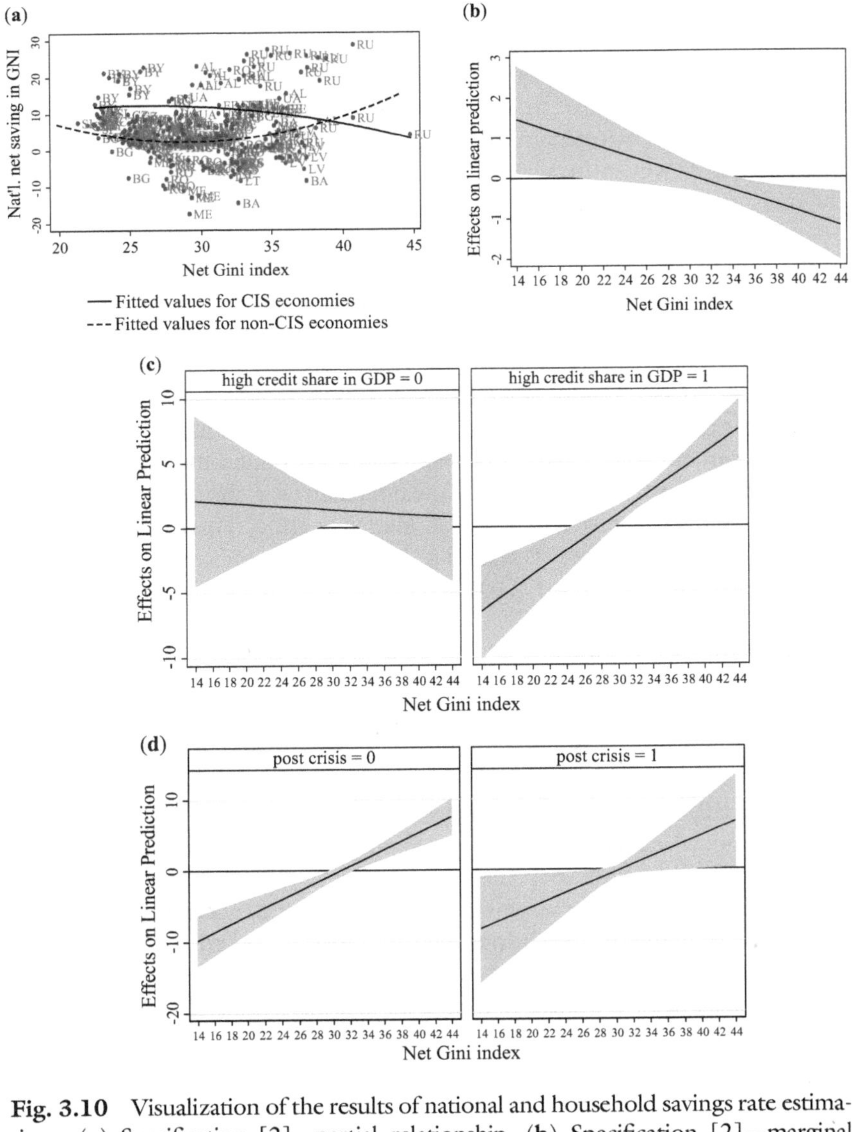

Fig. 3.10 Visualization of the results of national and household savings rate estimations. (**a**) Specification [2]—partial relationship. (**b**) Specification [2]—marginal effects. (**c**) Specification [5]—marginal effects. (**d**) Specification [6]—marginal effects
Source: The author's estimations

Specification [4] introduced an interaction term between the credit share of GDP (as an indicator of financialization) and the inequality indicator. The only (weakly) significant result stems from the national net savings rate. Similar to the findings of Bofinger and Scheuermeyer (2016), the main effect coefficients are positive, and the interaction term is negative. However, nowhere along the possible range of credit shares is the marginal effect of inequality on the national net savings rate significant. For specification [5], we split the countries into groups with high and low credit shares of GDP with the help of a dummy variable (based on the median value of the full sample of 35.4%) and interact it with both the Gini and the Gini^2. The only significant results stem from the estimation of the household gross savings rate (the respective subsample includes EU Member Countries from CEE, BAL, and SEE as well as Russia). It shows a significant U-shaped relationship between inequality and savings for countries and years with high levels of credit penetration and a mostly insignificant (and partly positive linear) result for the (few subsample) countries and years with low levels of financialization. However, looking at the marginal effects across the Gini index range for the case of high credit shares (see Panel (c) of Fig. 3.10), we can observe no significant results for Ginis between about 25 and 30 (where most CEE countries are). Basically, only Slovenia has a Gini below 25. Thus, the upward-sloping Keynesian effect range for Ginis between 30 and 40 is only relevant for SEE and BAL cases and Russia.

Finally, specification [6] tests a post-crisis dummy (from 2008 onward). The only significant result is the one for the household net savings rate (EU member states only). The period after the outbreak of the global financial crisis does not show many significant (marginal) results, which is a finding similar to the outcome in Bofinger and Scheuermeyer (2016). If at all, a slight Keynesian effect can be observed for the more equal economies. In the boom period before the crisis, a significant U-shaped relationship between household net savings and inequality can be observed again (see the marginal effects in Panel (d) of Fig. 3.10). However, the situation is quite complex. Indeed, it appears that it is especially the CEE countries—Slovenia and the Czech Republic (as well as the more developed SEE country Croatia)—that are driving the downward-sloping expenditure cascades effect in the lower inequality range before the outbreak of the global financial crisis. However, it must be noted that all of these economies recorded positive savings rates. On the other side of the inequality range, in the upward-sloping Keynesian effect area, one can find especially the Baltic countries. However, these had almost exclusively negative savings rates before the crisis. Thus, overall among the more-developed EU member states from CESEE, those with low levels of inequality displayed positive household net savings rates before the outbreak of the global financial crisis, while those with high inequality exhibited strong dissaving, which resulted in a more painful deleveraging process after the crisis outbreak. Hence, while observing in the boom period an expenditure cascades effect within the low inequality CEE and a Keynesian effect among the Baltic economies, when these two groups of low and high inequality countries are looked at as aggregates, we generally observe an overall expenditure cascades effect. Indeed, additional linear specifications for the current account balance show that, for the total sample before the outbreak of the global financial crisis, an expenditure cascades effect prevails, while after the crisis outbreak, a Keynesian effect can be detected—or rather a stronger deleveraging process in the more peripheral areas of the region. However, it must be noted that, overall, the econometric results of this section do not seem to be very robust to changes in the sample or the specification.

3.5 Conclusions

Overall, it can be said that financialization was particularly strong in the three small Baltic states, followed by countries from CEE and, at a certain distance, by economies of SEE and the CIS. This pattern can be observed in the deregulation indicator as well as in different indicators of foreign financial inflows. However, an important distinction can be made with regard to the structure of inward FDI stocks in the CESEE region. Economies from CEE and, to a certain extent, and with a lag, also economies from SEE were able to attract highly productive and export-oriented manufacturing FDI, while the Baltics and the CIS had a much stronger focus on domestically oriented banking, insurance, and retail trade service FDI that supported import activities more than exports. The strong influx of foreign funds into the financial sector has triggered, particularly in Russia and the Baltics, asset price volatility in the housing market—a bubble that partly burst after the outbreak of the global financial crisis. Similarly, the start of a shift from bank-based to market-based finance in a few countries of the region has been reversed in recent years. The repeating pattern of strong financialization up to the outbreak of the global financial crisis, especially in the Baltics and, to a certain extent, also in CEE, can again be observed with regard to the indebtedness dynamics of NFCs and households. The less-dynamic development of indebtedness in SEE and the CIS and the partial reversal in the Baltics and CEE after the outbreak of the global financial crisis leads to a certain alignment in financialization trends in CESEE.

A direct effect of the global financial crisis was the drying up of international capital flows and a rise in interest rates in CESEE countries. The growth of new loans to the private sector turned negative, and the refinancing of old loans became a problem. As a consequence, non-performing loans increased dramatically, especially in the more peripheral economies. Large shares of foreign currency loans also raised concerns about the stability of the financial system. A major problem characterizing the deleveraging process is the reversal of behaviour of the main economic agents in CESEE. The peripheral economies in particular have experienced a foreign-financed boom, with households, corporations, and the government being net borrowers in the aggregate. However, after the outbreak of the global financial crisis, the corporate sector became a net lender. Firms either sat on cash or paid back earlier debts. Investments were postponed; hence, domestic demand was dampened. As a consequence, earlier unsustainably high current account deficits often turned into surpluses. CEE economies that had received a larger chunk of export-oriented manufacturing FDI during the transition were partly able to avoid more extreme real adjustments, as in the Baltics and the Balkans, due to their stronger export base and more stable current account positions.

Finally, the differences in financialization, income distribution, and propensity to save, as well as the development of external (im)balances, were linked in an econometric exercise, the outcome of which showed a complex and not very robust picture. On the aggregate level, in samples, including those of most CESEE countries, we find negative linear effects between higher income inequality and the current account balance, particularly for the period before the outbreak of the global financial crisis; this indicates an overall expenditure cascades effect (where increasing consumption of higher income groups encourages additional consumption by poorer households). In the period after the outbreak of the crisis, a positive, Keynesian effect prevailed (where the individual propensity to save increases with personal income). Also, there are (statistically weak) signs that countries with higher inequality and more access to credit (especially the Baltics) experienced stronger dissaving over the full period of analysis. Apart from a weakly significant, hump-shaped, non-linear effect for the larger CESEE sample, in most cases these non-linear effects are only significant for the household savings rate indicators that are almost exclusively available for EU Member Countries—thus excluding most of the CIS and SEE countries. Here we find a U-shaped relationship between income inequality and savings rates, especially before the outbreak of the global financial crisis and where credit was abundant; hence, we see first an expenditure cascades effect where inequality is low and then a Keynesian effect where inequality is high. However, generally low inequality economies from CEE had positive saving rates, while high inequality countries from SEE and the Baltics were massively dissaving before the outbreak of the crisis; the latter group also experienced substantial financialization. In the wake of the global financial crisis, these (external) imbalances had to be adjusted in a painful deleveraging process.

Acknowledgments The author would like to thank Jan Hagemejer, Ichiro Iwasaki, Amat Adarov, Vladimir Gligorov, Peter Havlik, and Leon Podkaminer as well as all the participants of the IER-wiiw Joint International Research Project Workshop in Vienna on December 1 and 2, 2016, for their valuable comments and suggestions for improving the quality of the chapter. The author would also like to thank Tammy Bicket for language editing.

References

Árvai, Z. (2005). *Capital account liberalization, capital flow patterns, and policy responses in the EU's new member states* (Working Paper No. 213). Washington, DC: International Monetary Fund.

Becker, J., Ćetković, P., & Weissenbacher, R. (2016). Financialization, dependent export industrialization, and deindustrialization in Eastern Europe. In G. Cozzi, S. Newman, & J. Toporowski (Eds.), *Finance and industrial policy: Beyond financial regulation in Europe* (pp. 41–64). Oxford: Oxford University Press.

Bofinger, P., & Scheuermeyer, P. (2016). *Income distribution and aggregate saving: A non-monotonic relationship* (Discussion Paper No. 11435). London: Centre for Economic Policy Research.

Chinn, M. D., & Ito, H. (2006). What matters for financial development? Capital controls, institutions, and interactions. *Journal of Development Economics, 81*, 163–192.

Duesenberry, J. (1949). *Income, saving, and the theory of consumer behavior*. Cambridge, MA: Harvard University Press.

Frank, R. H., Levine, A. S., & Dijk, O. (2014). Expenditure cascades. *Review of Behavioral Economics, 1*, 55–73.

Gabor, D. V. (2010). (De)Financialization and crisis in Eastern Europe. *Competition and Change, 14*, 248–270.

Gabor, D. V. (2012). The road to financialization in Central and Eastern Europe: The early policies and politics of stabilizing transition. *Review of Political Economy, 24*, 227–249.

Karwowski, E., & Stockhammer, E. (2017). Financialization in emerging economies: A systematic overview and comparison with Anglo-Saxon economies. *Economic and Political Studies, 5*, 60–86.

Keynes, J. M. (1936). *The general theory of employment, interest, and money*. London: Macmillan.

Keynes, J. M. (1939). Mr. Keynes on the distribution of incomes and "propensity to consume": A reply. *Review of Economics and Statistics, 21*, 129.

Minsky, H. P. (1992). *The financial instability hypothesis* (Working Paper No. 74). Annandale-on-Hudson: The Jerome Levy Economics Institute of Bard College.

Nowotny, E., Ritzberger-Grünwald, D., & Backé, P. (Eds.). (2014). *Financial cycles and the real economy: Lessons for CESEE countries*. Cheltenham: Edward Elgar.

CHAPTER 4

Effects of the Global Economic Crisis on FDI Inflow in Eastern European Economies: A Panel Data Analysis

Taku Suzuki

4.1 Introduction

The reforms of social and economic systems in the Eastern European countries, including Transcaucasia, led to successful economic development and integration into the global economy, to a greater or lesser extent. Today, almost half of these countries have participated in the European Union (EU) and have received various economic benefits in several aspects, for example, financial support from highly developed EU countries, expansion of trading, liberalization of migration, and increased foreign direct investment (FDI). FDI is said to have contributed not only to enlarging economies (i.e., GDP) but also to improving the quality of these economies (i.e., industrial technology, etc.).

Despite those fruitful outcomes, the post-communist countries sometimes faced troublesome phases due to disturbances in the global market economy. Since the late 2000s, several economic shocks have hit the world financial markets. The first was the global financial crisis of 2008 (some consider this to have started in 2007). Nowadays, many economists consider

T. Suzuki (✉)
Faculty of Economics, Teikyo University, Tokyo, Japan

P. Havlik, I. Iwasaki (eds.), *Economics of European Crises and Emerging Markets*, DOI 10.1007/978-981-10-5233-0_4

this shock to have been the largest economic crisis of the twenty-first century and the worst since the Great Depression of the 1930s. The second was the Greek government debt crisis. This crisis is thought to have started in late 2009 or the beginning of 2010, and it spread widely around the world. What is worse, the repayment plan of the Greek government has been rescheduled several times, and, thus, the source of the next economic shock is potentially active. The third was the worldwide stock plunge in late 2014. The causes of this latest economic shock are numerous, and, in some cases, the outbreak process is said to have been a somewhat stepwise path. Although various theories and factors have been identified concerning this matter, the first factor is thought to be the Ukraine conflict, and the next step was falling oil prices caused by various factors, including economic sanctions against the Russian Federation. The third step was a depression of the emerging market concurrent with a plunging oil price. These economic shocks more or less damaged the inflow of FDI to developed and emerging economies; of course, the inflow of FDI to Eastern European countries was also strongly affected by these shocks.

With regard to the impact of the economic crisis on FDI, several studies examined the problems caused by economic shocks—including the global financial shock in the late 2000s—on FDI inflow. Some researchers analysed the current situation or the reasons for the decline. For instance, Arabi (2010) evaluated India's declining FDI inflow and its status in the world economy and made some recommendations regarding the government's strategy. He insisted that "the global economic crisis is an opportunity for India to deepen their economic ties" (p. 747) and to promote several policies, such as the enactment of a foreign investment promotion law, infrastructure investment, the strengthening of the Department of Industrial Policy and Promotion (DIPP) and the Foreign Investment Promotion Board (FIPB), and the establishment of an investment facilitation fund. Ledyaeva (2009) examined the determinants of FDI inflow in the Russian Regions by adopting a spatial autoregressive model. She used data around the Russian financial crisis in 1998 and specified some determinants of FDI, such as political risk, market size, and oil and gas resources. On the other hand, some researchers measured the impact of shocks on FDI inflow. For example, Stoddard and Noy (2015) confirmed the impact on inflow in developing and emerging economies by using Arellano–Bond GMM estimation with shock dummy variables. They used panel data of 34 countries from 1987 to 2009 and set a binary crisis index according to their own survey; they then detected that the banking crisis had a negative impact on FDI stock. Furthermore, Ucal et al. (2010) also estimated the impact on FDI inflow in 148 developing countries by using a generalized partially linear model with shock dummy variables. They focused on the impact of the 2008 financial crisis on FDI inflow and set binary shock variables in two ways: a shock dummy and a pre-shock dummy. With these, they confirmed that FDI inflow decreased after the collapse of Lehman Brothers and rose before the financial crisis hit the country.

These studies are very suggestive of further studies on the effect of global economic shocks on FDI inflow in Eastern European countries. However, I would like to point out some remaining tasks for further study. First, the differences in the size of the impact and the timing in the various areas have not been well examined. Usually, the same economic shock affects countries or areas to different extents and, sometimes, at different times. A global shock may affect country X immediately and hard, while affecting country Y hard but a little late, and affect country Z only slightly. Thus, differences in impact by area and in timing are to be considered in this study.

Second, some shocks originating for different reasons or countries are not rigidly distinct. Some preceding studies treated several shocks using a single binary variable, i.e., the shock index = 1 when that year is in any shock period, and = 0 otherwise. It may be that the impact of each shock on FDI inflow differs despite the fact that the magnitude of the crisis at the "seismic centre" is the same among those shocks. Therefore, a variable indicating economic shock should be created for each crisis.

Third, in previous studies, assumptions regarding shock variables are relatively simple, binary indices that sometimes fail to capture differences in the magnitude of the shock by year. Usually, the impact of economic shock lasts for several years and does not have the same magnitude throughout the crisis period. Accordingly, the use of a binary index is inadequate for capturing the declining impact year by year. Moreover, the pace of declining impact may differ with each economic shock. In other words, the pace of the declining impact of the 2008 financial crisis may not be the same as that of the subsequent Greek government debt crisis.

Based on these facts, this study pursues differences by areas, countries, and the shocks themselves by using an econometric method based on data of EU and non-EU member Eastern European countries. To achieve this purpose, I will take a general view of FDI inflow to Eastern European countries in Sect. 4.2. Afterwards, I will argue ways of setting up the shock variables and test hypotheses and then other control variables (in Sect. 4.3). In Sect. 4.4, I will show the models and results of empirical tests, before concluding this chapter in Sect. 4.5.

4.2 Overview of FDI Inflow to Eastern European Countries

Before the financial crisis, the world economy enjoyed the fruits of international transactions, including capital flow; however, the situation took a sudden turn after 2008. Besides the 2008 financial shock itself, other economic shocks partly deriving from this crisis hit the global economy several times in an ebb and flow. This situation was also true of Eastern European countries. Table 4.1 shows the change in the amount of FDI inflow to these post-communist emerging markets, including Caucasus countries that are "politically" regarded as Europe (however, Serbia, Montenegro, and Kosovo are excluded due to the unavailability of continuous data).

According to this table, the sum of FDI inflow to these countries continued growing until 2008, the year the crises began. They experienced consecutive increases in the amount of FDI inflow except in 2003, which was the year in which the Iraq War caused transitory investor anxiety. However, the Iraqi event affected FDI inflow in only eight out of 21 countries, and, thus, it can be said that this anxiety in the global market did not lead to the financial crises. Contrary to this pre-crisis period, some of these countries experienced sharp declines in FDI inflow in 2009, 2012, 2013, and 2014. Especially in 2009, the year of largest decline, 18 out of 21 countries experienced declines in FDI inflow; in the year of second largest decline, 2014, 12 countries experienced declines in FDI inflow. In 2012, 15 of 21 countries were damaged, although the declines were relatively smaller than those in 2009, 2013, and 2014. These facts demonstrate that the crises strongly hit these countries and sharply interrupted the trend of FDI inflow; the declines in their FDI inflow differ with each shock or crisis.

When focusing on the respective countries, we see some differences in the scale of damage to the FDI inflow. For example, the largest decline in 2009 was observed in the Russian Federation (−48103.4 million dollars),vfollowed by Romania (−8826.1), Bulgaria (−6469.8), Ukraine (−6097.0), and the less-affected countries, Azerbaijan (+459.2), Albania (+21.6), Estonia (+9.8), and Armenia (−183.7). Therefore, we can see not only the impact of the tremendous financial crisis but also increases in FDI even under the worst circumstances in the global economy. These disparities seem to be partly explained by the population size, i.e., countries with large populations tend to be affected more strongly, while those with

Table 4.1 FDI inflow to Eastern European countries, 2002–2014 (Million US dollar; Upper, FDI inflow; Lower, change from the previous year)

Year	*2002*	*2003*	*2004*	*2005*	*2006*	*2007*	*2008*	*2009*	*2010*	*2011*	*2012*	*2013*	*2014*
Albania	133.06	177.10	345.67	264.34	324.42	658.51	974.33	995.93	1050.71	876.27	855.44	1265.55	1109.96
	−73.37	44.05	168.57	−81.33	60.08	334.08	315.83	21.60	54.78	−174.44	−20.83	410.11	−155.59
Armenia	110.73	122.85	247.14	292.07	466.53	667.67	943.73	760.04	529.32	653.22	496.64	379.86	404.35[a]
	40.86	12.13	124.29	44.93	174.46	201.14	276.06	−183.69	−230.72	123.90	−156.58	−116.78	24.49
Azerbaijan	1392.44	3285.00	3556.10	1679.92	−583.99	−4748.88	14.09	473.31	563.00	1465.00	2004.60	2632.00	4430.40
	1165.93	1892.56	271.10	−1876.18	−2263.91	−4164.90	4762.97	459.22	89.70	902.00	539.60	627.40	1798.40
Belarus	247.10	171.80	163.80	306.60	357.10	1807.30	2187.90	1876.50	1393.40	4002.40	1429.30	2229.60	1827.60
	151.30	−75.30	−8.00	142.80	50.50	1450.20	380.60	−311.40	−483.10	2609.00	−2573.10	800.30	−402.00
Bosnia and	265.17	381.05	511.19	351.18	554.69	1819.24	1001.65	249.95	406.03	496.47	394.87	302.10	501.66
Herzegovina	146.31	115.88	130.13	−160.01	203.51	1264.55	−817.60	−751.70	156.08	90.44	−101.59	−92.77	199.56
Bulgaria	922.29	2088.53	3397.12	3919.97	7804.89	12388.86	9855.11	3385.35	1549.13	2945.13	1697.19	1837.23	1776.59
	113.86	1166.24	1308.59	522.85	3884.93	4583.97	−2533.75	−6469.75	−1836.22	1396.00	−1247.94	140.04	−60.65
Croatia	957.70[b]	1791.80[b]	1269.04[b]	1785.65[b]	3289.13[b]	4591.27[b]	5310.84[b]	3079.22[b]	1153.24[b]	1692.45[b]	1493.18[b]	921.56[b]	3678.16[b]
	−52.89	834.10	−522.76	516.61	1503.48	1302.14	719.57	−2231.62	−1925.98	539.21	−199.27	−571.62	2756.59
Czech	8482.05	2102.74	4974.50	11653.25	5462.63	10443.82	6451.00	2926.82	6140.58	2317.55	7984.11	3639.13	5492.00
Republic	2840.31	−6379.31	2871.76	6678.75	−6190.63	4981.20	−3992.82	−3524.19	3213.77	−3823.03	5666.56	−4344.98	1852.88
Estonia	288.73	928.00	957.12	2799.17	1334.41	2311.21	1829.68	1839.44	1508.54	1004.60	1564.94	545.94	507.03
	−250.56	639.27	29.12	1842.06	−1464.76	976.80	−481.53	9.76	−330.90	−503.94	560.34	−1019.00	−38.91
Georgia	160.21	334.65	492.33	452.75	1170.08	1750.24	1564.31	658.90	813.84	1048.23	911.29	948.94	1749.76
	50.37	174.44	157.68	−39.58	717.33	580.17	−185.93	−905.42	154.94	234.40	−136.95	37.65	800.82
Hungary	2993.57	2137.40	4265.73	7708.96	6817.55	3950.84	6327.19	1995.32	2192.81	6300.12	14409.22	3404.25	7489.95
	−942.48	−856.16	2128.33	3443.23	−891.41	−2866.71	2376.35	−4331.87	197.50	4107.31	8109.10	−11004.97	4085.70
Latvia	209.72	279.40	607.54	706.19	1663.87	2323.67	1264.09	93.88	379.39	1453.19	1109.08	903.12	595.20
	104.54	69.68	328.14	98.65	957.68	659.80	−1059.58	−1170.20	285.51	1073.80	−344.11	−205.96	−307.92
Lithuania	724.97	180.41	773.70	1028.09	1816.78	2015.01	1964.52	−13.72	799.60	1446.42	700.04	469.06	−156.71
	279.16	−544.56	593.29	254.39	788.69	198.24	−50.49	−1978.24	813.32	646.82	−746.38	−230.98	−625.78
Poland	4030.11	3982.31	12140.25	8203.22	14577.50	19836.22	12283.04	10039.32	12796.27	15925.14	12423.52	3625.46[a]	12531.02[a]
	−1549.15	−47.80	8157.94	−3937.03	6374.28	5258.72	−7553.18	−2243.72	2756.95	3128.87	−3501.62	−8798.06	8905.56
Republic of	84.05	73.75	146.20	190.70	258.47	541.26	711.46	208.33	207.90	288.21	195.07	242.74	200.58
Moldova	−19.39	−10.30	72.45	44.50	67.77	282.79	170.20	−503.13	−0.43	80.31	−93.14	47.67	−42.16

(*continued*)

Table 4.1 (continued)

Year	*2002*	*2003*	*2004*	*2005*	*2006*	*2007*	*2008*	*2009*	*2010*	*2011*	*2012*	*2013*	*2014*
Romania	1140.65	2196.30	6435.59	6152.30	10858.12	9732.81	13491.54	4665.45	3041.04	2362.92	3198.55	3601.36	3211.41
	−17.28	1055.65	4239.29	−283.29	4705.82	−1125.31	3758.73	−8826.09	−1624.41	−678.11	835.63	402.82	−389.95
Russian	3425.02	7754.76	15283.75	14375.05[a]	37441.57[a]	54921.85[a]	75855.70[a]	27752.26[a]	31667.97[a]	36867.77[a]	30187.66[a]	53397.14[a]	29151.66[a]
Federation	616.69	4329.74	7528.99	−908.70	23066.52	17480.28	20933.85	−48103.44	3915.71	5199.80	−6680.11	23209.48	−24245.48
Slovakia	5864.88	2975.67	4028.99	3109.64	5803.09	4017.25	4868.02	−6.08	1769.76	3491.29	2981.69	−604.08	−331.49
	3590.04	−2889.21	1053.32	−919.35	2693.45	−1785.84	850.78	−4874.10	1775.84	1721.53	−509.60	−3585.77	272.59
Slovenia	1569.68	271.18	675.46	561.65	706.28	757.29	1218.41	−475.83	105.37	1087.42	339.33	−151.18	1060.92
	1211.14	−1298.49	404.28	−113.81	144.63	51.02	461.12	−1694.24	581.20	982.05	−748.09	−490.51	1212.10
TFYR of		113.33	323.67	96.02	432.58	692.51	585.77	201.40	212.53	478.77	142.90	334.86	272.17
Macedonia			210.34	−227.65	336.56	259.93	−106.74	−384.37	11.13	266.24	−335.87	191.96	−62.69
Ukraine	693.00	1424.00	1715.00	7808.00	5604.00	9891.00	10913.00	4816.00	6495.00	7207.00	8401.00	4499.00	410.00
	−99.00	731.00	291.00	6093.00	−2204.00	4287.00	1022.00	−6097.00	1679.00	712.00	1194.00	−3902.00	−4089.00
Total	33695.11	32772.03	62309.88	73444.71	106159.69	140368.95	159615.38	65521.77	74775.43	93409.57	92919.62	84423.64	75912.21
	7404.23	−756.51	29793.83	13322.87	34020.19	33011.71	16983.12	−83908.97	9569.72	28011.74	−5889.21	−10250.53	−30204.53
Decrease	8	8	2	10	5	4	9	18	7	4	15	12	11

[a]Asset/liability basis
[b]Directional basis calculated from asset/liability basis

Source: UNCTAD

small populations tend to be affected less. Countries with large populations can attract FDI more easily and its backlash may also be larger. Hence, it may be a matter of FDI volatility.

However, a question remains: if this population size is taken into consideration, will these disparities disappear? The answer is, probably not. Table 4.2 shows the change in the per capita FDI inflow. As this table indicates, disparities do exist in another aspect. As to the amount of FDI inflow, the largest decline in 2009 is observed in the Russian Federation; however, the largest decline in per capita FDI inflow is observed in Slovakia (−903.2 dollars), followed by Bulgaria (−857.8), Slovenia (−833.0), and Lithuania (−614.5). On the other hand, countries that experienced large declines in FDI inflow had relatively small declines in per capita FDI inflow, other than Bulgaria; examples are the Russian Federation (−336.1), Romania (−423.0), and Ukraine (−132.0). In contrast, the list of less-affected countries is similar to that in the case of FDI inflow, such as Azerbaijan (+52.7), followed by Albania (+11.6), Estonia (+11.3), and Belarus (−32.4). Thus, another type of disparity emerges here. According to Table 4.2, the countries highly damaged in 2009 are relatively advanced market economies among the Eastern European countries, and CIS countries tend to be less damaged. This study will pay attention to this tendency as a key factor in explaining the differences in the per capita FDI inflow among countries and focus on it as a task in the next section.

As far as the timing is concerned, the peak negative impact by economic shock differs by country. For example, assuming that the decline in FDI between 2010 and 2012 is caused by the Greek government debt crisis, the peak impact in Armenia, Bulgaria, Croatia, and Romania was in 2010, while in Albania, the Czech Republic, and Estonia the peak was in 2011; in most of the others, the peak was in 2012. Surprisingly, Azerbaijan, Hungary, and Ukraine received no damage in this period. Although the difference by area or country group does not seem to be important in this example, the difference in timing seems to be worthy of examination.

As noted above, there should be some features in this trend of FDI inflow to Eastern European countries. Some countries seem to be damaged more while others are not. Other differences may also exist, not only in the magnitude of the shocks themselves, but also in the timing of the impact. Concerning these points, in the next section I will deepen the discussion and build the hypotheses and then discuss variables based on them.

Table 4.2 Per capita FDI inflow to Eastern European countries, 2002–2014 (US dollar; Upper, per capita FDI inflow; Lower, change from the previous year)

Year	*2002*	*2003*	*2004*	*2005*	*2006*	*2007*	*2008*	*2009*	*2010*	*2011*	*2012*	*2013*	*2014*
Albania	42.60	56.82	111.37	85.76	106.34	218.71	328.28	339.92	362.08	303.63	296.96	438.93	384.11
	−23.47	14.21	54.55	−25.61	20.58	112.37	109.57	11.64	22.16	−58.45	−6.67	141.97	−54.82
Armenia	36.34	40.46	81.67	96.88	155.40	223.44	317.22	256.24	178.61	220.09	166.75	126.95	134.51
	13.50	4.12	41.21	15.20	58.52	68.04	93.78	−60.98	−77.63	41.48	−53.34	−39.80	7.56
Azerbaijan	168.16	392.40	420.03	196.17	−67.42	−541.90	1.59	52.70	61.87	158.76	214.13	277.13	460.07
	140.52	224.24	27.63	−223.86	−263.59	−474.48	543.49	51.11	9.17	96.90	55.37	62.99	182.95
Belarus	25.15	17.60	16.89	31.80	37.22	189.13	229.67	197.42	146.80	421.85	150.60	234.76	192.37
	15.46	−7.54	−0.71	14.91	5.42	151.91	40.54	−32.25	−50.62	275.06	−271.26	84.17	−42.39
Bosnia and	69.63	99.82	133.61	91.61	144.51	473.71	260.86	65.13	105.87	129.55	103.14	79.01	131.41
Herzegovina	38.35	30.19	33.79	−42.00	52.90	329.20	−212.85	−195.73	40.74	23.68	−26.41	−24.13	52.40
Bulgaria	117.20	267.59	438.75	510.24	1023.65	1636.92	1311.63	453.80	209.14	400.41	232.37	253.32	246.70
	15.31	150.38	171.16	71.49	513.41	613.28	−325.30	−857.83	−244.66	191.28	−168.04	20.95	−6.62
Croatia	217.82	408.13	289.40	407.86	752.92	1053.74	1222.53	711.07	267.17	393.40	348.30	215.75	864.26
	−11.42	190.31	−118.73	118.46	345.05	300.82	168.79	−511.46	−443.90	126.23	−45.10	−132.56	648.51
Czech	829.52	205.91	487.12	1139.03	531.82	1010.97	620.41	279.81	584.45	220.01	757.13	345.09	520.93
Republic	278.80	−623.61	281.21	651.91	−607.20	479.15	−390.56	−340.60	304.64	−364.44	537.13	−412.04	175.84
Estonia	208.81	675.95	701.93	2064.80	988.91	1719.35	1365.50	1376.81	1132.46	756.44	1181.94	413.57	385.22
	−178.68	467.14	25.99	1362.87	−1075.89	730.44	−353.86	11.32	−244.35	−376.03	425.51	−768.37	−28.35
Georgia	34.60	73.13	108.82	101.17	264.17	399.06	360.17	153.28	191.49	249.79	220.17	232.43	433.67
	11.16	38.53	35.68	−7.65	163.01	134.89	−38.90	−206.89	38.20	58.31	−29.62	12.25	201.24
Hungary	294.41	210.76	421.63	763.57	676.45	392.57	629.53	198.84	218.96	630.72	1446.95	343.01	757.36
	−91.63	−83.65	210.87	341.94	−87.12	−283.88	236.96	−430.69	20.12	411.76	816.23	−1103.94	414.35
Latvia	90.52	122.17	269.19	317.02	756.61	1070.14	589.53	44.34	181.48	704.18	544.44	448.90	299.19
	45.67	31.65	147.01	47.84	439.59	313.52	−480.60	−545.19	137.14	522.70	−159.74	−95.55	−149.70
Lithuania	211.20	52.97	229.12	307.51	549.62	617.29	610.14	−4.32	256.05	471.06	232.07	158.26	−53.73
	82.31	−158.23	176.16	78.39	242.11	67.67	−7.15	−614.46	260.37	215.01	−238.98	−73.81	−211.99
Poland	104.80	103.57	315.70	213.27	378.85	515.22	318.83	260.41	331.73	412.63	321.77	93.88	324.47
	−40.24	−1.23	212.14	−102.43	165.57	136.38	−196.40	−58.41	71.31	80.90	−90.86	−227.90	230.59

Republic of	20.12	17.68	35.09	45.87	62.36	131.10	173.06	50.86	50.90	70.68	47.87	59.59	49.25
Moldova	−4.59	−2.45	17.41	10.78	16.50	68.74	41.95	−122.19	0.04	19.78	−22.80	11.71	−10.33
Romania	52.20	101.11	298.24	287.39	512.03	463.92	650.46	227.47	149.81	117.49	160.37	181.94	163.42
	−0.47	48.91	197.14	−10.86	224.64	−48.12	186.54	−422.99	−77.66	−32.32	42.88	21.57	−18.52
Russian	23.59	53.64	106.10	100.09	261.21	383.59	530.00	193.90	221.21	257.44	210.68	372.45	203.25
Federation	4.33	30.05	52.47	−6.02	161.12	122.37	146.42	−336.10	27.31	36.23	−46.76	161.77	−169.20
Slovakia	1089.02	552.63	748.29	577.44	1077.09	745.08	902.04	−1.13	327.32	645.18	550.58	−111.47	−61.13
	666.67	−536.38	195.66	−170.85	499.65	−332.02	156.96	−903.16	328.44	317.86	−94.59	−662.05	50.34
Slovenia	789.63	136.39	339.27	281.31	352.16	375.37	600.02	−232.93	51.34	528.12	164.49	−73.22	513.50
	609.31	−653.24	202.88	−57.95	70.85	23.21	224.65	−832.96	284.27	476.78	−363.63	−237.71	586.71
TFYR of	–	55.72	158.78	47.00	211.29	337.57	285.01	97.82	103.05	231.75	69.06	161.57	131.13
Macedonia			103.07	−111.78	164.29	126.29	−52.57	−187.19	5.23	128.70	−162.69	92.51	−30.44
Ukraine	14.47	29.98	36.39	166.85	120.51	213.86	237.09	105.08	142.29	158.47	185.37	99.61	9.11
	−1.92	15.51	6.41	130.46	−46.35	93.35	23.23	−132.01	37.20	16.19	26.90	−85.76	−90.50
Decrease	8	8	2	10	5	4	9	18	6	4	15	12	11

Source: UNCTAD

4.3 Hypothesis Development and the Selection of Variables

4.3.1 *Hypotheses and Economic Shocks as Independent Variables*

As mentioned above, Eastern European economies have been hit by several shocks that have affected FDI inflow since the late 2000s. These include the global financial crisis, which became apparent in September 2008, the Greek crisis in April 2010, and the worldwide stock plunge in late 2014, which was reputed to originate from various factors such as the Ukraine conflict and an emerging market depression concurrent with a plunge in oil prices. However, there may be some differences in the magnitude of the shocks themselves, their impact and timing by areas, and so on, as seen in the previous section.

It is not unusual to assume a difference in the magnitude of the shocks themselves; however, what are the background theories behind the differences in the size of impact and timing in each Eastern European country or area? More concretely, why is the size of the effect expected to differ by areas, as evidenced by drastic changes in EU members and relatively slight changes in non-EU members? It has often been said that the more deeply a country is embedded in the global economy, the larger the benefits but also the shocks from the global economy since the Asian financial crisis.[1] One of the reasons for this difference may be that the backward flow of FDI stock during a crisis is originally smaller in less-embedded countries. Therefore, it is no wonder that damage from an economic shock differs between EU members and other Eastern European countries.

Simultaneously, Eastern European countries are less embedded in the global economy than are Western developed countries, and it may take longer for financial shocks to affect FDI inflow. According to Koga (2009), the path of contagion of the financial crisis as concerns international banking is identified as being of three types. The first is the direct effect of the shock; i.e., the reversal of capital flow between donor countries in crisis and host countries. This type of contagion is thought to happen immediately. The second is the common lender effect, which means that the international banking system is more likely to be infected with a financial crisis: therefore, a country that shares the same lender with a crisis-stricken country is more likely to be affected.[2] The third is the herding effect, in which the crisis spreads through investor sentiment regardless of actual transaction relationships and their volume.[3] It is rational to think that the second and third types of contagion take relatively longer than the first type. Then, EU members in Eastern Europe that are less closely related to the international banking system and the global chain of capital flow than are OECD countries, may be hit by an economic shock after a certain time lag, due to the common lender effect and/or the herding effect rather than the direct effect. At this point, two hypotheses emerge that correspond to these insights from the overview and first remaining task mentioned in the Introduction (Sect. 4.1).

Hypothesis H_1 Shocks have a greater impact in countries that are more embedded in the EU (Eastern European countries admitted to the EU before the series of crises) than in those that are less embedded (those that were not EU members at the beginning of the series of crises).

Hypothesis H_2 FDI inflow may be reduced more drastically by lagged than by contemporaneous shock impacts.

To empirically test the above hypotheses and to investigate the second and third remaining tasks mentioned in the Introduction (Sect. 4.1)—namely, creating shock variables for each crisis and capturing the differences in the magnitude of shocks by year—measuring the shock in question and defining its period is crucial. As mentioned above, measuring shocks has not been well discussed. In previous studies, shock variables take the form of year dummy variables, and, due to problems I pointed out previously, this type of economic shock variable is not adequate for empirical examination. To capture the magnitude of the shocks in each year, this study tries to measure the size of shocks by my own calculations, using the gap between the highest price and the bottom of the stock market index in the period of crisis. In general, the stock market reflects the economy's business climate. In particular, indices of representative stocks, such as the NY Dow Jones Industrial Average, the London FTSE 100 Index, or the Frankfurt DAX, are thought to reflect the state of the global economy; hence, it is worthwhile to try to capture the magnitude of a global economic shock by the change in these stock market prices. Of course, the date of the beginning and ending, and identifying the top and bottom points in the stock market, are important for this method. With respect to these points, I have calculated each shock variable as introduced below.

First, define the crisis period as the time from the date of the "fatal" event for investors until stock prices hit bottom. Sometimes the date of the outbreak of the economic shock is different from its beginning in political history, so I will identify the economic beginning of each shock. With regard to the 2008 financial crisis, the "fatal" event occurred on September 29, 2008. It is a well-known fact that the background of this crisis included the collapse of the housing bubble and the subprime lending system in the United States. The influence of these events appeared in stock market movements in late July 2007, just before BNP Paribas closed its funds on August 9, 2007, gradually pulling down global stock market prices (e.g., the NY Dow Jones dropped 1923.6 points from August 8, 2007, to August 8, 2008, the Frankfurt DAX dropped 1044.28 points, and the London FTSE dropped 904.7 points) despite a temporary recovery in October 2007. Now, this day is generally regarded as the beginning of the credit crisis;[4] however, this crisis had not yet seriously harmed the real economy at that time. More than a year later, a sign of the next and biggest shock occurred, the collapse of Lehman Brothers Holdings Inc. on September 15, 2008. At first, the Dow Jones dropped just over 500 points but soon recovered 480 points. Thus, the influence of this crisis did not seem to be fatal until the Emergency Economic Stabilization Act of 2008 was rejected in the United States House of Representatives on September 29, 2008. On that day, Lehman Brothers Holdings Inc. passed the point of no return, and due to the adverse effects on other companies that had corporate bonds or investment trusts issued by Lehman Brothers and the resultant chain reaction, anxiety spread all over the world, bringing a huge financial shock that deeply harmed the world's real economy. Based on this fact, I have decided that the start date of this global economic shock is September 29, 2008, and the end of the period is March 9, 2009, when stock markets hit bottom and started to rise rapidly.

Second, in regard to the Greek government debt crisis, the start date is April 23, 2010. In general, the origin of the Greek crisis can be sought in late 2009 when George Papandreou's cabinet disclosed that data on government debt levels and deficits had been undercounted by the previous Greek government. At that time, the global stock market reacted only slightly to this revelation; for example, the Dow Jones index dropped temporarily before quickly recovering and continuing to rise. Although the stock market experienced a temporary drop in the latter half of January 2010, it continued its upward trend until Prime Minister George Papandreou formally requested a bailout for Greece by Troika (the EU, European Central Bank (ECB), and International Monetary Fund (IMF)) on April 23, 2010. At about that time, rating firms downgraded Greece's credit rating, and this crisis began to profoundly affect world stock markets. For example, the Dow Jones index fell 1200 points in a month and remained flat for three months. To make matters worse, this crisis brought a second dip in the following year and a third in 2012, although the crisis in the stock market seemed to be over at this time. In the first half of 2011, rating firms intermittently and repeatedly downgraded Greece's credit rating, which led to another plunge in the stock market; two months passed before a return to an uptrend. In 2012, the turmoil was caused by the unfortunate result of the election, in which no party won a majority of parliament seats. Although it is true that the problem of Greek government debt is unique and still unsolved, this crisis paused in the middle of 2012; therefore, I will identify the end date as June 4, 2012.

The third crisis in this study, the worldwide stock plunge of 2014, is slightly different from the previous two shocks in regard to the plurality of causes, as argued in the Introduction (Sect. 4.1). This crisis is thought to have derived from the Ukrainian unrest, falling oil prices, and depression in emerging markets. Considering the causes, this crisis seems to have begun on February 23, 2014; however, the fatal event in the economy occurred in late 2014, when the Dow Jones index dropped more than 1100 points in three weeks. Thus, I identified the dates of the start and end of the crisis as September 19 and October 16, 2014, respectively.

As the periods of the crises have been identified, the next step is to stipulate the rule for identifying the top and bottom of the crises. Using the gap between the bottom of the crisis period and the last peak one can capture the magnitude of the crisis through the period itself but may not capture the yearly decline in magnitude, and we cannot adequately accomplish the third task introduced in the previous section. Hence, in this study, the sizes of financial shocks in certain years during the crisis period are approximated by the gaps between the lowest price of the stock market and the highest price since the date the lowest price of the previous year occurred, or, in the case of the starting year of the crisis, just before the start of the crisis period. For instance, the bottom in 2008 was on November 20, and the last peak before this bottom was on September 26, just before the beginning of the period; the bottom in 2009 was on March 9, and the last peak between November 20, 2008 (the bottom in the previous year) and March 9 was on January 2, 2009.

For calculating, as mentioned before, there are several alternative stock market price indices. I chose the Dow Jones Industrial Average data because this index is the most representative one of the global economy and is also the most exogenous to FDI inflow to Eastern European countries; henceforth, it is used for the empirical analysis in this chapter. Needless to say, these shocks are distinguished to correspond with the second task stated in the Introduction and are named *Financial Crisis 2008*, *Greek Crisis 2010*, and *Stock Plunge 2014*. In addition to those shock variables, interaction terms with EU membership in the 2008 dummy (named *Add. Effect of ... to EU*), and their lagged variables, except for *Stock Plunge 2014*,[5] are introduced to correspond to the three tasks listed above.

4.3.2 Dependent and Control Variables

In addition to the above-mentioned shock variables, the dependent variable and some important control variables should be introduced in regression analyses. As for the dependent variable, data of per capita FDI inflow are best for the empirical analysis in this chapter. Usually, population affects and significantly determines the amount of FDI inflow, and, especially in cross-country cases, the effects of other factors are sometimes missed in regression analysis. In addition, this study will focus on disparities and other differences among these countries after eliminating the effect of population, as mentioned in the previous section. Therefore, to control the effect of population, I used UNCTAD's per capita FDI inflow data.

Moreover, some factors regarded as important in previous studies should be introduced to the regression analysis. With respect to this issue, Suzuki and Suganuma (2007) surveyed research on FDI and showed that some economic and political factors, as well as the endowment of natural resources, tend to have significant effects on FDI inflow. According to their literature review, several notable studies, such as those by Bevan and Estrin (2000) and Resmini (2000), found that the business environment, economic openness and standard of living, and market size are crucial factors for attracting FDI inflow. In addition to these factors, the regression analyses of these studies confirmed the positive effect of the endowment of natural resources on per capita FDI inflow. Consequently, these factors will be taken into consideration in this study.

For the business environment and economic openness index, the Worldwide Governance Indicator's Regulatory Quality Index [World Bank (a)] is used as a comprehensive index of these factors and named *Regulatory Quality*. At the same time, the interaction term between this index and the EU membership dummy is introduced to examine the differences between countries with EU membership (embedded countries) and others (named *Add. Effect of Regulatory Quality in New EU*). These variables may be affected by preceding economic shocks and may also reflect the remaining effect of past crises. Consequently, the effect of a newly occurring crisis may, to a certain degree, be distinguished from the continuing effect of previous crises by using these variables.

Next, due to the nature of dependent variable, the standard of living is supposed to be more important than market size for regression analysis; in this study, two indicators are used as an approximation of the standard of living. The first is the data of the Life Expectancy Rate at Birth provided by World Development Indicators [World Bank (b)]. This index reflects the quality aspect of the standard of living and is named *Standard of Living 1*. The second is the per capita GDP at a 2005 constant price [World Bank (b)]. This index reflects the quantity aspect of the standard of living. Usually, FDI inflow is thought to affect and partly determine the contemporary value of GDP, and perhaps this is true. However, investors cannot refer to the contemporary value of GDP in the process of making investment decisions. They can only refer to the previous value of GDP. Hence, it seems to be adequate to use lagged values of the per capita GDP for independent variables, named *Standard of Living 2*.

Regarding the effect of the natural resource endowment, I have calculated the total value of the proved reserves of oil and gas to quantify the attraction of natural resources for investors. This variable has been calculated based on data from BP (2016). This book of data contains the history of proven reserves of oil and gas as well as their price histories, i.e., the West Texas Intermediate and Henry Hub Natural Gas Spot Prices. Then, I have calculated the product of proved reserves and price (proved reserves multiplied by price) for oil and gas, and totalled them up. This sum of the values of useful fossil fuels, named *Resource Value*, can be considered to approximate the total value of nations' natural resources and, thus, their attraction to FDI inflow. This variable may reflect the depth of the world's depression, so it may be regarded as an indirect effect of an economic shock to resource-rich countries by another route.

Last, for further examination, I have set another shock variable to take into account specific political risks in these countries. In the latter half of 2013, President Viktor Yanukovych postponed signing the Ukraine–European Union Association Agreement, and this caused mass protests by proponents, known collectively as the Euromaidan. Because it was already obvious at that time that the problem was worsening, this was anticipated to affect FDI inflow. However, this shock was not economic or financial; therefore, its magnitude cannot be measured by the stock market price index. Thus, a pre-Ukrainian conflict variable, which captures the signs of political unrest in late 2013, is reluctantly introduced as a dummy variable, and so is the interaction term between this index and the EU membership dummy, named *Euromaidan Riots 2013* and *Add. Effect of Euromaidan Riots 2013 to EU*, respectively. However, the coefficient of this variable is not comparable to the aforementioned shock variables.

Definitions, sources, and statistics of these dependent and independent variables are summarized in Table 4.3.

Table 4.3 Definitions, sources, and summary statistics of variables

Variable name	*Definition*	*Source*	*Total*				
			Mean	*S.D.*	*Med*	*Max*	*Min*
Per Capita FDI	Per Capita FDI inflow to Eastern European countries	UNCTAD	328.641	336.081	229.395	2064.802	−541.902
Regulatory Quality	Business environment, which is expressed as the regulatory quality in the Worldwide Governance Indicators	World Bank (a)	0.348	0.705	0.487	1.675	−1.638
Add. Effects of Regulatory Quality to EU	Additional effects of BusEnv variables on EU member countries (CirMarket times EU membership dummy)	Author's Calculation based on World Bank (a)	0.445	0.511	0	1.674918	−0.072
Standard of Living 1	Life expectancy rate at birth	World Bank (b)	73.390	3.054	73.863	80.520	65.008
Standard of Living 2	Per capita GDP at the 2005 constant price	World Bank (b)	6434.957	4691.342	4882.323	20871.88	557.450
Resource Value	Total value of proved oil and gas (sum of proven reserves times market price)	Author's Calculation based on BP (2016)	38.222	169.406	0.000	1070.604	0.000
Financial Crisis 2008	Magnitude of the economic shock in the financial crisis period (2008.9.29–2009.3.9). Absolute value of the difference between the lowest price of the Dow Jones Industrial Average during the crisis period in each year and the highest price since the date of the lowest price in the previous year	Author's Calculation	467.573	1119.748	0	3590.810	0
Greek Crisis 2010	Magnitude of the economic shock in the Greek government debt crisis period (2010.4.23–2012.6.4). Absolute value of the difference between the lowest price of the Dow Jones Industrial Average during the crisis period in each year and the highest price since the lowest price of the previous year	Author's Calculation	327.976	606.219	0	1578.760	0

EU					Non-EU				
Mean	*S.D.*	*Med*	*Max*	*Min*	*Mean*	*S.D.*	*Med*	*Max*	*Min*
473.790	391.994	377.108	2064.802	−232.932	195.758	198.243	158.619	1222.526	−541.902
0.941	0.291	0.986	1.675	−0.072	−0.187	0.513	−0.183	0.925	−1.638
0.934	0.302	0.982	1.675	−0.072	0	0	0	0	0
74.524	2.325	74.206	80.520	70.866	72.358	3.273	72.990	77.830	65.008
9787.238	4157.197	9662.466	20871.88	2971.035	3387.429	2610.833	2683.882	11712.45	557.450
0.397	1.289	0.000	5.896	0.000	72.609	229.062	0	1070.604	0
467.573	1122.019	0	3590.810	0	467.573	1121.624	0	3590.810	0
327.976	607.448	0	1578.760	0	327.976	607.235	0	1578.760	0

(*continued*)

Table 4.3 (continued)

Variable name	*Definition*	*Source*	*Total*				
			Mean	*S.D.*	*Med*	*Max*	*Min*
Stock Plunge 2014	Magnitude of the economic shock in the emerging market depression period (2014.9.19–10.16). Absolute value of the difference between the lowest price of the Dow Jones Industrial Average during the crisis period in each year and the highest price since the lowest price of the previous year	Author's Calculation	89.423	310.340	0	1162.500	0
Add. Effects of Financial Crisis 2008 to EU	Additional effects of the Fncrisis variable on EU member countries (Fncrisis times EU membership dummy)	Author's Calculation	222.654	807.340	0	3590.810	0
Add. Effects of Greek Crisis 2010 to EU	Additional effects of the Grecrisis variable on EU member countries (Grecrisis times EU membership dummy)	Author's Calculation	156.179	449.367	0	1578.760	0
Add. Effects of Stock Plunge 2014 to EU	Additional effects of the Emshock variable on EU member countries (Emshock times EU membership dummy)	Author's Calculation	42.582	218.779	0	1162.500	0
Euromaidan Riots 2013	Effect of political unrest in the pre-Ukrainian conflict period (dummy variable)	Author's Calculation	0.077	0.267	0	1	0
Add. Effects of Euromaidan Riots 2013 to EU	Additional effects of the Preukrwar variable on EU member countries (Preukrwar times EU membership dummy)	Author's Calculation	0.037	0.188	0	1	0

EU					*Non-EU*				
Mean	*S.D.*	*Med*	*Max*	*Min*	*Mean*	*S.D.*	*Med*	*Max*	*Min*
89.423	310.969	0	1162.500	0	89.423	310.860	0	1162.500	0
467.573	1122.019	0	3590.810	0	0	0	0	0	0
327.976	607.448	0	1578.760	0	0	0	0	0	0
89.423	310.969	0	1162.500	0	0	0	0	0	0
0.077	0.268	0	1	0	0.077	0.267	0	1	0
0.077	0.268	0	1	0	0	0	0	0	0

4.4 Empirical Results

In this section, I will analyse the trend and its causes, focusing on economic shocks, based on data introduced in the previous section.

Figure 4.1 shows historical data of the per capita FDI inflow to countries without EU membership at the beginning of the series of crises[6] and to countries who were participating in the EU by 2008.[7] Panel (a) of this figure illustrates changes in the population-weighted average of countries' per capita FDI,[8] and Panel (b) shows the simple average of countries' per capita FDI.

At first glance, it seems obvious that new EU member states enjoyed privileges of membership, namely, higher standards of living and increased per capita FDI inflow before the crisis period. However, things suddenly changed after the collapse of Lehman Brothers Holdings Inc., the fourth-largest investment bank in the United States at that time. Countries with EU membership were hit harder by the shock and experienced sharp declines in FDI inflow. The largest decline from the global financial crisis among these countries occurred in 2009, the year after its beginning. Conversely, countries without EU membership felt less of a shock. Although they experienced a decline in FDI inflow in the year following the start of the crisis, the damage was far smaller than in Eastern European countries with EU membership. This outlook seems to be consistent with the hypotheses in this study.

Afterwards, FDI inflow to these new EU members recovered until 2012, despite the Greek government debt crisis, and fell again in 2013, in contradistinction to the slight change in non-EU member countries. This decrease may have been caused partly by the premonition of political conflict in Ukraine. This is not a financial shock, but it may have affected European countries. In addition, the changes in FDI inflow among them varied by country with respect to the speed and direction (plus or minus), regardless of EU membership. This may be the result of the worldwide stock plunge.

Keeping this trend in mind, I have conducted three types of regression analyses to confirm the robustness of the coefficient. The first is a traditional method for panel data, namely, fixed- or random-effects estimation (or pooling estimation), which is selected by statistical tests. The next model is multi-level regression, i.e., a regression model in which random effects are introduced to coefficients. This time, random effects are introduced to all coefficients, except for interaction terms, to examine whether differences in the impact on FDI inflow between EU participants and others

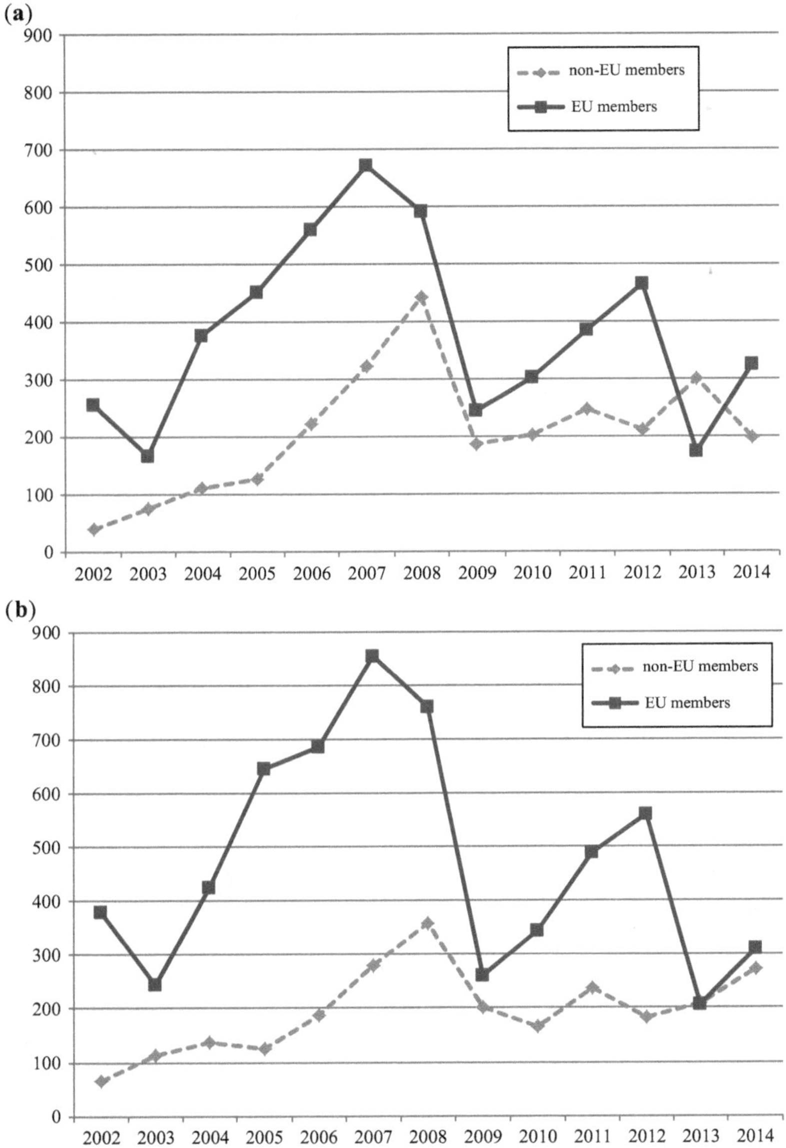

Fig. 4.1 Comparison of per capita FDI inflow between EU and non-EU members, 2002–2014. (**a**) Population-weighted average. (**b**) Simple average
Source: Authors' illustrations based on UNCTAD

in Eastern Europe are significant even if random differences in countries are assumed in the impact of the original variables. The third is the dynamic panel model. The matter of intertemporal choice for resource allocation may concern the theory of the impact of investors' decision-making on FDI, especially during a crisis, so may have to be taken into account. Thus, I employed Blundell-Bond's dynamic panel GMM estimation.

Before considering the regression analyses in detail, the problem of unit roots should be examined. As to this point, I have carried out two representative tests of the non-stationary process—the Levin-Lin-Chu test and the Im-Pesaran-Shin test. According to these tests, the null hypothesis that the data of the per capita FDI inflow to Eastern European countries is a unit root process is rejected at a 1% significance level by both statistical tests. Therefore, these regression models are proven to be adoptable for data in this study.

Estimation results following the above methodology are reported in Table 4.4. Statistical tests for model specification (the Breusch–Pagan test for random-effects vs. pooled OLS, the F-test for fixed-effects vs. pooled OLS, and the Hausman test for fixed-effects vs. random-effects) chose the random-effects model for *Standard of Living 1* (the life expectancy rate at birth) and chose the fixed-effects model for *Standard of Living 2* (the lagged value of the per capita GDP). In addition, I have used the remaining model with each standard of living variable, and, thus, have estimated a total of six equations.

As shown in Table 4.4, the results are roughly consistent with the hypotheses proposed in the previous section. The contemporaneous impact of the 2008 financial crisis did not indicate negative or significant signs in any equation, and neither did the additional shock term to embedded countries. Therefore, it can be said that the global financial crisis did not have an immediate negative impact on these countries, regardless of their EU membership status. However, the situation changes when we focus on the lagged impact of the 2008 financial shock. In fact, the concerned shock variable and its additional terms to EU members indicated negative and significant signs in all equations. The impact of the global financial shock of 2008 turned out to be serious, especially in embedded countries, as supposed in my hypotheses. In all equations, the absolute value of the coefficient of the lagged additional shock to EU members from the global financial shock exceeded the lagged shock itself. Therefore, it can be said that countries embedded in the global economy received at least twice as much damage as that of less embedded countries. In summary,

Table 4.4 Estimation results on the impact of economic shocks on per capita FDI inflow[ab]

Model	*[1]*	*[2]*	*[3]*	*[4]*	*[5]*	*[6]*
Estimator	*Random effects*	*Multi-level*[c]	*Blundell-Bond GMM*	*Fixed effects*	*Multi-level*[c]	*Blundell-Bond GMM*
Financial Crisis 2008	0.043***	0.042***	0.010	0.028*	0.039**	0.010
	(0.015)	(0.015)	(0.022)	(0.014)	(0.016)	(0.020)
Greek Crisis 2010	0.024	0.025	−0.015	0.010	0.026	−0.007
	(0.019)	(0.017)	(0.046)	(0.018)	(0.017)	(0.034)
Euromaidan Riots 2013	13.600	15.864	−74.811	−16.763	15.842	−50.501
	(50.484)	(43.937)	(120.750)	(47.497)	(41.728)	(79.539)
Stock Plunge 2014	0.024	0.030	−0.137	−0.027	0.020	−0.104
	(0.054)	(0.048)	(0.165)	(0.061)	(0.044)	(0.109)
Add. Effects of Financial Crisis 2008 to EU	0.006	0.007	0.006	−0.025	−0.011	0.004
	(0.025)	(0.027)	(0.026)	(0.033)	(0.030)	(0.030)
Add. Effects of Greek Crisis 2010 to EU	0.009	0.014	0.039	−0.006	0.001	0.032
	(0.039)	(0.037)	(0.083)	(0.035)	(0.037)	(0.083)
Add. Effects of Euromaidan Riots 2013 to EU	−316.026***	−312.642***	−291.436**	−376.844***	−349.762***	−290.554**
	(95.160)	(95.940)	(131.994)	(100.352)	(103.199)	(131.654)
Add. Effects of Stock Plunge 2014 to EU	−0.279**	−0.280**	−0.108	−0.360**	−0.323***	−0.109
	(0.127)	(0.121)	(0.158)	(0.144)	(0.123)	(0.171)
Financial Crisis 2008 (1)	−0.033***	−0.033***	−0.064***	−0.043***	−0.038***	−0.066***
	(0.011)	(0.010)	(0.019)	(0.014)	(0.010)	(0.017)
Greek Crisis 2010 (1)	−0.035	−0.034*	−0.105*	−0.056*	−0.040**	−0.096**
	(0.024)	(0.021)	(0.058)	(0.028)	(0.018)	(0.040)
Add. Effects of Financial Crisis 2008 to EU (1)	−0.089***	−0.089***	−0.067**	−0.099***	−0.091***	−0.062**
	(0.029)	(0.029)	(0.028)	(0.030)	(0.029)	(0.031)
Add. Effects of Greek Crisis 2010 to EU (1)	−0.034	−0.034	−0.009	−0.075	−0.052	−0.002
	(0.072)	(0.068)	(0.085)	(0.071)	(0.065)	(0.088)

(continued)

Table 4.4 (continued)

Model	*[1]*	*[2]*	*[3]*	*[4]*	*[5]*	*[6]*
Estimator	*Random effects*	*Multi-level*[c]	*Blundell-Bond GMM*	*Fixed effects*	*Multi-level*[c]	*Blundell-Bond GMM*
Regulatory Quality	114.768**	59.473	180.375	110.868**	89.054**	223.547
	(47.328)	(39.698)	(138.889)	(51.884)	(40.298)	(167.480)
Add. Effects of Regulatory Quality to EU	205.023*	277.874***	−30.274	−249.508	−19.424	−173.857
	(121.280)	(100.631)	(290.883)	(359.860)	(163.938)	(334.166)
Standard of Living 1	16.875	15.366**	36.083			
	(11.335)	(6.033)	(46.231)			
Standard of Living 2				0.098*	0.053***	0.028
				(0.050)	(0.021)	(0.023)
Resource Value	0.206***	0.213***	0.200	0.136	−0.024	0.197
	(0.053)	(0.036)	(0.283)	(0.128)	(0.088)	(0.316)
Lagged Dependent Variable			0.243**			0.225**
			(0.110)			(0.106)
Constant	−1007.197	−941.161**	−2339.244	−139.915	52.121	173.046**
	(794.867)	(429.137)	(3275.653)	(286.064)	(48.728)	(82.895)
N	271	271	251	271	271	251
R^2	0.534			0.576		
Adjusted R^2	0.504			0.511		
Akaike's Information Criterion (AIC)		3787.766			3777.668	
Bayesian Information Criterion (BIC)		3849.002			3838.904	
Hausman test (χ^2)	6.17			16.71**		

Notes:

[a]For more details on definitions and descriptive statistics of the variables used for estimation, see Table 4.3. ***, **, and * denote statistical significance at the 1%, 5%, and 10% levels, respectively

[b]Robust standard errors computed using the Huber-White sandwich estimator are reported in parentheses beneath regression coefficients

[c]Random effect is introduced to all coefficients except for additional effect variables

Source: Author's estimation

with respect to the 2008 financial crisis, my hypotheses seem to be supported statistically.

On the other hand, examination of the impact of the Greek government debt crisis brought different results from those of the 2008 crisis and were partly inconsistent with my hypotheses. In terms of the contemporaneous impact of this crisis, coefficients of the contemporaneous impact itself and additional impacts on EU members are not significant in any equation. Therefore, it can be said that the Greek shock did not have a negative impact immediately, as with the 2008 crisis. Regarding the lagged impact of this crisis, however, the results partly support my hypotheses. Actually, the lagged Greek shock variable indicated a negative and significant effect on FDI inflow in five of six equations; however, its additional term for EU members did not indicate a negative and significant sign in all equations. These results suggest a lagged impact on FDI inflow from the Greek economic shock, regardless of EU membership status, and there is no difference between them. In the case of the Greek crisis, my hypothesis H_1 is not supported, and hypothesis H_2 is partly supported.

In respect to the worldwide stock plunge in 2014, the coefficient of the contemporary impact of this shock did not indicate a significant sign; however, the additional shock to embedded countries indicated negative and significant signs in four of the six equations, and negative but insignificant signs in the dynamic panel GMM models. Hence, it can be said that hypothesis H_1 is supported on the whole. However, there is some difference between this economic shock and the former two crises. In the previous two crises, differences in the shock impact between embedded countries and others appeared in the lagged impact, and, contrary to this third shock, a contemporaneous shock did not affect either. It may be the case that investors, convinced of future crisis around the Ukrainian conflict or earlier, decided not to invest. This may mean that a worldwide stock plunge and its effect on these EU members were easier to forecast than previous shocks have been. Furthermore, the absolute value of totalled coefficients of this contemporary shock and its additional shock to EU members tended to be larger than those of lagged impact and additional lagged impact in the case of the two previous crises. Thus, it can be said that the magnitude of this shock may be smaller than the two previous shocks; however, the conductivity of this shock is higher than that in the preceding two cases. Unfortunately, hypothesis H_2 cannot be examined, due to data limitations (from 2002 to 2014).

In addition to these main shock variables, another shock variable, named *Euromaidan Riots 2013*, was examined in this study. This reflects the political risks in Ukraine and its negative effects on nearby countries in 2013, as explained before. As for this dummy variable, the results are similar to the case of the worldwide stock plunge in 2014; the contemporary impact of this shock is not significant, but the additional shock to embedded countries is negative and significant in all equations. Hence, in this case, hypothesis H_1 from this study is supported, in spite of the different nature of this shock, i.e., it is not an economic or financial but a political shock.

To summarize, the hypotheses in this study are fully supported in the case of the 2008 financial crisis and partly supported in the cases of the other crises.

Turning our attention to estimates of the control variables, the possibility that the business environment and openness, and its additional effect on embedded countries' standards of living and endowments of natural resources, affect FDI inflow is indicated to a greater or lesser extent as well as in previous studies. As for the business environment and economic openness, coefficients of the main and additional impacts on FDI tend to indicate positive and significant signs, except for the dynamic panel GMM model. It may be the case that the lagged value of the dependent variable reflects or contains the effect of the business environment and economic openness and correlates more strongly than these variables; thus, this business environment variable in a broad sense did not prove any significance. Assuming this, the business environment positively affected FDI, especially in embedded countries. These countries are more embedded in the global economy and, consequently, received more attention from investors than did other transition countries. On the other hand, investors might be somewhat suspicious of the certainty of the economies of these Eastern European countries with EU membership. Therefore, investors may be sensitive to the business environment, especially in these countries.

Similar to the business environment and economic openness index, coefficients of these standard of living variables on FDI tend to indicate positive and significant signs, except for the dynamic panel GMM model. Again, it may be the case that the lagged value of the dependent variable reflects or contains the effect of the standard of living and absorbs the effect of this independent variable. In general, however, it can be said that the effect of the standard of living on FDI inflow is roughly indicated, as it has been in preceding research in this study field.

The effect of the natural resources endowment indicated relatively weaker significance and robustness than did the effect of other variables, even when compared to the aforementioned independent variables other than shock variables. Regarding the coefficient of this variable, positive and significant signs are detected in only two of six equations. Thus, the endowment of natural resources should be assessed as less strongly determinant in this study.

4.5 Concluding Remarks

In this chapter, by empirical tests, I examined differences in the impact and timing of economic shocks between countries deeply embedded in the global market and those less embedded. I have pointed out remaining tasks for further study on the impact of economic crisis on FDI inflow and have created two hypotheses to correspond to these tasks, based on the trend of (per capita) FDI inflow to Eastern European countries, including the Caucasus area. The first hypothesis is that *shocks have a greater impact in countries that are more embedded in the EU than in those that are less embedded*, and the second one is that *FDI inflow may be reduced more by lagged than by contemporaneous shock impacts.*

As a result of empirical analysis using variables and methods discussed in Sect. 4.3, I have confirmed that global economic shocks in recent years have tended to affect FDI inflow with a time lag and are larger in embedded countries than in others. In other words, the more deeply a country is embedded in the global economy, the greater (the benefit and) the lagged shock from the global economy will be. The empirical results also suggest that the business environment and economic openness as well as the standard of living are important factors in attracting FDI, as shown in previous studies.

These results suggest not only the merits of economic liberalization and promotion of the market economy but also the risks of integration with the global economy. I do not mean to protest policies for globalization. Basically, I support the idea that the liberalization of investment and the provision of a sound business environment should be top priorities so that countries may benefit more from the global economy. Rather, I insist that the national economy should also be cautious regarding the side effects, the larger impact of economic shocks on FDI inflow.

In general, in a market economy system, preventing capital flight is often in contradiction with the system itself and sometimes turns out to be a sensitive problem. However, there are some countermeasures or advance preparations that countries can take against this problem, for example, additional multilateral currency swap arrangements, such as the Chiang Mai Initiative among Asian countries. Sometimes, a crisis causes a sharp decline in FDI inflow, and this leads to rapid currency depreciation; therefore, FDI further declines or capital flight happens. To prevent a cycle of these unfortunate events, reinforcement of the IMF, World Bank, ECB, and others should become a matter of course. Additionally, and just in case, the establishment of an extra framework/arrangement may be required, as long as it is worth the cost. This is merely one possibility, and I hope that government authorities will regard the risk of side effects and do their absolute best to avoid the next crisis.

Acknowledgments I gratefully acknowledge financial support from the Joint Usage and Research Center, the Institute of Economic Research, Hitotsubashi University. I thank Mario Holzner, Gabor Hunya, Ichiro Iwasaki, Andrea Szalavetz, and the other participants in the Vienna Project Workshop for their valuable comments and suggestions. In addition, I also thank Tammy Bicket for her editorial assistance. Needless to say, any remaining errors are my sole responsibility.

Notes

1. For example, see Schmukler et al. (2006).
2. For more detail, see Peek and Rosengren (1997, 2000).
3. See Chiang et al. (2007).
4. For example, see Edmonds (2010).
5. The data period ends in 2014, the year of a worldwide stock plunge. I excluded data on 2015 due to problems with the reliability of estimates; newly estimated FDI data often change significantly in the following year.
6. Albania, Armenia, Azerbaijan, Belarus, Georgia, the Republic of Moldova, the Russian Federation, TFYR of Macedonia, Ukraine, Bosnia and Herzegovina, and Croatia.
7. Bulgaria, the Czech Republic, Estonia, Hungary, Latvia, Lithuania, Poland, Romania, Slovakia, and Slovenia.
8. The amount of FDI inflow to a country group/total population of the country group.

References

Arabi, U. (2010). Implications of global financial and economic crisis on FDI flows: The Indian perspective. *Indian Journal of Economics and Business, 9*, 731–750.

Bevan, A., & Estrin, S. (2000). *The determinants of foreign direct investment in transition economies* (Discussion Papers No.2638). London: Centre for Economic Policy Research.

BP. (2016). *BP Statistical Review of World Energy June 2016*. London: BP p.l.c.

Chiang, T. C., Bang, N. J., & Huimin, L. (2007). Dynamic correlation analysis of financial contagion: Evidence from Asian markets. *Journal of International Money and Finance, 26*, 1206–1228.

Edmonds, T. (2010). *Financial crisis timeline* (Commons Briefing Paper No. SN04991). London: House of Commons.

Koga, M. (2009). *The worldwide spread of financial crisis and global activity of banks: Implications from existing studies* (Bank of Japan Review No. 2009-J-15). Tokyo: Bank of Japan. (in Japanese).

Ledyaeva, S. (2009). Spatial econometric analysis of foreign direct investment determinants in Russian regions. *The World Economy, 32*, 643–666.

Peek, J., & Rosengren, E. (1997). The international transmission of financial shocks: The case of Japan. *American Economic Review, 87*, 495–505.

Peek, J., & Rosengren, E. (2000). Collateral damage: Effects of the Japanese bank crisis on real activity in the United States. *American Economic Review, 90*, 30–45.

Resmini, L. (2000). The determinants of foreign direct investment in the CEECs: New evidence from sectoral patterns. *Economics of Transition, 8*, 665–689.

Schmukler, S., Halac, M., & Zoido-Lobaton, P. (2006). Financial globalization, crises, and contagion. In A. Morales Zumaquero (Ed.), *International macroeconomics: Recent developments* (pp. 207–225). Hauppauge: Nova Science Publishers.

Stoddard, O., & Noy, I. (2015). Fire-sale FDI? The impact of financial crises on foreign direct investment. *Review of Development Economics, 19*, 387–399.

Suzuki, T., & Suganuma, K. (2007). FDI to the transition countries and the role of the state. *Hitotsubashi Economics, 2*, 73–100. (in Japanese).

Ucal, M., Ozcan, K. M., Bilgin, M. H., & Mungo, J. (2010). Relationship between financial crisis and foreign direct investment in developing countries using semiparametric regression approach. *Journal of Business Economics and Management, 11*, 20–33.

UNCTAD. UNCTAD data center. Available at: http://unctadstat.unctad.org/wds/ReportFolders/ reportFolders.aspx

World Bank (a). Worldwide Governance Indicator. Available at: http://data.worldbank.org/data-catalog/worldwide-governance-indicators

World Bank (b). World Development Indicator. Available at: http://data.worldbank.org/data-catalog/world-development-indicators

PART II

The Czech Republic

CHAPTER 5

Employment in the Czech Republic: Trends During Economic Transition and the Global Recession

Daniel Münich and Klára Svitáková

5.1 Introduction

During the past quarter of a century, the Czech Republic has experienced three notable economic phenomena: economic transition, EU market entry, and Global Recession. A process of economic transition was launched in 1991, when the country was still part of federal Czechoslovakia, with the intention of turning the then centrally planned and almost fully nationalized economy—with centrally set salaries and administratively fixed prices for all goods and services—back into a functional market economy. The transition involved price liberalization, the removal of foreign trade barriers, and the loosening of the very rigid labour market and other business regulations. Several waves of privatization, involving everything from small shops to large companies, enabled a protracted transition into a European type of market economy integrated into the global markets, with a sizeable share of non-state and private economic sectors.[1]

In 1998, half way through that economic transition, internal financial and economic imbalances that were being fostered by political fragility and

D. Münich (✉) • K. Svitáková
CERGE-EI, Prague, Czech Republic

P. Havlik, I. Iwasaki (eds.), *Economics of European Crises and Emerging Markets*, DOI 10.1007/978-981-10-5233-0_5

business climate uncertainty became apparent, which gave rise to a domestic economic crisis. After a temporary economic downturn during which the most troublesome state-run banks were sold to Western banks, the Czech Republic began to restructure its institutions to fulfil the requirements for joining the European Union (EU). During the first few years of the new millennium, the country underwent further adaptation on several fronts. The EU required it to adopt modern institutions, laws and processes, and once this was complete the country entered the EU in 2004.[2] During the years that followed, on a wave of post-entry optimism, the country enjoyed an economic boom driven by flourishing international trade, and a sizeable influx of foreign direct investment (FDI). That economic boom translated into an overheated labour market, as we will see in greater detail later in this chapter. The good times came to an end with the worldwide economic crisis which began to affect the Czech economy in late 2008—its adverse impacts lasted until early 2014.

Figure 5.1 depicts the aforementioned long-term trends in the Czech economy's performance.[3] The long-term perspective enables us to benchmark the consequences of the recent Global Recession. During most of the

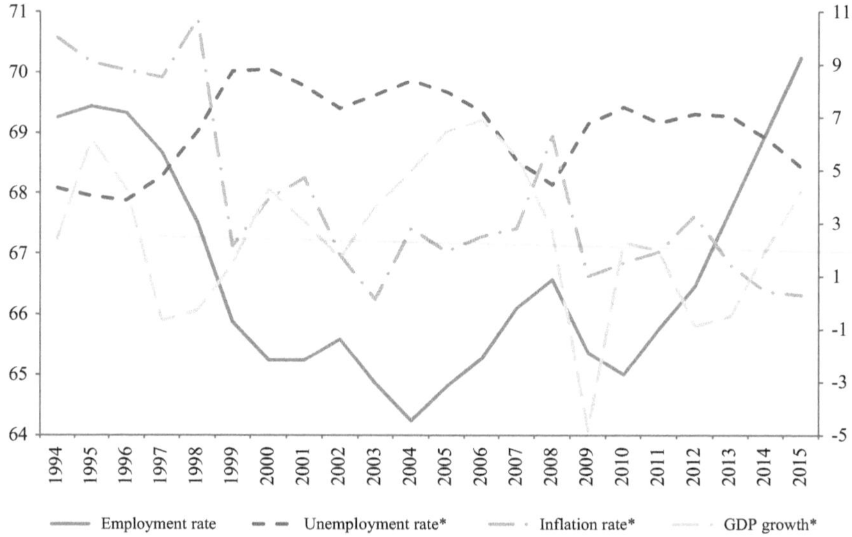

Fig. 5.1 Macroeconomic trends in the Czech Republic, 1994–2015
Note: Starred variables (*) are on the right axis Source: Authors' own computations using the Czech Labour Force Survey data and data from the Czech Statistical Office

time-span covered, the Czech Republic's economic performance, measured by GDP, followed EU-wide economic developments. The high degree of synchronicity between the Czech Republic and the EU stems from the important role international trade in manufacturing goods plays, in particular trade with its large, neighbouring German economy. The two economic booms at the beginning of the new millennium document this synchronicity with the EU's economic performance. The later of these two booms peaked during 2007–2008, and was followed by a swiftly emerging, deep and protracted economic crisis starting in late 2008, a temporary revival of economic growth in 2011, and a secondary recessionary downturn thereafter. Only once, in the second half of the 1990s, did the Czech economy experience a unilateral recession resulting primarily from internal structural economic imbalances, and political and policy decisions.

During the period examined, the employment rate in the Czech Republic followed a U-shaped trajectory. However, the difference between its overall minimum (64%) and maximum (70%) is rather small. On top of this there were employment rate fluctuations, related to the business cycle, which typically lagged 1–2 years behind GDP growth. Throughout the whole period the incidence of unemployment remained below 10%, quite low compared to most other EU countries. This was the case even during the recession in the late 1990s and during the most recent worldwide crisis (which we hereafter refer to simply as the 'crisis'). It should also be noted that the drop in GDP growth brought about by the economic crisis was substantial, reaching almost −5% in 2009, compared to +5% growth in 2007. However, the corresponding drop in the employment rate was relatively small and was exaggerated by its initially high levels in 2007–2008 when the labour market exhibited signs of overheating. The unemployment rate rose quickly during the crisis but did not reach the previous record level, which had been achieved in relatively good times during the first year of the new millennium.

While the Czech Republic's longer-term trends in general economic performance have already been the subject of detailed scrutiny by numerous studies,[4] much less is known about the long-term trends and impacts of these phenomena on employment, and in particular the structure of employment.[5] That is what this chapter sets out to investigate, noting that labour supply and its human capital content, together with physical capital accumulation, technological progress, and the quality of institutions and public governance, represents a key factor in economic performance and growth.

Unlike existing studies on the Czech Republic, we focus on working hours as a finer measure of labour supply, and on the contributions of typical demographic groups to the overall supply of hours worked. We pay special attention to the impact of the most recent crisis in the late 2000s and explore to what extent that crisis had a lasting impact on employment and its structure. Contrary to most other studies, we distinguish between shifts in employment caused by two different effects: (1) changes in labour market participation (the extensive margin); and (2) changes in work intensity (the intensive margin), i.e. the hours worked by those who work. This distinction is important if we are to capture the distribution of labour demand shocks among the working-age population and to account for possible changes in the demographic structure.

In the following section, we describe the Czech Labour Force Survey data used in our analysis, provided by the Czech Statistical Office (CSO). We proceed by investigating employment trends at the level of key demographic groups, distinguishing trends on the extensive and intensive margin. Doing so, we pay special attention to the comparison of the situation before, during and after the last economic crisis. In the concluding section, we summarize our key findings in the framework of broader socioeconomic developments and raise questions for further research.

5.2 Data

Since our analysis goes far beyond stylized aggregate statistical descriptors, we compute our indicators using original, individual level data from the Czech Labour Force Survey (LFS), collected by the CSO, which cover the period 1994–2015. The Czech LFS is a standard, representative, quarterly rotating panel of households consisting of about 50,000 respondents each quarter. In our analysis we deal only with the subpopulation of individuals aged 15–64, i.e., those who are likely to interact with the labour market. To obtain statistics representative at the country level we used corresponding population weights supplied by the CSO.

All LFS respondents aged 15–64 are classified as being either employed, unemployed or out of the labour force. The employment and unemployment rates we present are constructed based on this information. All employed individuals report positive *weekly hours usually worked* and most of them report positive *hours actually worked* in their main job during the reference week. The aggregate weekly hours *usually* worked are consistently greater than aggregate weekly hours *actually* worked in each period.

Following Blundell et al. (2013), we use the hours actually worked.[6] For individuals with multiple jobs, hours actually worked in a second job during the reference week are also reported. The sum of the weekly hours actually worked in the main job and the weekly hours actually worked in the second job across all employed respondents, multiplied by 52 weeks, gives us the total hours worked per year. Dividing by the corresponding population size gives us the mean number of hours worked annually per individual, while dividing by the number of employed people gives us the mean hours worked annually per worker; these are our two main variables of interest.

During 1994–1997 the LFS data was collected based on seasonal[7] rather than calendar quarter periodicity.[8] For these early years, the data points for the calendar quarters were constructed artificially by joining LFS samples from two consecutive seasons using weights created appropriately to match the calendar quarters. As our resulting time-series are deseasonalized,[9] this data limitation of the LFS data series has a negligible impact on the resulting patterns.

5.3 Empirical Analysis

5.3.1 Trends in Aggregate Employment

We begin our exposition of employment trends in the Czech Republic by reviewing its most aggregated indicators shown in Fig. 5.2. To provide easier insight, all variables are measured relative to their levels in 1994 (100%). Note that the unemployment rate is on the right-hand axis. The working-age population 15–64 years of age grew steadily until about 2010, before beginning to decline. At its peak, that population was 7.5% larger than its 1994 level. These relatively sizeable changes in the population were primarily driven by its diverse age structure. In particular, relatively large cohorts born during the baby booms of the communist regime in the 1960–1970s dominated the working-age pool during the 1990s. The economic transition and associated societal changes that followed the Velvet Revolution in 1989 were accompanied by a huge decline in fertility. Many young women postponed maternity and the average number of children per woman also fell, mainly due to the growing opportunity costs of raising children. As a result, the number of children born dropped by 30% between 1990 and 1996. This huge drop in fertility undoubtedly contributed to the decline in the working-age population that started 20 years later, as seen in Fig. 5.2.

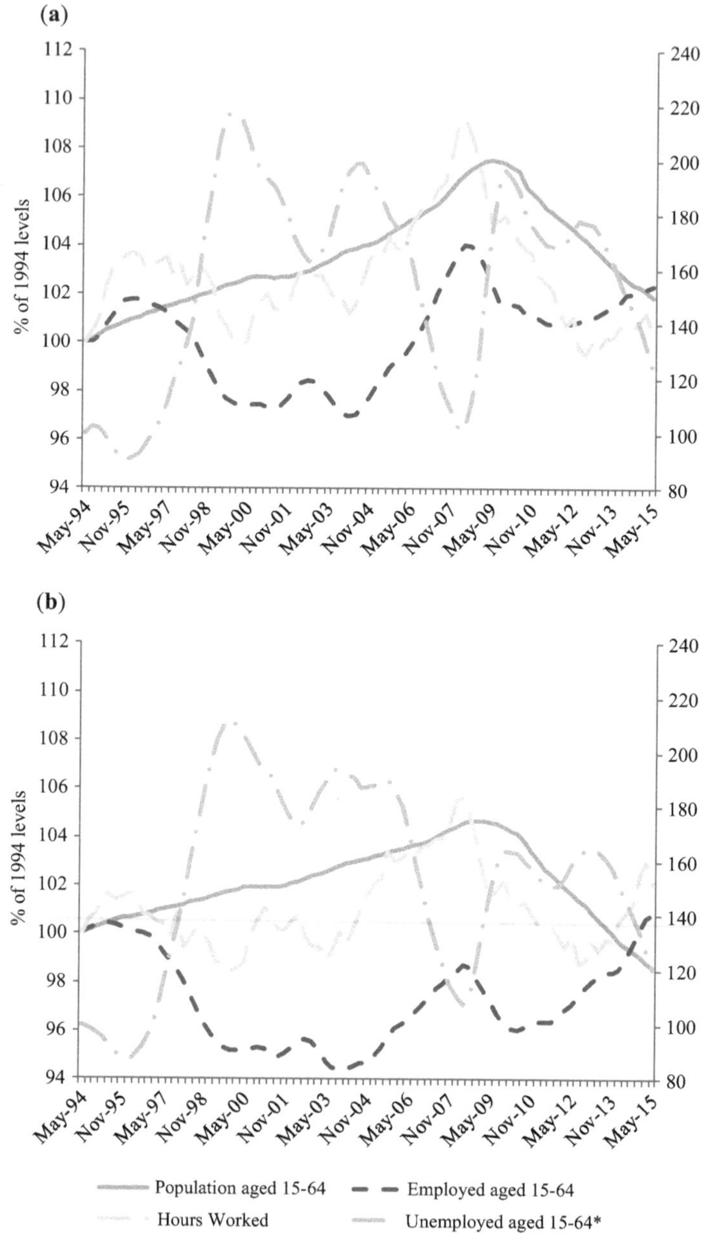

Fig. 5.2 Labour market trends in the Czech Republic, 1994–2015. (**a**) Men (**b**) Women
Note: Starred variables (*) are on the right-hand axis
Source: Authors' own computations using the Czech Labour Force Survey data

Throughout the whole period international migration levels were relatively low; the Czech Republic maintains one of the lowest shares of foreigners. The average net annual migration inflow during 2000–2015 was just 20,000 individuals per year, representing 0.2% of the whole population. The working-age population peak in 2010 was partly driven by a temporary immigration wave from Ukraine attracted by overheated labour demand during the pre-crisis years 2007–2008, when the net immigration flow reached an historical record of 80,000 individuals per year.

Despite these changes in the size of the working-age population during a relatively short historical period, the total number of hours worked per annum by the population of men and women 15–64 years of age remained rather stable. The swift adverse impact of the economic crisis, and the boom that preceded it, are both notable. The primary driving force behind the fluctuations in total hours worked were changes in employment (the extensive margin) which can be inferred from the substantial degree of correlation between employment changes and changes in total hours worked. However, some discrepancies in these patterns indicate that changes to the mean hours worked by working individuals (the intensive margin) also played a role. The recent post-crisis years have seen growth both in overall employment levels and in total hours worked, despite a declining population size. Although the trends for men and women show similar patterns, the women's trends exhibit less volatility. In addition, the world economic crisis affected women less, and in 2015 women supplied relatively more hours of work than men, using the year 1994 as an overall benchmark.

Figures 5.3, 5.4, and 5.5 depict long-term trends in the mean annual hours worked by the population of 15–64 year olds, the employment rate (extensive margin), and the mean annual hours worked per worker (intensive margin), separately for men and women, respectively. We begin by describing the aggregate trends before turning to age specific patterns.

As shown in Fig. 5.3, for men there was a mild downward long-term trend in the total hours worked per person, accompanied by relatively small business cycle fluctuations (the solid line). The long-term pattern for women is effectively trendless, and the effects of the business cycle, including the most recent economic crisis, are quite small. Behind these rather stable mean hours worked lie more salient trends in employment rates,[10] i.e. the extensive margin, as shown in Fig. 5.4, and in the mean hours worked per worker, i.e. the intensive margin, as shown in Fig. 5.5.

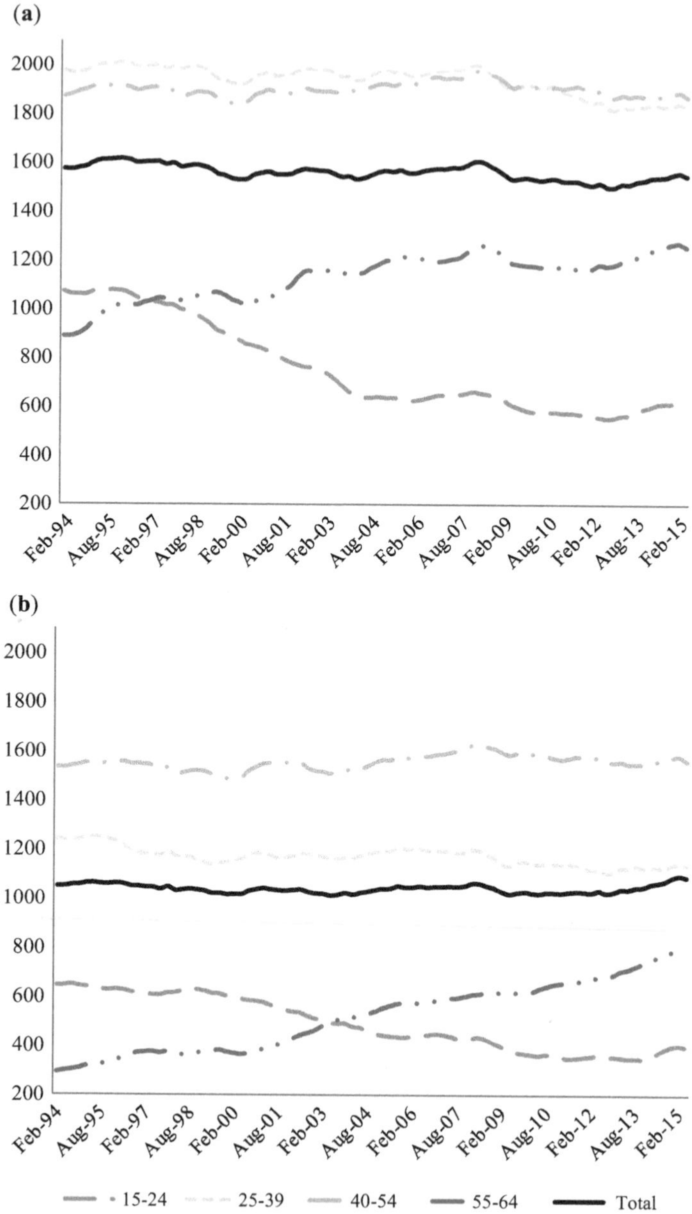

Fig. 5.3 Mean annual hours of work per individual, by gender and age. (**a**) Men (**b**) Women

Source: Authors' own computations using the Czech Labour Force Survey data

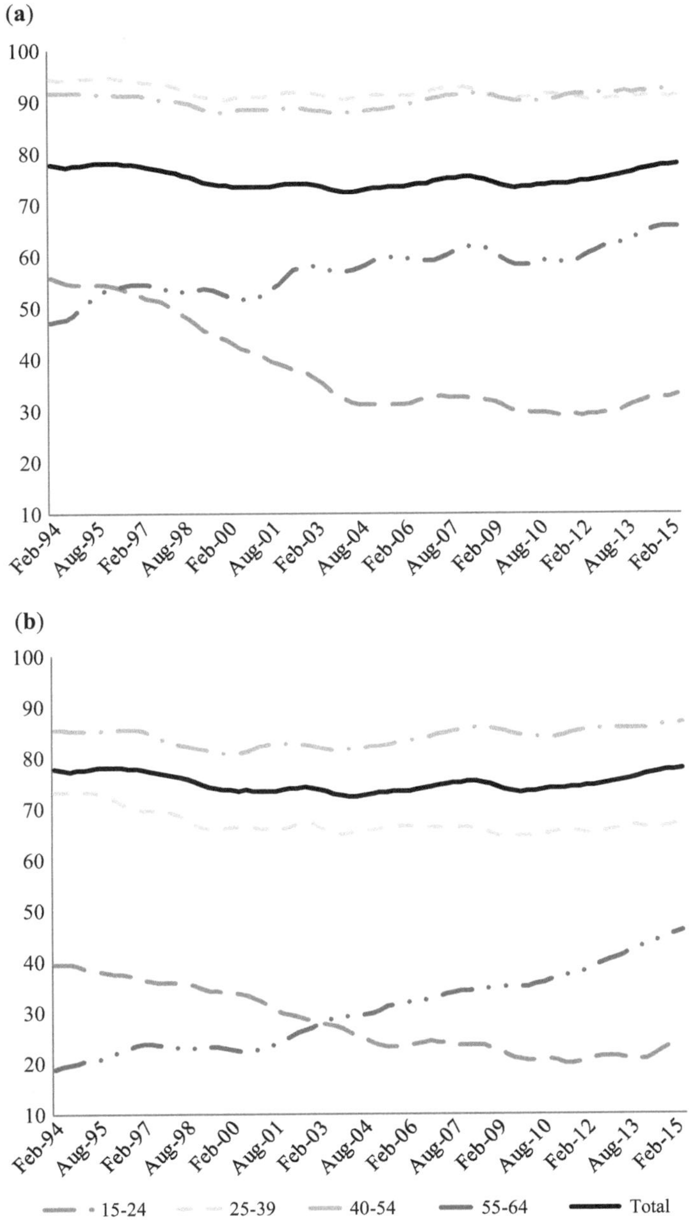

Fig. 5.4 Employment rate, by gender and age. (**a**) Men (**b**) Women
Source: Authors' own computations using Czech Labour Force Survey data

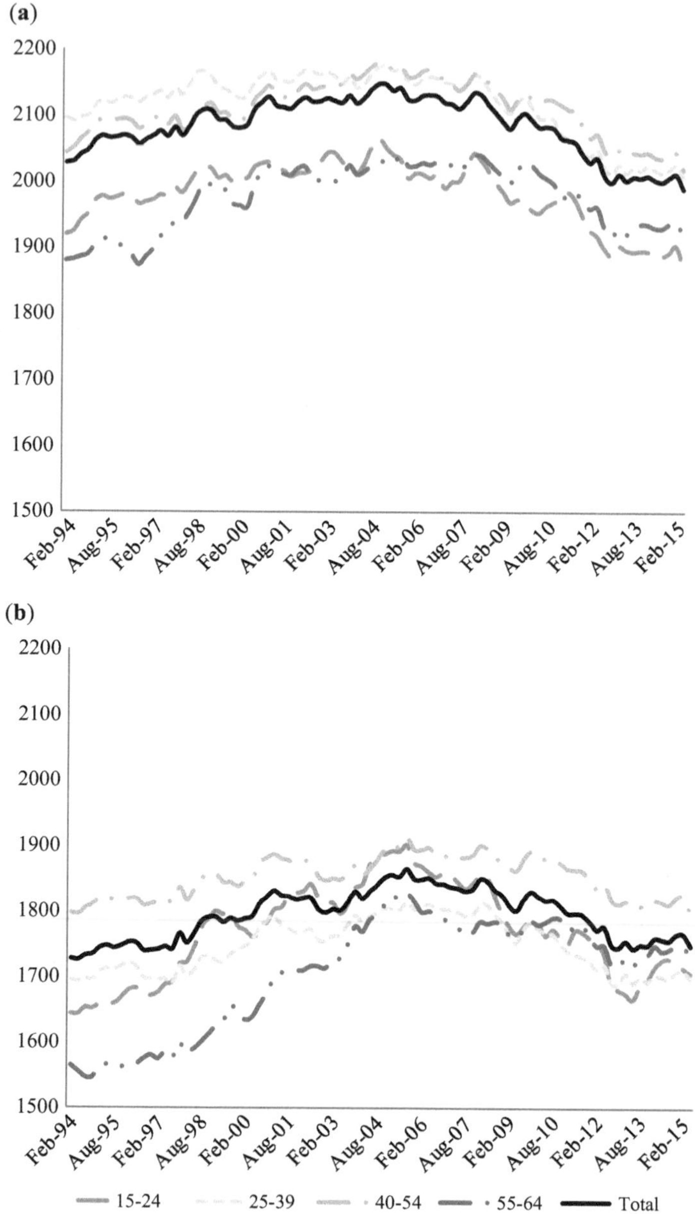

Fig. 5.5 Mean annual hours of work per worker, by gender and age. (**a**) Men (**b**) Women
Source: Authors' own computations using the Czech Labour Force Survey data

The latter shows humped-shaped profiles which are similar across all age groups and both genders. The average hours worked per worker increased from 1994 to reach a maximum at the brink of the economic crisis in 2008. Since then, both during and after the crisis, they have experienced a rather steep decline with notable convergence closing the differences between individual age groups. More interestingly, in the most recent years, the mean hours worked per worker across all age groups sit in a very narrow range of between 1882 and 2050 hours per year in the case of men and 1660–1830 in the case of women (full-time work corresponds to about 2000 hours per year). In 2015, the mean annual hours worked by working men was notably below 1994 levels for all age groups except the oldest one, while mean hours of working women reached levels quite similar to 1994 levels.

We also observe that the long-term shifts on the intensive margin in Fig. 5.5 were obviously more heterogeneous in the case of women. While the youngest and oldest working women increased their mean working hours, the mean hours worked by women in the intermediate age groups was about the same in 2015 as in the early 1990s. There is an evident gender difference in the mean working hours of those who worked in 2015 but this represents a mere 14%. This is because the dominant share of Czech working women worked full-time; part-time jobs were in low supply throughout the period studied.

The U-shaped trends in the employment rate in Fig. 5.4 and the inverse U-shaped trend in the mean hours of work per worker in Fig. 5.5 worked against each other to result in a rather stable trend in the mean hours worked per individual in the economy as a whole. Similarly, the aggregates conceal mutually compensating demographic trends at both ends of the age distribution, which we will discuss in the next subsection.

The recent economic crisis coincided with a growing employment rate but declining mean working hours among those who work, resulting in relatively stable mean hours of work per individual and the above-mentioned compensating effect. One possible explanation for this combination of effects is the added worker phenomenon, when originally non-employed household members start working to compensate for their spouses' salary losses resulting from the crisis. However, it is not entirely clear whether the decline in the mean hours worked per worker was due to the crisis or whether it was driven by other longer-term factors.

5.3.2 *Trends in the Employment Structure*

Once we narrow our focus to look at age specific trends in employment, we see quite distinct patterns in the mean hours worked per person at both ends of the age distribution, as seen in Fig. 5.3. While the number of mean hours worked among the youngest group (15–24 years old) had dropped to almost half its 1994 level in 2005, the mean hours worked among the oldest group (55–64 years of age) had increased by about one-third over the same period. Noting the similarity of the age specific trends between Figs. 5.3 and 5.4, we can conclude that the trends in hours worked per person were primarily driven by changes on the extensive margin. The economic crisis only had a minor, temporary impact. The pace of growth in the mean hours worked by older women remains high even in 2015; we discuss this in more detail below.

Furthermore, the diverging trends between women aged 25–39 and those aged 40–54 are notable. This phenomenon is related to an ongoing trend of shifting maternity towards higher ages, as mentioned above.

5.3.3 *Young Generations and Extending School Attendance*

The employment trends among the youngest population group, those aged 15–24, deserve special attention. The steady long-term decline in the mean hours worked per person in this age group exceeds any discernible effect from the recent economic crisis. Instead, this decline was driven by a steady increase in the duration of initial education. In particular, during the last quarter of a century growing proportions of Czech pupils entered primary school at the age of seven rather than six, a fourth grade at the end of lower secondary school was reintroduced, four-year upper-secondary programmes became more widespread and the proportion of shorter apprenticeship programmes (2–3 years long) shrank; this was accompanied by a huge expansion in access to tertiary education (colleges and universities) from 15% of an age cohort in the 1990s to about 50% in 2015. This latter trend was the result of several complementary phenomena: (1) persistently high private financial returns from tertiary education; (2) growing demand for tertiary educated employees in public and state institutions; (3) expansion in the capacity of incumbent public universities; (4) the growth of private colleges (since 1998); and (5) the establishment and expansion of regional public universities and colleges. The rise in university enrolment was reinforced by the fact that despite the division between undergraduate and postgraduate level studies,[11] most undergraduate level students now continue to Master's level. It should also be noted that despite its lower level of economic development and rather low spending on schooling, the Czech Republic's initial schooling has an above average duration within the OECD and the average young person therefore finishes full-time study at a relatively late age. Overall, the huge expansion and extension of initial schooling during the past 25 years has translated into a significant decline in total youth employment (as shown in Figs. 5.3 and 5.4) via lower participation and fewer mean hours worked by those who work. To what extent the increased duration of initial schooling will pay off in the future in terms of a more productive labour force to compensate for the public and private opportunity costs of the longer study period is yet to be seen.

5.3.4 *Extending Life Expectancy and the Statutory and Effective Retirement Ages*

The developments on the upper side of the age distribution are also notable; these were driven by a complex mix of factors. The statutory and effective retirement ages were set at very low levels in the late 1990s, in line with the rather low life expectancy of the population in a socialist country managed by a communist regime. That relatively low life expectancy (excluding very low infant mortality) was related to the health burdens resulting from a large share of employment being in heavy industries, unhealthy lifestyles, highly polluted air, and the lower quality of the health care system. Over time, thanks to steady improvements on all of these fronts, the country saw steady increases in life expectancy, and these were accompanied by increases in the statutory and effective retirement ages. According to a recent study by Bakalová et al. (2015), the Czech population's age-health profile has been improving substantially and moving closer to that of Western European countries. These trends translated into an increase in employment among the older population, 55–64 years of age, as can be seen in Figs. 5.3 and 5.4.

A closer look at the mean hours worked per person reveals that the upward drift in the oldest group was initially less pronounced for women than for men but that around the year 2000 it started to grow much faster for women. In 1994, a large share of women of this age had already retired. As shown in Fig. 5.4, between 1994 and 2015 the employment rate among women in this age group more than doubled, and Fig. 5.5 documents that their work intensity grew by far the most, by about 200 hours per year over the past two decades.

5.3.5 Changing Occupational Mix

The Czech economy's occupational structure has been characterized historically by a large share of employment in manufacturing at the expense of employment in private services. Overall, from the early 1990s we observe a steadily declining share of employment in low-skilled occupations[12] in Fig. 5.6 and a growing share of occupations requiring higher skills in Fig. 5.7. Again, the similarity between the trends in employment shares and shares of hours worked per person (not shown here) indicates that occupational adjustments mainly took place on the extensive margin of labour supply.

The crisis that emerged in late 2008 had discernible impacts on the occupational composition. While long-term trends in some occupations were almost unaffected, such as *craft & related trade workers, plant & machine operators*, some others were substantially affected such as *service & sales workers* (+), *elementary occupations* (−), *technicians* (−), and *managers* (−). The crisis fostered a decline in employment in *elementary occupations* and increases in *services & sales*. The latter was the only low-skilled occupational group to experience a notable increase in its share of employment after the crisis. As for occupations requiring middle and higher skills, the crisis brought a sizeable (about 30%) drop in the share of female *technicians & associated professionals* accompanied by a growing share of women among *professionals* and *clerical support workers* as shown in Fig. 5.7. Overall, the employment shifts from low-skill jobs towards occupations requiring middle and higher skills were more pronounced for women, both before and after the crisis. The crisis had a markedly adverse impact on managers, in particular male managers. This suggests that the crisis forced firms to restructure their internal managerial practices toward greater management efficiency. However, in absolute terms, the decline in the number of managers was rather small, since this occupational category represents only a small share of the population.[13]

5.3.6 Persistently Low Unemployment

From the beginning of the economic transition in the early 1990s, through the resurrection of the market economy and later on, the Czech Republic managed to maintain very low unemployment rates, even in times of deeper economic downturn in the late 1990s and during the crisis in the late 2000s. The unemployment rate remained well below 10% most of the time, and the country ranked among the EU and OECD countries with

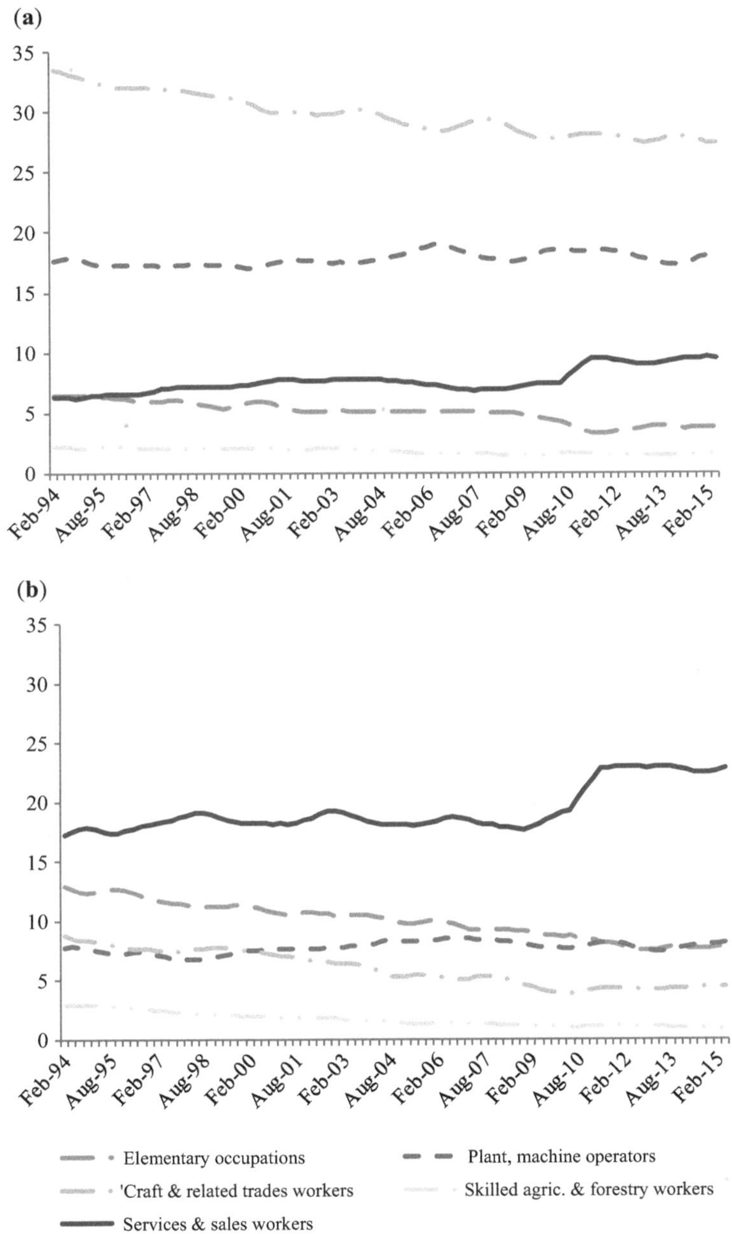

Fig. 5.6 Occupational share in total employment—lower skills. (**a**) Men (**b**) Women
Source: Authors' own computations using the Czech Labour Force Survey data

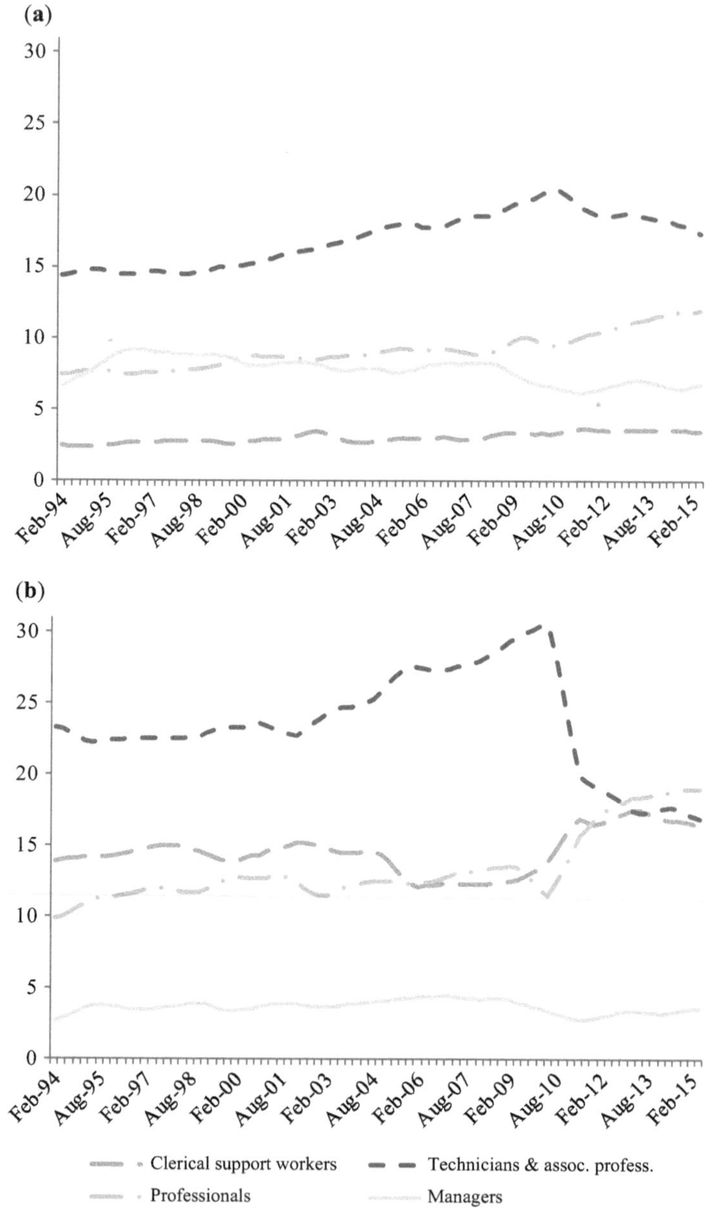

Fig. 5.7 Occupational share in total employment—higher skills. (**a**) Men (**b**) Women
Source: Authors' own computations using the Czech Labour Force Survey data

the lowest incidence of unemployment. Most of its unemployment was of a frictional character: individuals who lost or left jobs and spent a while searching for a new position. The long-term unemployed, who are more disconnected from regular work, typically represented about 30–40% of all unemployed. This implies that unemployment fluctuations had a rather minor impact on total employment.[14]

The first signs of the most recent economic crisis were seen in late 2008, before it fully erupted during 2009–2010. Layoffs and firms' postponement in hiring new labour resulted in swiftly growing unemployment. Nevertheless, from a longer-term perspective and when taking into account the extraordinary economic boom that preceded the crisis, Fig. 5.8 documents that the economic crisis had a relatively minor impact, temporarily affecting the long-term declining trend in the unemployment rate that is visible from the early 2000s onwards.

The association of the unemployment rate with business cycle fluctuations is obvious but there are also a few other patterns of interest. First, the incidence of unemployment was significantly higher among youngsters (as shown in Fig. 5.8) and those with primary education (as shown in Fig. 5.9) than among the other groups. Needless to say, these two demographic groups are of a relatively small size and their contribution to overall unemployment was thus rather small. Second, the incidence of unemployment varies markedly more among women, across the age groups in Fig. 5.8 and educational groups in Fig. 5.9, than among men. Third, the economic crisis had a more adverse impact on men, and on those with lower educational attainment in particular. Interestingly, neglecting the extraordinary but temporary drop in the unemployment rate during the boom of 2006–2007, women fared somewhat better during the crisis than they had done during the early 2000s.

By 2015, the impact of the crisis seems to have been erased and unemployment patterns returned to those before the crisis. The only notable exceptions are the youngest women, men 15–39 years of age and the low skilled who still face a relatively higher incidence of unemployment.

Figures 5.10 and 5.11 shed light on the trends in unemployment rate for the major occupational groups.[15] The crisis had an immediate negative impact on all occupations requiring low and medium skills, with *plant and machine operators* and *elementary occupations* being the most adversely affected in absolute terms. In 2015, the incidence of unemployment on middle- and low-skilled occupations resembles the situation preceding the crisis. For the higher-skill occupations in Fig. 5.11, we observe that the

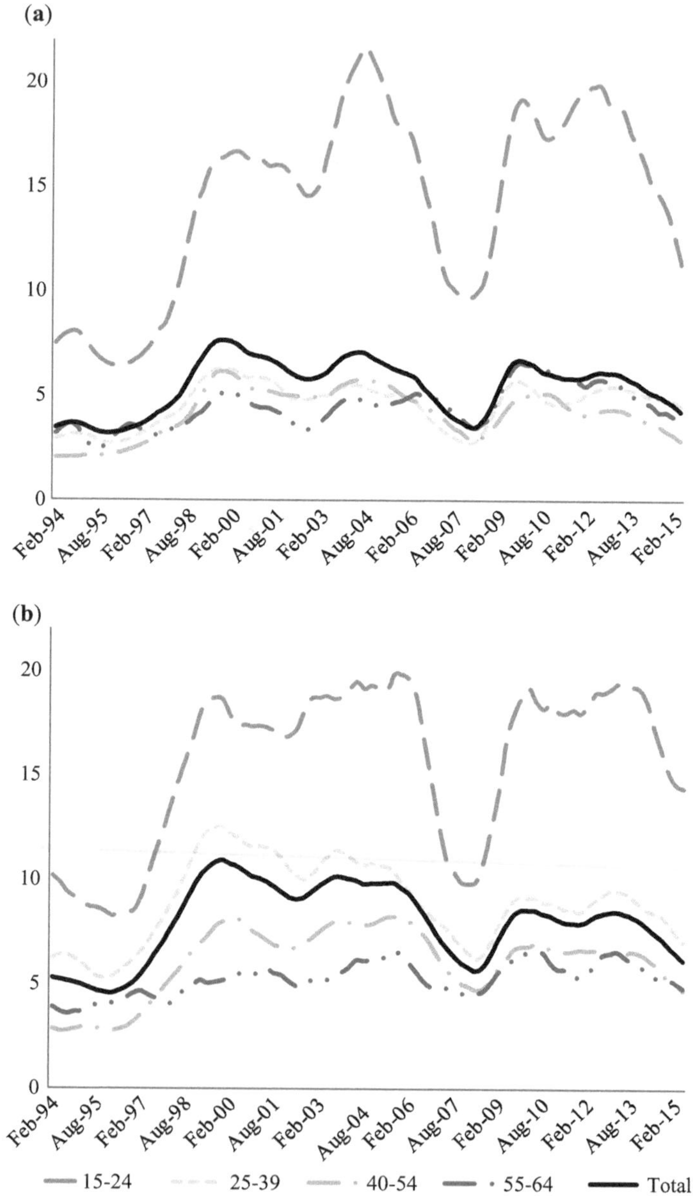

Fig. 5.8 Unemployment rate, by gender and age. (**a**) Men (**b**) Women
Source: Authors' own computations using the Czech Labour Force Survey data

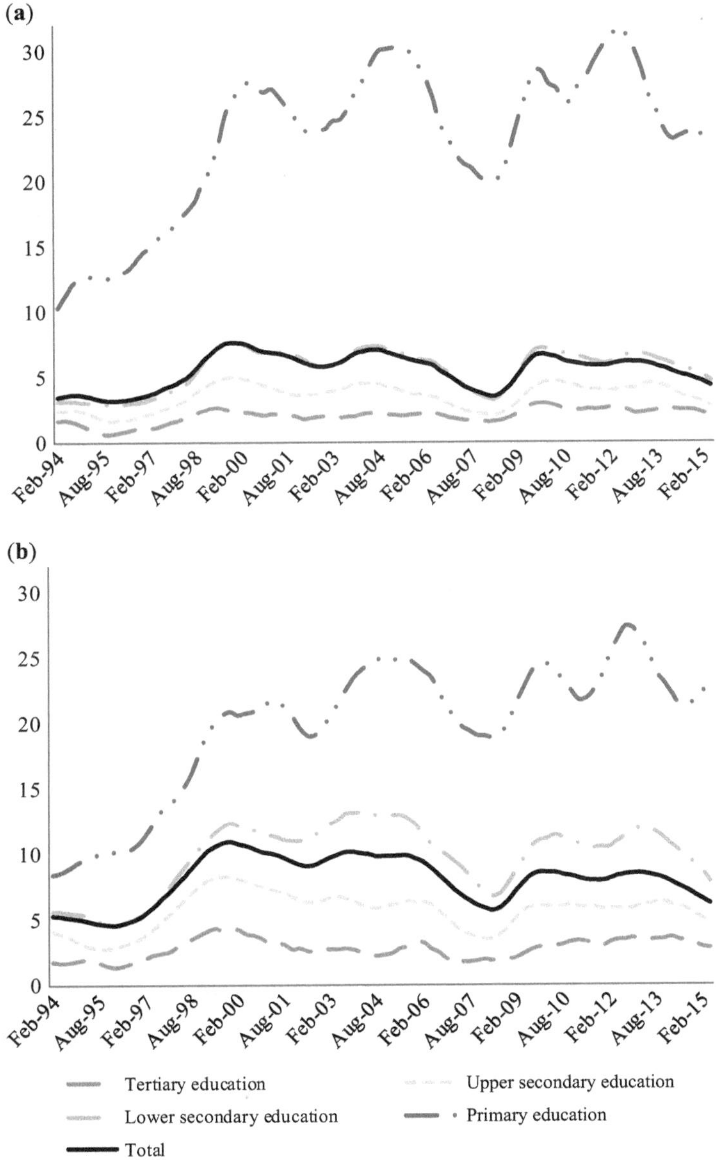

Fig. 5.9 Unemployment rate, by gender and education. (**a**) Men (**b**) Women
Source: Authors' own computations using the Czech Labour Force Survey data

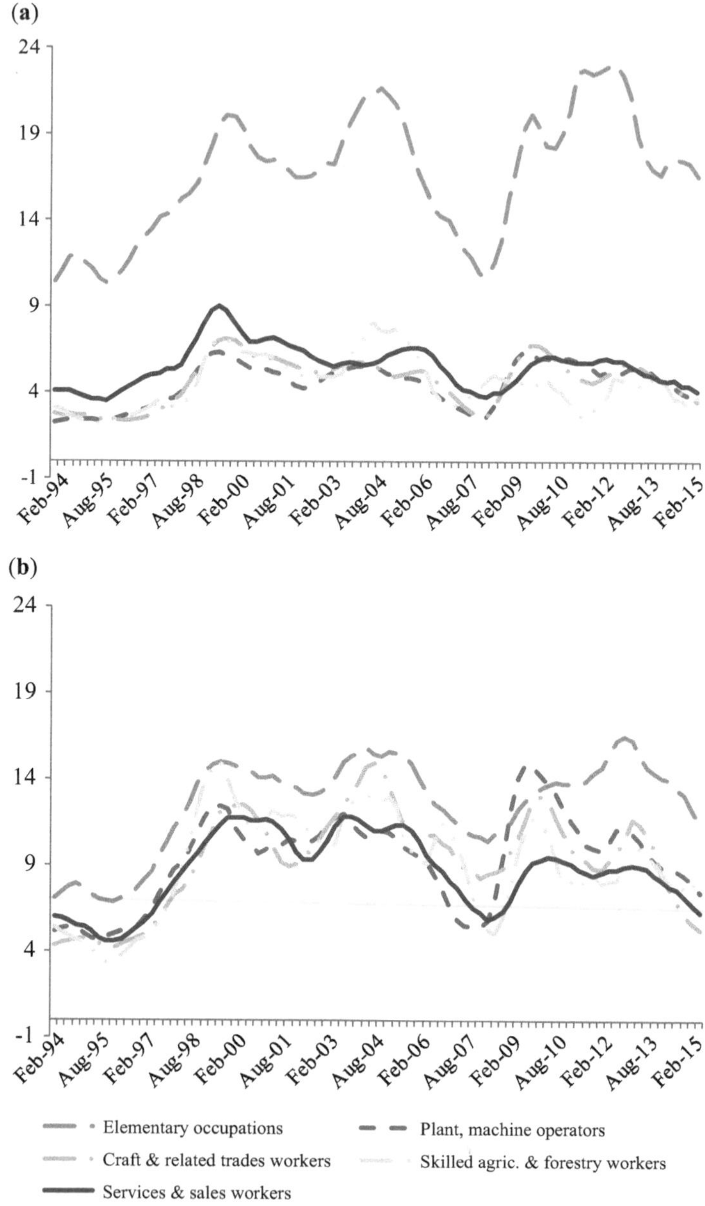

Fig. 5.10 Unemployment rate, by low-skilled occupations. (**a**) Men (**b**) Women
Source: Authors' own computations using the Czech Labour Force Survey data

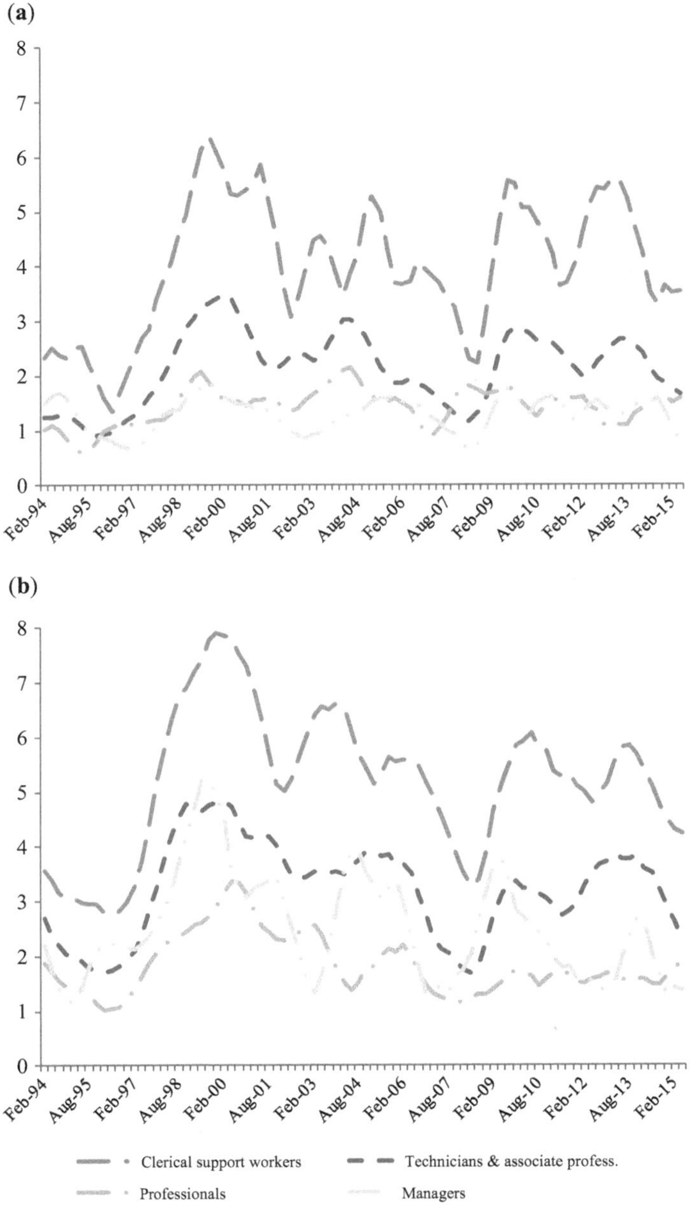

Fig. 5.11 Unemployment rate, by higher-skilled occupations. (**a**) Men (**b**) Women
Source: Authors' own computations using the Czech Labour Force Survey data

crisis had a swift adverse impact on all occupations except *professionals*. While the rapid rise of unemployment among *managers* was only temporary, unemployment among *technicians* and *clerical support workers* remained high for an extended period of time and only began to decline in 2014. Overall, the incidence of unemployment among lower-skilled occupations exhibited much greater sensitivity to the business cycle and remains considerably more heterogeneous (note the different scales).

5.4 Concluding Discussion

Since the 1990s, the Czech economy has exhibited a high degree of dependence on economic developments in the EU and among its major trade partners. The total supply of labour in the economy was supported by a growing working-age domestic population until the end of the first decade of the new millennium. Positive net immigration played little part in this. Despite volatile aggregate economic developments, the total hours worked in the Czech economy remained rather stable, with the exception of stylized business-cycle fluctuations.

Our detailed insight reveals that particular age groups experienced substantial changes during the period studied, and that there were sizeable shifts on the intensive and extensive labour supply margins. The changes on the intensive margin were smaller than those on the extensive margin, but helped to accommodate the adverse impact of the recent economic crisis, which hit the country in 2008. The relatively smaller shifts on the intensive margin were related to an extraordinarily short supply of part-time work arrangements in the economy, for both men and women. One possible explanation for this situation is an exceptionally large share of employment in manufacturing, where shift-work schedules predominate. Another possible explanatory factor is that extraordinarily high social security contributions are imposed even on medium and lower salaries, so that part-time work (which is lower paid) does not pay off due to the fixed costs of work, such as commuting time and related travel costs.[16] The lack of part-time jobs limits the choice for most individuals of either full-time work or no work at all, which in turn reduces the scope for labour supply adjustments on the intensive margin (hours of work).

The youngest (15–24) and the oldest (55–64) groups in the population experienced substantial changes on the extensive margin of labour supply. Having opposite signs and being of similar size, these effects compensated for each other over time to a large extent. While the developments on the lower tail of the age distribution were primarily driven by the steadily growing average duration of initial schooling, the developments on the upper tail were mainly driven by the steadily improving health of the ageing population and growing work opportunities due to the changing occupational mix towards jobs requiring less physically demanding work.

The global economic crisis's adverse impact on employment was notable but was relatively well accommodated. Its impact looks larger because the economy and labour market were overheated in the period just preceding the crisis. The crisis mainly brought about temporary fluctuations, which do not seem to have been particularly severe in the light of the more pronounced longer-term trends. The crisis's impact on unemployment was considerable but temporary and, at its peak, the unemployment rate did not reach the country's historical maximum. In 2015, the only noteworthy impact persisting from the crisis seems to be the shift in the occupational structure of employment. Men with a lower education in manual occupations requiring middle to low skills experienced the most adverse impact. Some other occupations were also affected and the persisting trends in employment and unemployment suggest some underlying restructuring was initiated by the crisis.

Besides changes in the total population as a result of its age structure and labour demand fluctuations, employment trends in terms of mean hours worked per person emanated from the microeconomic behaviour of individuals, who make decisions not only about whether to work or not but also about the number of hours they work. This involves a plethora of factors, such as the level and structure of pay, incentives provided by the tax-benefit system, the external and internal flexibility of work arrangements, alternatives for time-use, and personal preferences. Our short exposition in this chapter does not aspire to identify the individual contributions from these factors; that remains a challenge for further research.

Acknowledgements Daniel Münich's research was supported by the Czech Grant Agency via grant P402/12-G130. The data used for the analysis were originally collected and provided for research by the Czech Statistical Office (CSO). We acknowledge valuable expert advice on the data by Ondřej Nývlt and Daniel Chytil, from the CSO. The usual caveats apply.

Notes

1. For a detailed overview and analysis of the economic transition, see Švejnar (1995, 2002).
2. See Hanousek et al. (2007), Pizzati and Funck (2002), Flek et al. (2004), Gottvald (2001).
3. GDP and inflation data were retrieved from the Czech Statistical Office.
4. See Bičáková and Kalíšková (2016), Bruggemann and Trenkler (2007), Pytlíková and Filipová (2017).
5. For a cross-sectional insight into key employment patterns see Večerník (2007).
6. The trends of both variables are rather similar, so most of our conclusions hold for usual working hours as well.
7. Seasons: Spring, Summer, Fall, Winter.
8. The first season is considered to include December, January and February, the second—March, April, May, etc.
9. To remove seasonal fluctuations (quarterly) from the graphs, we used moving averages of quarterly indicators. The moving average at time t is computed as an average across the current value, one quarter lag, and two lead periods.
10. The employment rate is defined as the share of employed individuals in the population of an age-specific demographic group.
11. This division is part of the so-called Bologna process, a collective effort on the part of the public authorities and stakeholders, including the European Commission, to introduce a three-cycle system (bachelor/master/doctorate), to enhance flexibility and foster simpler recognition of tertiary qualifications.
12. A change of occupational classification in the data was introduced in 2011 (from KZAM to ISCO). However, the classification remained the same at the first digit level, so only the first digit level is used in this study. The only disparity between the two classifications at the first digit level was in the category of *armed forces*, which disappeared from the data after 2010. The *armed forces* category is therefore not shown in our graphs.
13. For more on the employment of managers see Jurajda and Paligorova (2009).
14. Further details about unemployment trends in the Czech Republic from an international perspective can be found in Münich and Švejnar (2007).
15. The occupation-specific unemployment rate is constructed as the share of unemployed in the labour force (employed and unemployed), where employment counts individuals currently employed in a particular occupation and unemployment counts those currently unemployed who report their last employment within the given occupation.
16. A more detailed exposition of income tax distribution in the Czech Republic is provided by Dušek et al. (2013).

References

Bakalová, J., Boháček, R., & Münich, D. (2015). *A comparative study of retirement age in the Czech Republic* (IDEA Study 3/June 2015). Prague: CERGE-EI.

Bičáková, A., & Kalíšková, K. (2016). Occurrence and rise of unemployment of women with pre-school children: The case of the Czech Republic. *Politická Ekonomie, 64*, 695–712.

Blundell, R., Bozio, A., & Laroque, G. (2013). Extensive and intensive margins of labour supply: Work and working hours in the US, the UK and France. *Fiscal Studies, 34*, 1–29.

Bruggemann, R., & Trenkler, C. (2007). Are Eastern European countries catching up? Time series evidence for Czech Republic, Hungary and Poland. *Applied Economic Letters, 14*, 245–249.

Dušek, L., Kalíšková, K., & Münich, D. (2013). Distribution of average, marginal and participation tax rates among Czech taxpayers: Results from a TAXBEN model. *Czech Journal of Economics and Finance, 63*, 474–504.

Flek, V., et al. (Eds.). (2004). *Anatomy of the Czech labour market: From over-employment to under-employment in ten years?* Prague: Karolinum Press.

Gottvald, J. (2001). Czech labour market flows from 1993 to 2000. *Prague Economic Papers, 10*, 129–144.

Hanousek, J., Kočenda, E., & Švejnar, J. (2007). Origin and concentration: Corporate ownership, control and performance in firms after privatization. *Economics of Transition, 15*, 1–31.

Jurajda, Š., & Paligorova, T. (2009). Czech female managers and their wages. *Labour Economics, 16*, 342–351.

Münich, D., & Švejnar, J. (2007). Unemployment in East and West Europe. *Labour Economics, 14*, 681–694.

Pizzati, L., & Funck, B. (2002). *Labor, employment, and social policies in the EU enlargement process: Changing perspectives and policy options*. Washington, DC: World Bank.

Pytlíková, M., & Filipová, L. (2017). Czech Republic. In G. Razzu (Ed.), *Gender inequality in Eastern European labour market: Twenty-five years of transition since the fall of communism* (pp. 44–76). Routledge: Abingdon.

Švejnar, J. (Ed.). (1995). *The Czech Republic and economic transition in Eastern Europe*. London: Academic Press.

Švejnar, J. (2002). Transition economies: Performance and challenges. *Journal of Economic Perspectives, 16*, 3–28.

Večerník, J. (2007). The Czech labour market: Historical, structural and policy perspectives. *Prague Economic Papers, 16*, 220–236.

CHAPTER 6

FDI and Ownership in Czech Firms: Pre- and Post-crisis Efficiency

Jan Hanousek and Evžen Kočenda

6.1 Introduction, Motivation and Relevant Literature

The social and economic reforms of the 1990s in Central and Eastern Europe (CEE) helped these countries create competitive market economies and more efficient enterprises through firm restructuring, privatization, and institutional reforms (Aussenegg and Jelic 2007). In this respect, ownership structures have become a key determinant of corporate performance in CEE countries (Estrin et al. 2009). Following the transition from a command to a market system and quite soon after their successful integration into the European Union (EU), CEE countries had to face another challenge in the form of the global financial crisis in 2008 (referred to hereafter as the GFC or "crisis"). How did local firms perform as transition ended, European integration was ongoing, and then during and after the merciless crisis? We focus on one CEE country, analysing the corporate

J. Hanousek (✉)
CERGE-EI, Prague, Czech Republic

E. Kočenda
Institute of Economic Studies, Charles University, Prague, Czech Republic

P. Havlik, I. Iwasaki (eds.), *Economics of European Crises and Emerging Markets*, DOI 10.1007/978-981-10-5233-0_6

performance of Czech firms in terms of their efficiency and how this efficiency has been determined by various firm characteristics, ownership structures, the presence of foreign direct investment (FDI), and the effect of the GFC.

6.1.1 Global Financial Crisis and Czech Firms

The GFC affected many countries and the Czech Republic was no exception. As many readers might not be familiar with the economic development in Central and Eastern Europe, in the following sub-section we describe how the Czech economy and firms were negatively affected by the crisis, and support our account with relevant details. We believe that such a description helps readers better understand our research aim and approach.

The rationale for the analysis of the impact of the global financial crisis on the efficiency of Czech firms is straightforward. The Czech Republic, having a medium, open, and export-driven economy (with exports taking as much as an 80% share of the country's output), was clearly not spared from the adverse consequences of the global turmoil starting in 2008. In fact, the crisis spilled over to the Czech Republic from the economies of the Eurozone which, being the most important trading partners for Czech firms, experienced a sharp drop in demand during the onset of the GFC. On the other hand, before 2008, the rather strong dependency on the EU facilitated the solid growth of the Czech economy after EU accession in 2004, with expansion being led in particular by booming exports (Fidrmuc and Martin 2011).

The GFC, however, led to a double recession in the Czech Republic. As Vazac (2011) documents, after the negative external shock of 2008, the GDP first declined in 2009 as it was pulled down by falling investment and exports, despite a sizable drop in the value of the Czech currency. The second recession struck in 2012, as subdued demand and government spending cuts choked the nascent economic recovery of 2010 and 2011. Fiscal policy indeed had a rather procyclical impact, as the right-wing government cut benefits and public investment as well as public sector expenditure. Moreover, the second recession induced a decrease in real wages in the non-manufacturing sectors and slower wage growth in the manufacturing sector, which left the Czech economy in a protracted period of low demand and threat of deflation (Myant 2013).[1] It was not until 2014 that the economy turned around, thanks in part to the weak-koruna policy pursued by the Czech central bank.

However, changes in the economic environment were not negative for all firms. Large and young firms as well as those selling on foreign markets in fact experienced an upswing in demand in the aftermath of the GFC. On the other hand, construction firms, foreign-owned firms, and firms facing strong competition were hit by the economic downturn (Babecký et al. 2015). Other key industries of the Czech economy (automotive, engineering) along with traditional industries (steel, glass, textile) as well as services also had to cope with a decreasing number of orders and worsening payment abilities of customers. Thus, Czech firms typically scaled down their operations and postponed planned investments as the impact of lower revenues kicked in. Access to credit might also have been somewhat restricted but there was no credit crunch in the Czech Republic as the Czech banking sector, restructured in the late 1990s after a banking crisis, went through the crisis relatively unscathed.

6.1.2 *Determinants of Firm Efficiency*

"What determines firm efficiency?" is a central question in economics and finance. The seminal literature suggests that primary determinants of firm efficiency are capital structure and ownership (Jensen and Meckling 1976; Jensen 1986), while other firm, market, and cultural characteristics play a role as well (Leibenstein 1966; Diaz and Sanchez 2008). However, the existing empirical literature on the link between capital structure, ownership structure and firm performance and/or efficiency is fragmented (see Weill 2008; Dilling-Hansen et al. 2003 among others); only recently, more comprehensive findings have become available (Hanousek et al. 2015). Further, the related literature almost uniformly suggests that foreign ownership improves firm performance better than domestic ownership. In many instances, empirical evidence supports this argument in CEE countries. The positive spillover effects of foreign ownership in the form of FDI on firm performance in CEE is shown by Hanousek et al. (2011) and further reported at the microeconomic level by Djankov and Hoekman (2000) and Hanousek et al. (2012) for Czech firms and, for example, by Javorcik (2004) for Lithuanian firms.

However, the literature remains largely silent on the effects of particular ownership structures on firm efficiency in the Czech Republic and CEE. Further, much of the work targeting the early stage of transformation frequently uses small and often unrepresentative samples of firms. It also often combines data from different accounting systems, and has access to limited data on firm ownership, treating ownership as a relatively simple categorical concept (e.g., private versus state, state versus foreign, domestic private outsider versus domestic private insider). Additionally, it is often unable to distinguish the exact extent of ownership by individual owners, or even relatively homogeneous groups of owners. These shortcomings prevent many studies from providing accurate evidence on the effects of various ownership categories on technical efficiency as well as corporate performance. The exception is a study by Hanousek et al. (2012) that employs a variety of firm characteristics and ownership categories to analyse the performance of Czech firms, but does not address the challenge of the recent GFC.

Hence, we take a comprehensive perspective in this chapter and offer the following contributions. We use an exceptionally sizeable dataset of Czech firms in both the manufacturing and service sectors, from 2001 to 2012. Our approach employs a stochastic production frontier model and shows in detail how key firm characteristics plus specific ownership structures affect firm efficiency. We further analyse the development of firm efficiency before the recent global financial crisis (2001–2008) and later (2009–2012).

We analyse links between ownership structure, firm characteristics, and firm performance primarily from the agency theory perspective. For example, ownership theory predicts a conflict of interest between owners and managers. Owners are interested in firm performance and strive to maximize profits, whereas managers are tempted to pursue selfish strategies—low effort level, high compensation, empire building—to maximize their own utility, resulting in a lower market value of the firm (Jensen and Meckling 1976). As agency conflicts could be mitigated by monitoring, the presence of large shareholders is positively correlated with firm performance because larger owners have stronger incentives to monitor and influence managers to protect their investments (Shleifer and Vishny 1997). At the same time, large shareholders might use their control rights to maximize their own utility rather than the firm's value at the expense of minority shareholders. In the case of less concentrated ownership, conflict between shareholders and managers could also result in conflicts among shareholders.

The composition of our dataset follows strict requirements for data quality in terms of coverage (number of firms) and detail on ownership structures. Further, by dividing our sample into subsamples we detect and analyse the impact of the economic crisis after 2008. In addition, our dataset enables us to trace the true development of ownership structure over time in unprecedented detail. In each firm in the sample, we can detect ownership concentration, its domestic or foreign origin, and the degree to which owners control the firm. Following legal standards, we distinguish several ownership categories that provide owners with different degrees of control, including potential coalitions of owners.

The firms under research constitute the bulk of the economic activity in the Czech Republic, which makes our analysis stronger because the potential bias due to focusing on specific sectors is negligible. However, at the same time we are able to distinguish the two-digit industrial sectors in which the firms operate and aggregate our results across two key sectors: manufacturing and services. Further, in our analysis we include additional firm and market characteristics (size, leverage, and market concentration) and, hence, we can provide substantially richer results in terms of how these characteristics potentially affect firm efficiency.

In this study, we want to evaluate the efficiency effect of FDI via foreign ownership as well as the effects of various degrees of ownership concentration. We employ the stochastic production possibility frontier approach introduced by Aigner et al. (1977) and Meeusen and van den Broeck (1977) to analyse the effect of ownership by using a model for panel data and time-varying technical efficiency from Khumbhakar (1990) and Battese and Coelli (1995). The methodology is well established in the empirical literature. We adjust our methodology in such a way that all the parameters of the production function account for the specific two-digit (NACE) industries in which firms operate. Effects at a high level of detail are derived from this setup. Within our methodology, we also address the potential problem of unobserved (fixed) firm heterogeneity, including the endogeneity of firm ownership with respect to its efficiency.

The reminder of this chapter is structured as follows: The methodology is described in Sect. 6.2. In Sect. 6.3 we introduce the data, the specific development of Czech firms, describe firm and market characteristics and ownership categories, and formulate our hypotheses. In Sect. 6.4 we present our empirical results and conclude in Sect. 6.5.

6.2 Modelling Approach

We analyse the drivers of a firm's efficiency in two steps by employing stochastic frontier analysis (SFA). First, we derive a firm's efficiency from the stochastic production possibility frontier. Second, we relate the technical efficiency of the firm—defined as the distance from the efficiency frontier—to several factors shown in the literature to have an effect: firm-specific characteristics (size, capital structure, and degree of competition) and ownership structure. Thus, our model consists of two specifications: (1) describing the efficiency frontier with the help of a production function; and (2) modeling the determinants of efficiency.

We perform the estimation on a series of short panels with fixed effects that enables easy identification, requires the least restrictive assumptions, alleviates the potential problem of unobserved (fixed) firm heterogeneity, lowers potential estimation bias, and accounts for the endogeneity of firm ownership structures with respect to efficiency. The estimation itself is performed using the maximum likelihood one-stage procedure originally designed by Battese and Coelli (1995). Similarly to Weill (2008), we obtain efficient estimates that are free of potential correlation among variables.

6.2.1 *Firm Efficiency*

To perform the SFA we first formulate the production function. The general production function $y_t = f(x_t; \beta)$ relates inputs (x) to the resulting output (y), which is produced efficiently. However, as the production involves some degree of inefficiency, the production function is modified to $y_t = f(x_t; \beta) \cdot TE_i$. The firm's technical efficiency TE_i represents the non-negative ratio of observed output to the maximum feasible output and lies within the interval (0,1] as the firm's output is assumed to be positive. If a firm employs all inputs efficiently ($TE_i = 1$), it achieves an optimal output while TE_i smaller than one indicates a degree of inefficiency. Efficiency is assumed to be a stochastic variable with a distribution common to all firms and can be written as $TE_i = \exp\{-u_{it}\}$; since if $0 < TE_i \leq 1$, then $u_{it} \geq 0$. Further, a firm's output is also assumed to be subject to various random shocks (from machinery breakdown to bad weather) that are denoted as $\exp(v_{it})$. The production function is then written as: $y_t = f(x_t; \beta) \cdot \exp(-u_{it}) \cdot \exp(v_{it})$. After taking the natural log of both sides we obtain: $\ln y_{it} = \beta_0 + \sum_{j=1}^{k} \beta_{jit} \ln x_{it} + v_{it} - u_{it}$. In this general specification v_{it} is a pure noise component and a two-sided normally distributed variable, while u_{it} is the non-negative technical inefficiency component showing the distance from the efficiency frontier. Both terms form a compound error term with an *a priori* unknown distribution. To account for changes in technical inefficiency over time we estimate a time-invariant technical inefficiency model separately in a series of three short panels (2001–2004, 2005–2008, and 2009–2012). The time dimension is then brought in by merging the results from the short panels. This approach enables easier estimation and any potential bias is fairly moderate; for more details see Hanousek et al. (2015).

We employ the mainstream Cobb-Douglas production function with two-digit NACE sectors. This represents a less-restrictive production function than other options, is robust (Chirinko et al. 2010), and has been shown empirically to fit Czech data (Hájková and Hurník 2007) as well as those from other CEE or CIS countries (e.g., Brown et al. 2006). Formally, our model of the efficiency frontier of I firms ($i = 1,\dots, I$) in J two-digit NACE sectors ($j = 1,\dots, J$) over T time periods ($t = 1,\dots, T$) is specified as follows:

$$\ln y_{it} = \sum_{j=1,\dots,J} \left[\beta_{0j} + \beta_{1j} \ln c_{it} + \beta_{2j} \ln l_{it} \right] \cdot \mathrm{ID}_{itj} + \phi_t + v_{it} - u_{it}. \quad (6.1)$$

In specification (6.1) $\ln y_{it}$ is the natural log of the value of the production of firm i at time t, measured as firm operational revenues (sales). Then $\ln c_{it}$ is the natural log of the capital of each firm measured as working capital and $\ln l_{it}$ is the natural log of the firm's labour, measured as the number of employees. A common intercept for all firms is denoted by β_0.

Further, it has been shown that ownership structures in firms are often industry specific (Thomsen and Pedersen 1998). Therefore, we employ industry-sector dummies to capture the specific effects of various sectors so that these effects do not interfere with ownership effects. Hence, ID_{ijt} represents a vector of dummy variables to associate each firm with the specific industry sector j it operates in. We further interact dummy variables for each of the 45 two-digit NACE industries with both inputs (capital and labour) to control for industry-specific effects. We also include in specification (6.1) yearly time dummies (ϕ_t) that control for time-specific effects (country-wide economic development and business cycles) that are equal for all firms but vary over time. Finally, the random error is denoted as v_{it} and $u_{it} \geq 0$ represents inefficiency; producer effects are required to be non-negative because they represent the degree of inefficiency.

6.2.2 *Drivers of Firm Efficiency*

In the second step, we follow the estimation approach outlined in Hanousek et al. (2015) and model firm efficiency (u_i) as a function of (1) a set of key market and firm characteristics used widely in the literature and (2) detailed firm ownership structure. Formally, the model for each period (pre-crisis and post-crisis) is specified as follows:

$$u_{it} = \alpha_i + \beta_1 \text{Size}_i + \beta_2 \text{Age}_i + \beta_3 \text{Debt}_i + \beta_4 \text{DebtLInfo}_i$$
$$+ \sum_{C}^{c=1} \delta_c \text{HHI}_c + \sum_{J}^{j=1} \gamma_j \text{OWN}_{it}^{j} + \sum_{K}^{k=1} \xi_t I(\text{industry} = k) + v_{it}, \quad (6.2)$$

for all $i = 1,\dots, N$ (*firm index*); $t = 1,\dots, T$ (*time index*); $c = 1,\dots, C$ (*market competition categories*); $j = 1,\dots, J$ (*ownership categories*); and $k = 1,\dots, K$ (*double-digit industry categories*). Let us note that model (6.2) is estimated separately for the periods 2001–2008 and 2009–2012 to consider the potential effects of the crisis.

In specification (6.2), we account for several factors potentially affecting corporate performance. The *Size* of the firm is measured as (the log of) total assets and captures the effect of firm size on inefficiency, based on the hypothesis that larger firms lose momentum to improve their efficiency (e.g., Diaz and Sanchez 2008). *Age* is defined as the number of years from a firm's incorporation and measures the effect of a firm's age on efficiency under a prior that younger firms might be eager to compete via higher efficiency or be less efficient due to not yet being established. *Debt* (leverage) defined as Total Debt/Total Assets (in per cent) captures the effect of the capital structure, as firms may finance a project by their own resources or by loans and thus become more indebted. Based on free-cash-flow theory (Jensen 1986), projects financed by loans must meet the market interest rate and hence they are likely to be more profitable than projects financed by internal funds (free cash flow). On the other hand, according to the pecking order hypothesis, projects are financed according to a pre-committed schedule (Myers 1977). As in our dataset we also have firms for which we have limited information on their leverage so we include a special dummy *DebtLInfo* in order not to lose track of these mostly small firms.

We also account for the degree of competition that is defined by market concentration in the industry in which firms operate. Based on the *x*-inefficiency theory (Leibenstein 1966), low competition provides a protective environment leading to higher corporate inefficiency. Hence, a less concentrated industry provides more competition and should lead to increased efficiency (Dilling-Hansen et al. 2003). To operationalize the above concept, we include the Herfindahl-Hirschman index (HHI) of industry concentration. From the regulatory perspective of the different (local) levels of industry concentration we employ the HHI based on the scale used by the U.S. Department of Justice and the Federal Trade Commission (2010) for assessing low, moderate and high industry concentration levels. If a firm belongs to an industry with high competition (low concentration) or low competition (high concentration), in each case the HHI variable in (6.2) takes a value of one and zero otherwise. The effect of moderate competition (a moderately concentrated industry) is captured by a constant term. A specific variable captures the proportion of a firm on the sector concentration measured by HHI; a higher proportion means that a firm faces lower competition.

In specification (6.2) we account for a possible shift in the mean of technical efficiency (parameter μ) caused by the GFC-affected economic conditions from 2009 onwards. Our data provide a sign of a structural break and since the effect of the GFC is one of our key topics, we allow for a different (post-crisis) mean from 2009 onwards. For this reason, we also do not report an overall effect for the whole time span of our data as the coefficients would be meaningless due to the structural break.

Finally, we account for the effects of diverse ownership structures over time. The ownership structure $\left(\mathrm{OWN}_{it}^{j}\right)$ is defined in year t for each firm i to account for a specific ownership category j (domestic, foreign, and unknown domicile owners). To account for unobserved firm-level heterogeneity, the model is estimated by using fixed effects that are captured by coefficient α_i.

To summarize, coefficients γ_j associated with the ownership effect estimated via panel fixed-effects specification (6.2) represent (changes in) ownership effects. The employed variables of the ownership structure also distinguish the extent of ownership concentration along with the extent of control over a firm. The ownership categories require a more detailed explanation, and therefore we elaborate more on them in Sect. 6.3.1. The estimation results of (in)efficiency regressions (6.2) should be interpreted in terms of coefficients' values: larger coefficients associated with specific ownership categories mean that under a particular ownership type, a firm moves further from the efficiency frontier. More details are provided in Sect. 6.5, where we present our results.

6.3 Data, Variables, and Hypotheses

6.3.1 *Data and Ownership Categories*

The dataset contains unique firm-level unbalanced panel data for the period 2001–2012 constructed from several updates of the Amadeus database. The total number of firm*year observations is 1,021,607.

Descriptive statistics of the firm-level balance-sheet data used in (6.1) and (6.2) are summarized in Table 6.1. The turnover (sales) of firms exhibits a similar standard deviation as that of inputs, meaning rather constant returns to scale of the Czech firms' production. In all parameters, except for leverage, an increase can be witnessed during the post-crisis period. Only leverage exhibited a marginal decline, an understandable feature given unfavourable economic conditions associated with the GFC. A marked increase in labour after the crisis should be associated with improving conditions of large firms, while smaller ones experienced some decline in labour force.

Ownership variables are defined with respect to country-specific legal rules as in Gugler (2003). As shown in Hanousek et al. (2007), holders of

Table 6.1 Descriptive statistics: firm level data

Group	*Variable*	*Mean*	*Std. Dev.*	*Min*	*Max*
Period 2001–2008	Log (total assets)	12.27	2.22	3.66	23.92
	Log (fixed assets)	11.39	2.52	3.66	23.60
	Log (working capital)	10.85	2.50	3.64	20.79
	Log (turnover)	12.53	2.56	3.59	23.25
	Leverage	0.13	0.25	−0.05	1.10
	Number of employees	39.74	241	1	38,923
Period 2009–2012	Log (total assets)	12.14	2.23	3.89	24.09
	Log (fixed assets)	11.50	2.42	3.92	23.90
	Log (working capital)	10.76	2.47	3.88	20.73
	Log (turnover)	12.21	2.49	3.87	23.38
	Leverage	0.14	0.25	−0.05	1.10
	Number of employees	30.39	173.47	3	10,000

Notes: The descriptive statistics corresponds to the sample used for the regression analysis. It means that the period 2001–2008 represents 466,041 observations, while period 2009–2012 covers 555,566 observations. The total number of firm*year observations is 1,021,607

different concentration thresholds have, under Czech law, different opportunities to influence corporate governance. Majority ownership represents a high degree of concentrated ownership, while minority ownership can be viewed as a form of moderately dispersed ownership (not reaching 10%). Based on the above distinction of ownership concentration, we define several specific ownership categories which are described in Table 6.2. Rather than using exact percentage stakes, we opt for dummy variables that differentiate various ownership categories. All ownership categories are exclusively defined both for domestic and foreign owners as

Table 6.2 Definition of ownership categories

Type	*Condition*	*Description*
Majority ownership	More than 50% of shares	Grants the owner the right to staff management and supervisory boards, alter and transfer the firm's assets, make crucial strategic decisions at general shareholder meetings
Controlling non-majority ownership	An owner holds a stake in a firm that is lower than 50%, but this stake is greater than the sum of all the remaining stakes that can be identified	Provides the owner with effective control of the company
Combined controlling minority ownership	Two owners whose combined stake exceeds 50%	These two owners cannot individually control the firm or act against each other, not having enough voting power. However, they may coordinate their steps and control the company via their combined voting rights
Blocking minority ownership	A minority owner holds a stake higher than the threshold of 33% legally required by Czech law	Enables a strong minority owner to pursue its own interests and to potentially contest the decisions of a majority owner
Legal minority ownership	A minority owner with a stake higher than 10%	Reflects the situation in firms where other owners are confronted with at least one non-marginal owner pursuing its own interest. The law entitles the holder of the legal minority stake to call general shareholder meetings and obstruct decisions by delaying implementation through lengthy court proceedings

well as those without a known domicile. The categories of foreign ownership defined below are based on stakes above 10% and are considered to represent FDI ownership.[2] A constant captures the dispersed or unknown ownership of a firm that represents a negligible (about 3%) proportion in our sample.

6.3.2 Testable Hypotheses

Based on our data and prior assumptions we formulate four hypotheses to be assessed. Their formulation is grounded in the literature and the key arguments are also shown below.

Hypothesis 1. H_0 *Firm characteristics do not affect a firm's efficiency.*

Hypothesis 1 accounts for the possibility that large firms might be less efficient than smaller firms (Diaz and Sanchez 2008), that more leveraged (indebted) firms might be more efficient than those using internal funds (Jensen 1986), and that firms operating in a highly-concentrated industry with a low-competition environment might suffer from higher inefficiency.

Hypothesis 2. H_0 *Ownership concentration or the extent of control has no effect on firm efficiency.*

Hypothesis 2 indirectly examines the agency problem arising from the separation of ownership and control. Because of this, a concentrated ownership structure might lead to higher firm efficiency, since it results in a superior monitoring of managers (Shleifer and Vishny 1997). On the other hand, large owners may engage in self-dealing, which can reduce efficiency. Further, minority ownership should not improve a firm's efficiency as control is very likely to be missing in such an ownership structure. On the other hand, even a minority owner, or a pair of minority owners with a sufficiently high stake, could control a firm. Further, legal minority owners might not represent an excessive threat to a majority owner's control but can exert an important monitoring influence. Blocking minority owners might affect a firm's efficiency via the implicitly influential decisions of the majority owner, or they may oppose decisions of majority owners instead of monitoring, which may decrease firm efficiency. Finally, owners might form coalitions of the so-called block owners, and thus be able to exert a noteworthy disciplinary impact (Dilling-Hansen et al. 2003) or in contrast refuse to cooperate. The null hypothesis is formulated in a general way so that it allows testing of various degrees of ownership concentration to capture, for example, the diminishing extent of control.

Hypothesis 3. H_0 Foreign ownership (through FDI) does not improve a firm's efficiency.

Hypothesis 3 is related to the trade literature where it has been argued that foreign owners have better access to technology and therefore multinational firms established through FDI and owned by foreign owners should be more efficient (Temouri et al. 2008). Similarly, Estrin et al. (2009) show that efficiency in foreign-owned (privatized) firms in new EU member countries is higher than in domestically owned firms.

Hypothesis 4. H_0 The global financial crisis does not affect a firm's efficiency.

Hypothesis 4 examines the effect of the GFC since a crisis can be disruptive to a firm's operation. Our prior assumption is that during the crisis, firm efficiency suffers due to generally difficult conditions and related obstacles specific to Czech firms that we highlighted in Sect. 6.1.1.

6.4 Empirical Results

The key results for how firm efficiency is determined by firm characteristics, competition, ownership types, and the financial crisis are presented in Table 6.3 for all Czech firms. Further, in Table 6.4, we present results for a subset of large firms, defined according to EU rules as those with 50 or more employees. The results are reported separately for pre-crisis (2001–2008) and post-crisis (2009–2012) periods.

Coefficients associated with the distance from the efficiency frontier for a specific variable and specific period should be interpreted in the following manner. A fully efficient firm would have a distance from the efficiency frontier equal to zero. Hence, a positive value of a statistically significant coefficient associated with a variable indicates that this variable moves a firm away from the efficiency frontier. For example, a positive coefficient associated with a particular type of ownership category indicates that the

Table 6.3 Efficiency of the Czech firms

General characteristics	*Period (2001–2008)*	*Period (2009–2012)*
Size (log of total assets)	0.001***	0.001***
	(0.000)	(0.000)
Age of the firm (in years)	0.002***	0.002***
	(0.000)	(0.000)
Leverage (debt/total assets)	−0.007***	−0.010***
	(0.000)	(0.000)
Missing leverage information (0/1)	0.032***	0.032***
	(0.009)	(0.009)
Low competition	−0.005***	−0.013***
	(0.002)	(0.003)
High competition	0.031***	0.010***
	(0.002)	(0.002)
Firm market share (per cent)	0.001***	0.002***
	(0.000)	(0.000)
Majority – domestic	−0.011***	0.007***
	(0.003)	(0.000)
Majority – foreign	0.013***	0.024***
	(0.001)	(0.000)
Control (no majority) – domestic	0.001	0.039***
	(0.008)	(0.002)
Control (no majority) – foreign	−0.001	0.019***
	(0.002)	(0.001)
Combined control – domestic	0.018***	0.032***
	(0.006)	(0.006)
Combined control – foreign	0.010	0.029***
	(0.008)	(0.001)
Blocking minority – domestic	−0.008	−0.015***
	(0.006)	(0.001)
Blocking minority – foreign	0.019***	0.005***
	(0.001)	(0.001)
Legal minority – domestic	0.002	−0.003***
	(0.007)	(0.001)
Legal minority – foreign	0.015***	0.005***
	(0.002)	(0.001)
Constant	0.768***	0.777***
	(0.003)	(0.004)
Industry fixed effects	Yes	Yes
R^2	0.076	0.243
Number of observations	466,041	555,566

Notes: Coefficients show the effects of each ownership category or firm characteristic to moving a firm towards or away from the efficiency frontier: the smaller the coefficient is, the more each specific factor contributes to firm efficiency. ***, **, and * denote significance at the 1%, 5%, and 10% levels, respectively. Standard errors are shown in parentheses. Base category: Medium competition, Dispersed/Unknown ownership

Source: Authors' estimation

Table 6.4 Efficiency of the Czech large firms (number of employees ≥50)

General characteristics	*Period (2001–2008)*	*Period (2009–2012)*
Size (log of Total assets)	0.010***	0.005***
	(0.000)	(0.000)
Age of the firm (in years)	0.001***	0.001***
	(0.000)	(0.000)
Leverage (debt/total assets)	−0.052***	−0.057***
	(0.003)	(0.003)
Missing leverage information (0/1)	0.025***	0.021**
	(0.009)	(0.010)
Low competition	0.010**	−0.001
	(0.004)	(0.005)
High competition	−0.001	0.005
	(0.003)	(0.004)
Firm market share (per cent)	0.001***	0.001***
	(0.000)	(0.000)
Majority – domestic	−0.005	0.018***
	(0.007)	(0.002)
Majority – foreign	−0.018***	0.015***
	(0.003)	(0.001)
Control (no majority) – domestic	−0.013	0.021***
	(0.016)	(0.007)
Control (no majority) – foreign	0.019	0.008***
	(0.013)	(0.002)
Combined control – domestic	0.000	0.026*
	(0.000)	(0.014)
Combined control – foreign	0.000	0.019***
	(0.000)	(0.005)
Blocking minority – domestic	0.008	0.010**
	(0.012)	(0.004)
Blocking minority – foreign	0.001	0.003
	(0.010)	(0.002)
Legal minority – domestic	0.015	0.005
	(0.014)	(0.005)
Legal minority – foreign	−0.011	0.009***
	(0.011)	(0.002)
Constant	0.652***	0.759***
	(0.008)	(0.008)
Industry fixed effects	Yes	Yes
R^2	0.138	0.232
Number of observations	39,823	33,046

Notes: Coefficients show the effects of each ownership category or firm characteristic to moving a firm towards or away from the efficiency frontier: the smaller the coefficient is, the more each specific factor contributes to firm efficiency. ***, **, and * denote significance at the 1%, 5%, and 10% levels, respectively. Standard errors are shown in parentheses. Base category: Medium competition, Dispersed/Unknown ownership

Source: Authors' estimation

specific ownership category is associated with a lower contribution to firm efficiency; the larger the coefficient, the greater distance and inefficiency it represents. However, even in the case of two positive coefficients, when their values decrease between two periods, we are able to identify an improvement in efficiency. On the other hand, a negative and statistically significant coefficient associated with a specific category indicates that the category helps to move a firm closer to the efficiency frontier: the firm becomes more efficient as the coefficient becomes smaller. For example, in the case of the inequality between two coefficients (i.e., $\gamma_1 > \gamma_2$), the ownership type associated with the coefficient γ_2 has a smaller distance from the efficiency frontier and, hence, contributes to firm efficiency more than the ownership type associated with the coefficient γ_1. To summarize, when comparing the effects of two different ownership categories, we simply observe the value of the associated coefficients: the smaller the coefficient, the greater the contribution to a firm's efficiency and vice versa. A similar interpretation applies to firm characteristics, as well.

6.4.1 *Effect of Firm Characteristics and Market Competition*

Our results related to Hypothesis 1 show that the overall effect of the size of firms is statistically significant but very small. The effect is consistently associated with an essentially neutral impact on efficiency as witnessed by small, positive, and statistically significant coefficients (Tables 6.3 and 6.4). All firms exhibit an unchanged effect on size before and after the crisis (Table 6.3). On the other hand, for large firms the impact is somewhat better during the post-crisis period (Table 6.4). However, the effect of firm size must be regarded as narrow in economic terms since the associated coefficients are quite small. In any event, based on our findings, we infer that the size of a Czech firm cannot be associated with better efficiency in general.

Overall, the age of firms is also consistently statistically significant as well as small, and with a negligible effect in improving efficiency; this feature is invariant with respect to the crisis. Moreover, the coefficients' values do not materially differ whether for all, or just large, firms (Tables 6.3 and 6.4). Hence, the age of the firm does not allow for much variety in inference, but the fact that it does not improve efficiency should not be exaggerated, as the effect is rather small economically.

The effect of capital structure on firm efficiency is found to be quite strong, as the respective coefficients are large, negative, and statistically significant overall. This means that from the aggregate point of view the more leveraged firms get closer to the efficiency frontier. Still, an interesting observation can be inferred from the differences between firms and periods. The improving impact of leverage is evident from the negative and significant coefficients that also differ before and after the crisis (Table 6.3). Based on the coefficients' values, we infer that large firms are driving the result (Table 6.4). This finding is quite interesting as it shows that debt helps large firms to improve their efficiency to a greater extent. This finding is also intriguing in that it does not conform to prevailing common wisdom on the damaging effects of the GFC. We further shed more light on this issue as in our dataset we also have firms for which we do not have complete information on their leverage. In order not to lose track of these (chiefly small) firms we include a special dummy (missing leverage information). Based on the coefficients we see that firms with limited information on their capital structure do not exhibit an improvement in efficiency and this is invariant over both periods (Table 6.3). A similar result is evidenced for large firms but here the impact is lower and decreases after the crisis (Table 6.4). Also important is the fact that both effects are economically significant. Our evidence yields support for the Jensen (1986) hypothesis on the positive effect of capital structure in general. On the other hand, in firms where proper information on capital structure is missing, we find quite the opposite effect. The question remains whether improper reporting on leverage is not already an indication of firms' poor efficiency.

Finally, we infer the impact of a low- versus high-competition environment. The overall effect is mixed in the sense that manufacturing firms do not have statistically significant coefficients (Table 6.3) while firms in services do (Table 6.4). Since we differentiate between high and low competition the results are interpreted with respect to the moderate competition category. Hence, we have two broad results. A low-competition environment exhibits a mild, economically significant contributing effect to firms' efficiency and a high competition environment does not (Table 6.3). This finding goes against the *x*-inefficiency hypothesis. The judgement for large firms is precluded by the general lack of statistical significance; on the other hand, coefficients are quite small anyway (Table 6.4). Further, the contributing effect of low competition increases during the post-crisis period, while the non-improving effect of high competition decreases its impact. An additional inference can be made with the help of the dummy variable that captures the effect of the proportion of a firm in the sector's concentration measured by the HHI. For both groups of firms, we observe that the larger proportion of the concentration (that a firm captures) does exhibit a lesser contribution to improving an individual firm's efficiency (Tables 6.3 and 6.4). This means that when firms face less competition on an individual level, this buffer does not improve their efficiency. However, caution should be exercised because the effects are very small in terms of economic impact. To sum up our results, we do not find any evidence for the *x*-inefficiency hypothesis on the individual or aggregate levels.

6.4.2 *Effect of Ownership*

We now proceed with an assessment of Hypothesis 2, which is on the effect of different ownership categories as defined in Table 6.2. The overall observation is that all ownership categories produce economically significant effects, while their statistical significance varies, and sometimes a lack of statistical significance prevents more elaborate assessment.

The key *Majority ownership* category clearly shows its ability to affect improvements in efficiency. Domestic majority owners improve the efficiency of firms during the pre-crisis period more than foreign owners in general (Table 6.3). Foreign majority owners, on the other hand, exhibit quite a contributory effect in large firms before the crisis (Table 6.4). However, it is evident that both domestically and foreign controlled firms are further from their efficiency frontier during the post-crisis period, albeit domestic owners exhibit a better record (Tables 6.3 and 6.4).

The ownership category which enables control of the firm without a majority (*Controlling non-majority ownership*) does not allow for assessment before the crisis, as the coefficients are statistically insignificant (Tables 6.3 and 6.4). During the post-crisis period, firms under this ownership category are not close to their efficiency frontier and, thus, the category exhibits a similar pattern to majority ownership. Still, there is a difference because firms under domestic ownership are markedly further from their efficiency frontier than those under foreign control.

Combined controlling minority ownership consistently shows the least contributory effect to efficiency when compared to the previous two categories. Coefficients are positive and larger than those of the two categories enabling control of the company, which means that under such ownership firms are even further from their efficiency frontier (Tables 6.3 and 6.4). In all (Table 6.3) as well as just large (Table 6.4) firms, foreign owners perform slightly better than domestic ones, albeit such a comparison can be made only during the post-crisis period. It seems as if foreign minority owners of Czech firms form marginally better efficiency-improving coalitions than domestic owners. The result is in opposition to the earlier findings of Hanousek et al. (2012), although their result was obtained solely for the pre-crisis period. Further, the difference in distance from the efficiency frontier is not large for domestic or foreign-owned firms and, therefore, the result does not point to particularly strong differences between the two categories.

Two categories of control (*Majority ownership* and *Controlling non-majority ownership*) may have problems executing control with the presence of non-marginal minority owners. As discussed earlier, the holders of *Blocking* and *Legal minority* ownership rights may exert their power by questioning or obstructing some decisions of the otherwise controlling owners. In firms where domestic owners possess blocking and legal minority rights, efficiency improvements exhibit an economic effect during the post-crisis period (Table 6.3). On the other hand, foreign owners with blocking minority rights do not show a particularly beneficial effect, albeit that some improvement is visible after the crisis. An assessment of large firms is limited by mostly statistically insignificant coefficients; nevertheless, evidence points to the low non-contributory impact of both categories (Table 6.4). Taken together, there is non-negligible evidence of the positive disciplining effect on firm efficiency when a controlling owner must account for the presence of domestic minority shareholders. This finding is in line with related empirical studies showing that majority owners can alter their behaviour when a strong minority owner is present in the firm, for example in the case of dividend payments (Gugler 2003).

In sum, majority owners are found to be the most beneficial ownership category with respect to a firm's efficiency when compared with other categories that enable control of the firms. In this respect our results are in favour of agency theory, as they show that a concentrated ownership structure leads to higher firm efficiency via the superior monitoring of managers (Shleifer and Vishny 1997). Further, minority ownership itself does not seem to improve a firm's efficiency decisively, as truly strong control is very likely to be missing in such an ownership structure. An economically significant effect is evidenced also when minority owners discipline stronger owners via their legally grounded powers. On the other hand, owners in a coalition-like position seem to be unable to exert a noteworthy disciplinary impact.

6.4.3 Effect of Foreign Ownership

The effect of foreign ownership (Hypothesis 3) differs according to its type or ability to control. In the case of *Majority ownership*, domestic owners seem to contribute more to their firms' efficiency than foreign owners (Table 6.3) but foreign owners improve efficiency better in really large firms (Table 6.4). However, when foreign owners are able to control firms without a sheer majority stake (*Controlling non-majority ownership*) then their contribution to reducing inefficiency is larger than that of domestic owners. This effect is especially pronounced in large firms (Table 6.4). When two owners are able to form a majority (*Combined controlling minority ownership*), then this category exhibits a worse impact than the previous two categories, but foreign owners perform slightly better than domestic owners. When foreign owners are equipped with blocking or legal minority rights, they do not seem to exert any notable disciplining effect on controlling owners.

In sum, despite the fact that foreign majority owners perform worse than domestic owners, the effect of foreign ownership is strongest when a foreign owner controls a firm without needing a majority of voting power. This result resonates with an earlier finding that foreign-owned firms in Europe involved in multinational operations do better in financial performance than purely domestic units (Mathur et al. 2004). The results also indicate that coalitions of foreign minority owners are not necessarily overly helpful in improving the efficiency of Czech firms. A corollary to our finding is a documented link between technological progress in new EU countries and foreign direct investment (Uzagalieva et al. 2012), intensive trade links (Hanousek and Kočenda 2014), and further space for deepening trade and international production networks (Frensch et al. 2016). All those features involve foreign ownership in new EU firms and those in the Czech Republic in particular, due to its high level of interconnectedness within EU production and trade structures.

6.4.4 Effect of the Crisis

Our results show that the effect of a firm's characteristics and ownership categories changes over time before and after the crisis. However, the assessment of Hypothesis 4 is conditional on the statistical significance of the coefficients' pairs in both periods. From our findings, we infer that the effect of the GFC can be considered mildly positive in general. At the same time, the effect is unbalanced. While the effect of firms' characteristics remains unchanged or changes little, the effect of ownership is more pronounced. During the post-crisis period, ownership as a controlling device exhibits worsening efficiency across the key categories. However, ownership as a disciplining device exhibits a limited scope of efficiency improvement after the GFC, mainly thanks to domestic owners equipped with blocking and legal ownership rights.

In order to provide more solid assessment, we performed a series of tests to further assess the (in)efficiency development before and after the GFC. The results indicate that the crisis period tends to lower average inefficiency of firms. For example, average inefficiency (distance from the best performing firm) was 0.842 (median 0.871) in 2001 but after 2009 average inefficiency equals 0.814 (median 0.813). Given that we have more than half a million observations in each period, the above difference is quite economically significant.

We also computed difference in inefficiency for each existing firm in the periods 2001–2008 and 2009–2013—we obtained a (quasi) pair *t*-test accounting for the time invariant firm characteristics. The resulting test of the differences in firms' inefficiency between both periods is not large but fully statistically significant (0.003, *t*-stat. 51.6). This result brings evidence that an improvement in efficiency, albeit an economically small one, occurred in individual firms during the post-crisis period.

In general, the findings show that a period of financial distress pushed some less efficient firms to become more efficient in order to survive. It also seems that firms were losing efficiency due to a lack of pressure from their majority owners, but a limited improvement effect can be traced to owners with secondary control potential. Another possible explanation for the cases of poorer efficiency is via the important trade channel. Since Czech firms are heavily engaged in international trade, especially within the EU (Hanousek and Kočenda 2014; Frensch et al. 2016), a worsening of trade patterns during the GFC might negatively impact firms' efficiency as well. After all, the regular international trade flows were severely affected during the GFC (Chor and Manova 2012) along with capital inflows to new EU countries (Globan 2015). Specifically, before 2008 the solid economic growth was led by the expanding exports from Czech firms to the EU. However, the GFC affected firms when it quickly spilled over to the Czech Republic from important Eurozone trading partners, who themselves experienced a sharp drop in demand during the onset of the GFC (Fidrmuc and Martin 2011).

6.5 Conclusion

Our analysis deals with questions as to how size, age, competition, capital structure, ownership type, and the global financial crisis impact the efficiency of Czech firms. To answer these questions, we employ a stochastic frontier approach, using a large and detailed dataset, and cover the time span 2001–2012.

We show that larger Czech firms cannot be associated with better efficiency in general and that their age has only a negligible impact. The impact of capital structure on firm efficiency is shown to be strong and pronounced in large and more leveraged firms that tend to improve efficiency after the crisis. We also find that higher competition is not fruitful with respect to efficiency, either on the individual or aggregate level.

Further, we show that majority owners are most contributive with respect to firm efficiency when compared to other categories we analyse. Interestingly, minority owners with legally grounded power are able to impose significant efficiency improvements. Remarkably, the effect of foreign ownership is strongest when foreign owners control firms with less than a majority of voting power. In contrast, improvement is missing when minority owners have to share control over a firm.

Finally, we demonstrate that the impact of the crisis is not balanced but can be regarded, in general, as marginally positive in terms of efficiency. The firms' characteristics change only a little between pre- and post-crisis periods with the exception of the firm's capital structure: large and more indebted firms improve efficiency after the crisis. The effect of ownership is more pronounced. The worsening impact of the crisis is evidenced for controlling ownership categories. However, minority owners exhibit a limited disciplining effect to improve efficiency after the GFC.

Acknowledgements We benefited from valuable comments we received from Václav Brož, Richard Frensch, Mario Holzner, Ichiro Iwasaki, Andrei Yakovlev, and participants at several presentations of this study. The research is part of the international project "Economics of European Crises and Emerging Markets" organized by the Institute of Economic Research, Hitotsubashi University, and the Vienna Institute for International Economic Studies (wiiw) and financially supported by the Suntory Foundation. The usual disclaimer applies.

Notes

1. Indeed, the base wage was changed less frequently than before the crisis and a certain share of firms froze wages; wage growth materialized typically in very small or large firms as well as those with a foreign owner (Babecký et al. 2015).
2. Based on the official definition, if "the direct investor owns at least 10% of the voting power (in a firm)" (OECD 2008, p. 17), then the firm is considered a direct investment and the foreign domicile of the direct investor constitutes the FDI. Since we can identify from our data specific ownership stakes of 10% and up, the majority and minority control categories can be distinguished according to domicile, and provide information about FDI ownership.

References

Aigner, D., Lovell, C., & Schmidt, P. (1977). Formulation and estimation of stochastic frontier production functions. *Journal of Econometrics, 6*, 21–37.

Aussenegg, W., & Jelic, R. (2007). The operating performance of newly privatised firms in Central European transition economies. *European Financial Management, 13*, 853–879.

Babecký, J., Galuščák, K., & Žigraiová, D. (2015). *Labour market adjustment since the global financial crisis: Evidence from the survey of Czech firms?* (Research and Policy Note No. 1/2015). Prague: Czech National Bank.

Battese, G. E., & Coelli, T. J. (1995). A model for technical inefficiency effect in a stochastic frontier production function. *Empirical Economics, 20*, 325–332.

Brown, J. D., Earle, J. S., & Telegdy, Á. (2006). The productivity effects of privatization: Longitudinal estimates from Hungary, Romania, Russia, and Ukraine. *Journal of Political Economy, 114*, 61–99.

Chirinko, R. S., Fazzari, S. M., & Meyer, A. P. (2010). A new approach to estimating production function parameters: The elusive capital–labor substitution elasticity. *Journal of Business and Economic Statistics, 29*, 587–594.

Chor, D., & Manova, K. (2012). Off the cliff and back? Credit conditions and international trade during the global financial crisis. *Journal of International Economics, 87*, 117–133.

Diaz, A., & Sanchez, R. (2008). Firm size and productivity in Spain: A stochastic frontier analysis. *Small Business Economics, 30*, 315–323.

Dilling-Hansen, M., Madsen, E., & Smith, V. (2003). Efficiency, R&D and ownership: Some empirical evidence. *International Journal of Production Economics, 83*, 85–94.

Djankov, S., & Hoekman, B. M. (2000). Foreign investment and productivity growth in Czech enterprises. *World Bank Economic Review, 14*, 49–64.

Estrin, S., Hanousek, J., Kočenda, E., & Svejnar, J. (2009). Effects of privatization and ownership in transition economies. *Journal of Economic Literature, 47*, 699–728.

Fidrmuc, J., & Martin, R. (2011). FDI, trade and growth in CESEE countries. *Focus on European Economic Integration, 1*, 70–89.

Frensch, R., Hanousek, J., & Kočenda, E. (2016). Trade in parts and components across Europe. *Czech Journal of Economics and Finance, 66*, 236–262.

Globan, T. (2015). From financial integration to sudden stops? New evidence from EU transition countries. *Czech Journal of Economics and Finance, 65*, 336–359.

Gugler, K. (2003). Corporate governance, dividend payout policy, and the interrelation between dividends, R&D, and capital investment. *Journal of Banking and Finance, 27*, 1297–1321.

Hájková, D., & Hurník, J. (2007). Cobb-Douglas production function: The case of a converging economy. *Czech Journal of Economics and Finance, 57*, 465–476.

Hanousek, J., & Kočenda, E. (2014). Factors of trade in Europe. *Economic Systems, 38*, 518–535.

Hanousek, J., Kočenda, E., & Svejnar, J. (2007). Origin and concentration: Corporate ownership, control and performance in firms after privatization. *Economics of Transition, 15*, 1–31.

Hanousek, J., Kočenda, E., & Maurel, M. (2011). Direct and indirect effects of FDI in emerging European markets: Survey and meta-analysis. *Economic Systems, 35*, 301–322.

Hanousek, J., Kočenda, E., & Mašika, M. (2012). Firm efficiency: Domestic owners, coalitions, and FDI. *Economic Systems, 36*, 471–486.

Hanousek, J., Kočenda, E., & Shamshur, A. (2015). Corporate efficiency in Europe. *Journal of Corporate Finance, 32*, 24–40.

Javorcik, B. S. (2004). Does foreign direct investment increase the productivity of domestic firms? In search of spillovers through backward linkages. *American Economic Review, 94*, 605–627.

Jensen, M. (1986). Agency costs of free cash flow, corporate finance, and takeovers. *American Economic Review, 76*, 323–329.

Jensen, M., & Meckling, W. (1976). Theory of the firm: Managerial behavior, agency costs and capital structure. *Journal of Financial Economics, 3*, 305–360.

Khumbhakar, S. C. (1990). Production frontiers, panel data, and time-varying technical inefficiency. *Journal of Econometrics, 46*, 201–211.

Leibenstein, H. (1966). Allocative efficiency vs. 'x-efficiency'. *American Economic Review, 56*, 392–415.

Mathur, I., Singh, M., & Gleason, K. C. (2004). Multinational diversification and corporate performance: Evidence from European firms. *European Financial Management, 10*, 439–464.

Meeusen, W., & Van den Broeck, J. (1977). Efficiency estimation from Cobb-Douglas production functions with composed error. *International Economic Review, 18*, 435–444.

Myant, M. (2013). The impact of the economic crisis on collective bargaining in the Czech Republic. *European Review of Labour and Research, 19*, 185–194.

Myers, S. (1977). Determinants of corporate borrowing. *Journal of Financial Economics, 5*, 147–175.

OECD (Organization for Economic Co-operation and Development). (2008). *OECD benchmark definition of foreign direct investment* (4th ed.). Paris: OECD.

Shleifer, A., & Vishny, R. W. (1997). A survey of corporate governance. *Journal of Finance, 52*, 737–783.

Temouri, Y., Driffield, N. L., & Higón, D. A. (2008). Analysis of productivity differences among foreign and domestic firms: Evidence from Germany. *Review of World Economics, 144*, 32–54.

Thomsen, S., & Pedersen, T. (1998). Industry and ownership structure. *International Review of Law and Economics, 18*, 386–404.

U.S. Department of Justice and the Federal Trade Commission. (2010). *Horizontal merger guidelines*. Available at: https://www.ftc.gov/sites/default/files/attachments/merger-review/100819hmg.pdf

Uzagalieva, A., Kočenda, E., & Menezes, A. (2012). Technological innovation in new European Union markets. *Emerging Markets Finance and Trade, 48*, 51–69.

Vazac, R. (2011). Czech Republic: Crisis postponed: Navigation to recovery. In J. Jungmann & B. Sagemann (Eds.), *Financial crisis in Eastern Europe* (pp. 109–175). Wiesbaden: Gabler Verlag.

Weill, L. (2008). Leverage and corporate performance: Does institutional environment matter? *Small Business Economics, 30*, 251–265.

PART III

Hungary

CHAPTER 7

Impacts of the Crisis on the FDI-Led Development Model in Hungary: Emergence of Economic Patriotism or Shift from the Competition State to Patronage?

Miklós Szanyi

7.1 Introduction

Despite the profound success in developing the Central European economies over the past 25 years, the Hungarian and Polish governments have started to openly question the applicability of various elements of the foreign direct investment (FDI)-led development model of the "competition state". They took measures to curtail the activity of multinational firms that have played an important role in the successful process of modernizing the region. This chapter attempts to explain the rationale of this policy using the political economy approach. It defines economic policy changes as shifts in the power relations of national elites and highlights selective advantage and punishment measures that are often labelled economic patriotism. However, economic patriotism is interpreted in this chapter as the application of covert discrimination policies for the benefit

M. Szanyi (✉)
Institute of World Economics, Centre for Economic and Regional Studies of the Hungarian Academy of Sciences, Budapest, Hungary

P. Havlik, I. Iwasaki (eds.), *Economics of European Crises and Emerging Markets*, DOI 10.1007/978-981-10-5233-0_7

of spatially defined interest groups. The discussed policies are targeted rather at closely defined companies. They are not regarded here as tools of economic patriotism but rather of state clientism, a departure from the competition state toward a patronage state.

7.2 Development of Business-Polity Relationships in the CEE Transition Process: Patterns of the Competition State

The transition process in Central and Eastern Europe (CEE) was developed based on the interplay of local political forces and the international advising institutions whose recommendations stemmed from neoliberal concepts. The aim of shaping social processes that would mainly support the emergence of a local bourgeoisie was an important aspect of the transition process. The most important catalyst of the changes was the process of privatization. Liberal concepts of ownership change, and privatization emphasizes the political impacts of the process. The reduction of state property was regarded as a crucial element of institution building, mainly because of its role in reducing the chances of the survival of paternalism between managers of state-owned enterprises and politicians at various levels (Boycko et al. 1996; Rapaczynski 1996). The liberal concept emphasized liquidating the power position of incumbent management in order to make the transition process irreversible (Frydman and Rapaczynski 1994). Concerning practical implementation, the general concept did not make strong recommendations, for example, in favour of foreign investors. Therefore, the practice of privatization varied among CEE countries. However, privatization was a key issue of the transition process in all transition countries.

Political economic approaches to the privatization process soon directed attention to the empirical fact that incumbent management's influence and economic power could not be eliminated (Stark 1996; Stark and Bruszt 1998). Nevertheless, fears of reversing the transition process proved to be unfounded. Instead, new power networks evolved that included old and new players from the economy and from polity as well. New types of alliances were established; new elites were created. While the penetration of multinational business was very rapid in the markets of transitioning economies, adjustment processes of local companies and entrepreneurs lagged behind (Szanyi 1996). Therefore, market power shifted very quickly away from local firms to foreign companies. Foreign penetration increased to unusually high levels.

The process of economic restructuring was also reflected in the relationships between business and polity. Both foreign and domestic business organized into various interest groups. Drahokoupil (2008) analysed the emergence and impact of the new elite around foreign-owned companies. He regarded this elite as the ultimate winners of the transition process in CEE, especially in the Visegrad four (V4) countries (as compared with the position of the incumbent technocratic-managerial elite and the new entrepreneurs). He called this elite "foreign investors with their comprador intellectual allies", and he claimed "the domestic comprador forces rather than their foreign allies had...a major role in domestic politics" (p. 361). The rise of this sector was intertwined with the consolidation of the "competition state", the main aim of which was to insert the local economy into the structures of global capitalism. Based on the strategic-relational state theory, Drahokoupil et al. (2008) argued that the social relationships of production, institutions, and ideas constitute "a (strategically selective) environment that provides advantages to some actors and certain strategies over others" (p. 363). If this environment is determined by one or another type of elite, the advantages will be received by actors bound to the given ruling elite.

The dominance of one or another elite may or may not be politicized and bound to parties in power. In this regard, we find observations for both solutions. Drahokoupil (2008) argued that the political support of the competition state went beyond party divisions in CEE. Thus, the connected "comprador elites" might work under the rule of various political parties. Post-crisis experience showed more partisan approaches toward foreign investors in CEE economies, most importantly in Hungary (Stark and Vedres 2012) and Poland. Schoenman (2014) made the type of business-polity connections conditional upon political and economic uncertainty and upon the strength and degree of organizations of networks (lobbying platforms). According to him, elites may or may not act in non-partisan ways in relation to polity, depending on their level and strength of organization and the level of political uncertainty of the ruling parties. In this approach, the dominance of a certain type of elite may be challenged when determinants change. Moreover, Schoenman (2014) found different patterns of business-polity co-operation in the various CEE countries.

Local business developed representative organizations; however, direct links between businesspeople and politicians also persisted over time. The incumbent management of pre-transition state-owned enterprises as well as small-scale entrepreneurs formed local businesses. Some analysis of the

Hungarian business elite showed that most influential entrepreneurs had some kind of pre-transition career, either as party members and chief or second line managers of state owned enterprises (SOEs) or small-scale entrepreneurs (Laki 2002). It also turned out that local entrepreneurs could not keep pace with the dynamic development, the superior technological and market competences, and the wealth of multinational competitors (Laki and Szalai 2013). Typically, influential Hungarian entrepreneurs maintained good personal relationships with politicians and frequently also became officers of various parties. Therefore, the representation of Hungarian business in polity was much more based on personal linkages than on representative organizations.

Be it a temporary or long-lasting phenomenon, business-polity elites do whatever they can to stabilize their privileged positions. State and corporate functions of the elites are integrated through personal ties, institutional channels, material benefits, and recruiting patterns. There is a frequent personnel exchange between business, polity (state, regional, and local administration), and supporting institutions (consulting firms, developing agencies, law offices, etc.). Many people hold several positions in various areas. Interactions between the state and business are usually institutionalized. Due to important agency problems, the flow of material benefits between government and business is also frequent, giving way to rent seeking and corruption. Last but not least, personal careers usually combine positions in various areas of business-polity interplay. The recruitment system gives preference to broader professional experience that includes both business and government positions. While Drahokoupil (2008) provided evidence regarding the establishment of FDI-based elites in various CEE countries, other authors have described a similar process featuring local business (Schoenman 2014; Naczyk 2014; Stark and Bruszt 1998; McDermott 2002).

Elites exercise influence through personal contacts and by using communication platforms of business networks. Depending on the main message of their study, authors describe particular sets of business networks. Drahokoupil (2008) highlighted FDI-related networks and emphasized FDI dependency. Naczyk (2014) interpreted the sharp turn in the orientation of government policies in Hungary and Poland from FDI support toward preferences for local businesses. He described, therefore, mainly local business networks and mechanisms of the polity-local business interplay. Transparency International Hungary (2014) drew attention to the fact that after 2010, in an effort to thwart FDI dependence, the then-new

Hungarian government closed the usual communication interfaces toward multinational business. Simultaneously, it allowed local business interest groups to exercise more influence on government decisions.

Schoenman (2014) compared the Polish, Romanian, and Bulgarian experiences with business-polity exchanges. He found that these were more institutionalized in Poland than in the other two countries, where even if formal representative organizations existed, they were overshadowed either by wealthy businesspeople (oligarchs), who used them to lobby for their own business interests, or by influential politicians. He also claimed that broad networks (with substantial membership) were less partisan and, thus, in any political setting, their lobbying power was greater than personal contact-based lobbying. Business-polity networks that are based on the activity of broad representation can lobby for broadly distributive advantages in exchange for political support. Narrow networks, where personal contacts play a dominant role, create "selective advantage" institutions and distribute benefits to targeted recipients who are supporters of the ruling political party.

Schoenman (2014) stated that this dichotomy of the business-polity network structure works differently with high or low levels of political uncertainty. When political uncertainty is high and polity needs the (material and moral) support of broad business co-operation, a kind of concertation characterizes business-polity relations. In the case of high uncertainty and narrow networks, influential oligarchs may capture the state (as in pre-Putin-era Russia or Bulgaria). Political uncertainty is usually high in transition economies; nevertheless, there may be periods of less uncertainty (as in Hungary after 2010 or in Romania during the 1990s). In environments with little uncertainty, broad business networks may engage in new corporatist co-operation with the state. However, if business is less organized, polity may dominate the relationship and pick winners of selective advantage measures. Schoenman calls this *patronage*; however, the term *business capture* (see Yakovlev 2006) can be also applied in this setting.

We may conclude here that the organizational network of business-polity relations differs to a large degree among CEE countries. Meanwhile, business representation has formal institutions in each of these countries. Their membership, bargaining power, and embeddedness vary. The representation of multinational businesses is usually strong and well organized—in countries where FDI has been strong. The characteristics of local business representation are very different and are shaped by local political, economic, and social development factors. They are definitely less effective than the characteristics of the representation of FDI-based elites and are usually less broad and are often partisan. Additionally, personal business-polity relationships may also be important, in some countries even determining or giving way to business or state captured positions.

7.3 Economic Patriotism

FDI-bound elites dominated the first two decades of transition in CEE, even in countries with less significant FDI stock. The neoliberal concept was reinforced by the international advising community, which favoured well-established multinational players over weak local companies, investors, or interest groups. The classic concept of free competition and its general impact on overall well-being determined transition policies with corrections in favour of local institutions and the development of infrastructure. The massive transfer of finances and knowledge has flown into the CEE region, largely contributing to the modernization processes of these countries. The CEE region, especially the V4 countries, became integrated parts of the European economic space. Foreign penetration is dominant not only in market supplies, but also in local production. The share of foreign-owned (mostly multinational) companies is over 50% in the majority of economic sectors in terms of production, investments, and exports. Many observers regarded this high foreign share to be excessive. Szentes (2005–2006) wrote about unhealthy asymmetric interdependence, and Nölke and Vliegenhart (2009) developed the "Dependent Market Economy" concept in the framework of the Varieties of Capitalism literature.

The 2008–2009 crisis delivered extraordinary shocks to most developed market economies, which required rapid crisis management steps of various kinds that did not fit into the framework of the neoliberal concept. Many forms of increased state intervention were applied temporarily (nationalization, cash transfers to bail out important firms); others remained in place for longer (e.g., stimulating demand through increased public spending). However, even in the worst days of the crisis, governments refrained from applying "classic" protectionist policy tools, such as devaluing currencies or restricting imports. This fact reflects the different level of today's world economic integration as compared with the time of the Great Depression as well as accumulated policy experience since then. Thus, we may conclude that crisis management practice itself remained influenced in many areas by the neoliberal concept. Many of the temporarily applied steps have been withdrawn.

However, few governments in CEE countries have gone against the current; they did not limit state economic intervention but rather continued and even increased it after the crisis shocks eased. The most striking examples are Hungary and Poland. Poland was reported to have undertaken steps aimed at strengthening statist policies in the field of state property management. Many of these steps had already been taken by the Civic Platform-dominated government after 2010 (Naczyk 2014). The new right-wing populist government simply continued and expanded these policies. Hungary entered open conflict with a series of policies that ran against various EU regulations. However, Mihályi (2015) pointed out that in certain delicate issues, social-liberal Hungarian governments of the 2000s also pursued interventionist policies.[1] Thus, the departure from the neoliberal suit started before the crisis in Hungary. These facts allow the conclusion that in some CEE countries, politicians have started questioning the dominant neoliberal policy agenda in general and have increasingly favoured interventionist policies. The tendency can be regarded as a reaction to the far-reaching application of neoliberal policies that produced strong dependencies in economies, starting from the time of direct state control at the beginning of the transition process.

Increased state intervention is currently referred to as *economic patriotism* (Clift and Woll 2012; Naczyk 2014). Clift and Woll (2012) made a clear distinction from classic *economic nationalism*, whose roots trace back to Adam Smith and Friedrich List. The main difference lies in economic patriotism's limited toolkit. This means that governments do not go back to outright protectionist measures but use covert tools to positively discriminate in favour of domestic players, or they use liberalization measures selectively. The goal is to regain control over open markets. The term itself was first used in 2005 by Dominique de Villepin, then French prime minister, who called the defence of local prerogatives in integrated markets *economic patriotism* (Clift and Woll 2012). They also stated that the conflict over pursuing special political economic interests of the citizenry in conditions of complex economic, legal, and regulatory interdependence had started well before the 2008 financial crisis. Having no exclusive control over large parts of economic governance and facing deepening international trade and competition policy regulation, governments needed creative policy strategies.

I use the definition of *economic patriotism* given by Clift and Woll (2012) as "economic choices which seek to discriminate in favor of particular social groups, firms or sectors understood by the decision-makers as insiders because of their territorial status. Economic patriotism entails a form of economic partiality: a desire to shape market outcomes to privilege the position of certain actors. Unlike economic *nationalism*, economic patriotism is agnostic about the precise nature of the unit claimed as *patrie*. It can also refer to supranational or sub-national economic citizenship" (p. 308). An important feature of this approach is that it uses territorial references to political economic space in the definition rather than policy content. Thus, it can handle a wide range of state intervention, including selectively applied liberal economic policies (Helleiner and Pickel 2005). The novelty of the present-day economic patriotism over old-fashioned economic nationalism and mercantilism is that it is a response to the reconfiguration of economic governance and market interdependence. Governments become creative to assure traditional economic policy objectives using new means. They can today transfer their particular objectives from the national to the supranational level. For example, the EU can reinforce liberalization within the EU for the sake of protection from the outside. On national and subnational levels, we can distinguish between defending existing local production advantages and creating these in the process of integrating markets.

Paradoxically, deregulation and liberalization may themselves serve the creation of new types of discrimination (Levy 2006). Deregulation involves not only the removal of restrictions but also active reregulation that can be designed to promote particular outcomes. The need for reregulation provided politicians with new means of continued influence over the economy to obtain territorially beneficial outcomes. As Clift and Woll (2012) stated, economic patriotism represents a shift from measures of classic protectionist trade barriers to less direct measures, such as discriminatory product and process standards or state subsidies (as part of an overall aid policy). Alternatively, practices may also prefer selective liberalization in strategic sectors or the introduction of competition rules that prohibit standards common abroad and other restrictions. These forms of protectionism cannot be easily detected, and their usage had already spread parallel with the mass-scale liberalizationprocess (e.g., within World Trade Organization (WTO) negotiations) during the 1990s.

As seen from the analysis above, the roots of practices that gave rise to the concept of economic patriotism are not new; moreover, they characterize all market economies, not just CEE countries. What is new is the way of selling the idea more openly, taking on deliberate conflicts with institutions that safeguard the neoliberal concept. Occasionally, other governments also pursued policies that openly contradicted, for example, the EU's liberal competition policy rules. Clift and Woll (2012) interpreted these clashes as political messages to electorates that lacked serious intentions of realization. We can see similar attempts but on a larger scale from the Hungarian and, more recently, the Polish governments. They are aware of the impossibility of implementation under the current EU framework regulations; nevertheless, they would like to send political messages to both their electorates and Brussels. However, the number of new noncompliant measures can seriously undermine classic market economic institutions and erode the rule of law in these countries.

The other, more important purpose of economic patriotism in CEE is the real reconstruction of power relations. In this sense, the practice of the Hungarian and Polish governments goes beyond the rationale described above. Evidence from Hungary shows that selective measures have been applied in favour of particular agents. This is in contrast with the notion that economic patriotism uses broadly distributive measures in favour of groups of actors determined territorially. The aim of such steps is not the general preference of citizenry but the promotion of selected clients—selected members of the local elite who were considered losers in the power competition during the transition process.

This aim is more likely to be achieved if the new (local business-bound) elite has no strong organizations. Our previous analysis showed that local business associations in Hungary were rather weak, especially when compared with the lobbying platforms of foreign investors. Moreover, their leadership has always been politically determined; thus, these organizations could not strongly enforce the interests of their members. Weak, politically influenced networks and strong personal links between influential business people and polity make the Hungarian business elite easy prey for the state. Using selective advantage measures does not serve the interest of elites as a whole, but only selected clients. This practice cannot be regarded as an example of economic patriotism. The concept of economic patriotism is, rather, used as a politically advantageous selling label for predatory practices of the state.

The application of covert protectionism is sometimes justified with historical (not repeatable today) success stories of the classic East Asian developmental state. However, an important element of these was regulated competition in protected internal markets first and in global markets later. Patronage states kill market competition altogether. Clients are protected in domestic markets from foreign and domestic competition alike.

Without competition, however, economic agents rely solely on maintaining good relations with their patrons and do not enter the difficult path of innovation and activity sophistication. The result is declining competitiveness, deteriorating product and service quality, decreasing income generation, and overall impoverishment. The concept of economic patriotism never negated the role of competition as a driving force of market economies. The political practice of the patronage state eliminates competition and cannot be regarded, therefore, as an example of economic patriotism.

7.4 Departure from the FDI-Led Model to Patronage: Empirical Evidence from Hungary

7.4.1 *Evolution of the FDI-Led Model*

Hungary is a small, open economy that started the transition process from socialism to the market economy in 1989. The establishment of minority foreign ownership in the form of joint ventures was already legally allowed under communism in 1972, and a USD 400 million stock of investments had been accumulated as of 1989. Moreover, regular contacts with world markets and foreign firms allowed the accumulation of some network capital in the Hungarian economy and became an important lever of Hungary's internationalization process. More significant FDI started to arrive in the country after 1991, when the privatization process was directed toward sales to foreign investors. When the privatization process decelerated at the end of the 1990s, large-scale greenfield investments started to uphold yearly FDI inflow levels in the range of €3–4 billion (see Table 7.1). Later, the expansion of existing capacities also gained momentum. This is shown by the increasing share of reinvested profits in the source structure of FDI stock increments (Antalóczy et al. 2011).

Hungarian FDI statistics clearly demonstrate the outstanding role of foreign investments. During the years of the transition process, most of the largest multinational companies established a direct presence in Hungary in the form of affiliated companies. The foreign presence has been especially strong in the automotive and electronics industries of manufacturing, as well as in retail trade, banking and financial services, telecommunications, and media. These are typically the most globalized businesses. The establishment of Hungarian affiliates in these areas reflects the successful integration of the Hungarian economy in global production

Table 7.1 Inward FDI in Hungary (net inflow, reinvested profits, loans, €bn)

Year	*FDI change*	*Capital inflow*	*Reinvested profits*	*Loans*
1995	3695.7	3562.7	−163.6	296.5
1996	2625.0	1745.9	397.3	481.8
1997	3681.1	2010.2	1155.0	515.9
1998	2988.1	1371.8	1009.2	607.1
1999	3106.3	1434.9	1054.2	617.3
2000	2998.4	1509.6	1135.0	353.8
2001	4390.7	1096.3	1478.7	1815.7
2002	3185.1	1156.7	1911.4	116.9
2003	1887.5	−664.1	1787.6	764.0
2004	3438.7	1081.6	2227.4	129.6
2005	6172.1	3966.2	1917.9	288.0
2006	5454.4	1475.3	1358.6	2620.4
2007	2852.1	844.0	2274.5	−266.4
2008	3086.8	2301.4	895.1	−109.8
2009	1289.1	2821.6	−191.8	−1340.8
2010	1231.6	2814.0	−186.1	−1396.3
2011	1557.5	430.0	1225.9	−98.4
2012	3942.1	1915.9	1462.0	564.1
2013	1871.8	2202.7	1491.0	−1821.9
2014	4504.5	87.3	3682.7	734.5

Source: Hungarian National Bank

networks. I regard this development as a key determinant of structural development, technological modernization, investment activity, and economic growth in Hungary (see Table 7.2).

7.4.2 Positive and Negative Impacts and Criticisms of the FDI-Led Development Model

The strong influence of multinational companies in the Hungarian economy can be illustrated by several figures. They have contributed much to national investments,[2] creating a massive body of highly productive manufacturing and service bases. The uneven spread of FDI is also very visible. In hot spots such as Komárom, Győr, and Székesfehérvár, various parts of the larger Budapest agglomeration's new industrial districts have been created or old ones renovated. Foreign companies produce 70% of manufacturing production and 48% of manufacturing employment. Their shares in retail trade, banking and financial services, and telecommunications are

Table 7.2 Share of foreign-owned companies in sales, employment, and gross investments in Hungary (selected economic branches, %)

		2008	*2012*
(a) Sales			
	Manufacturing	64.9	69
	Energy supply	74.4	67.5
	Trade	44.6	45.4
	Infocommunications	62.7	67.7
	Total non-financial	50.1	53.3
	Financial	53.8	70.1
(b) Employment			
	Manufacturing	44	47.7
	Energy supply	51.5	51.9
	Trade	21.5	24
	Infocommunications	29.8	37
	Total non-financial	23.8	26.1
	Financial	46.9	45.1
(c) Gross investments			
	Manufacturing	67.8	78.3
	Energy supply	61.6	65
	Trade	49.4	41.3
	Infocommunications	74.2	79
	Total non-financial	49.6	55.3

Source: Central Statistical Office

also exceptionally high. Since foreign firms, especially those in manufacturing, are partners in international value chains, they are by definition export oriented. More than 80% of total manufacturing exports are delivered by the foreign-owned sector. In other V4 countries, foreign ownership participation is similarly important.

We can evaluate the strong presence of multinational business in various ways. My perspective considers development trends of the entire transition period up to now. As compared to the starting point, the current economic structure of Hungary is more developed with a large share of high- and medium-high tech manufacturing production and highly efficient service sectors. This extraordinary change in the economic structure would not have been possible without the strong investment activity of foreign firms. It is important to recognize that global markets are dominated by firms that are also present in Hungary. Barriers to entering the global markets are extraordinarily high; penetration is extremely difficult, even for the most innovative small firms. Inserting V4 economies into the system of global value chains is hardly imaginable without the effective role of global players of the markets.

On the other hand, we can see clear drawbacks as well. The strong presence of multinational firms produced dual structures in V4 economies. Foreign firms have relatively few contacts with local companies in their main area of production activity. Local suppliers usually do not enter their value chain. The reasons for this are manifold. First, existing technological links of co-operation in the value chain are not likely to be replaced by new entrants because of the high costs of entry. Second, local firms only gradually attain technological capabilities and financial and logistical capacities for co-operating with global business. At the time of FDI penetration of the V4 economies, local firms were not fit for co-operation (Antalóczy et al. 2011). Nevertheless, after 2000, the scope of the essential contribution by local firms to the global value chains started to increase. Due to the 2008–2009 crisis and recession, cost-cutting considerations became even more important, moving multinational firms towards more intensive local sourcing. V4 countries launched support programmes to enable local firms to co-operate with multinational companies (Kalotay and Sass 2012).

Another important issue that has been widely discussed is the extent of positive externalities stemming from multinational firms (spillover effects). Most studies tried to measure the externalities using various measures of productivity, assuming that the aggregate impact of spillovers will increase the productivity of local firms. The results have been mixed and not very convincing. A meta-analysis of the related literature indicated that a larger part of the findings supported the idea of measurable productivity increases (Iwasaki and Tokunaga 2014). There are methodological and also logical explanations for the lack of positive results (Szanyi 2002).

Critics of the FDI-based development model drew attention to systemic problems that could be far more important than the low level of positive impacts. Nölke and Vliegenhart (2009) wrote an important paper in which they tried to conceptualize the CEE economic model (DME model). They selected the role of FDIs in shaping the structure of the establishing market economies of the V4 countries. They argued that the large share of multinational companies in the production and trade of these economies strongly influenced the development of other economic and social subsystems as well. Their impact on national innovation and education systems was negative because their operation did not need high-end input from these systems. Furthermore, strong bias was exercised in a variety of national policies, since tax relief for multinational companies deprived governments of financial tools, and also because their operation was largely independent of national policies.

However, foreign investments and the activities of multinational companies have also been criticized politically. With such criticisms, populist parties hoped to receive social support and votes in elections. Using terms such as *luxury profits* of foreign firms, treating profit transfers as attacks against national property, and treating predetermined tax revenue expectations as the state's justified claims against foreign firms have earmarked populist sentiments articulated in Hungarian and Polish mass media. Similar statements have served as moral justification and political and social support for unfriendly changes in regulations and tax policies. This means that political expectations of sharing a bigger part of the potential benefits of global economic integration were enforced by measures that reached beyond the usual action sphere of policies and market institutions.

7.4.3 Some Selective Advantage and Disadvantage Measures in Hungary

While the main focus of the Hungarian government after 2010 was supporting domestic business ventures, the strongly embedded Hungarian economy continued relying on the activity of multinational firms. Populist political attacks were targeted against selected branches and even companies. Critical arguments (when applied at all) lost their general character when they were translated into policy measures. The Hungarian government identified a group of companies that it then did not treat well. Meanwhile, other companies and branches received further (mainly political) support.[3]

Banks and financial institutions were repeatedly accused of unfair practices toward customers. They were also thought to realize above-average profits. The foreign presence in the Hungarian banking sector was unusually high (80%), which also annoyed the government. Actions were taken to change all of this. The Hungarian government was one of the first governments to introduce sector-specific extra taxes (on turnover and transactions). Additionally, banks had to bear much of the cost of compensating private debtors with (non-performing) foreign exchange debt. These changes in regulations and new taxes brought banks into the red when they still had problems with recapitalization after the 2007–2008 financial crisis. The government blamed owners of private pension funds for the low level of returns. Pension claims were then "secured" by the government when claims of private pension accounts from the compulsory insurance system were taken and rechannelled into the pay-as-you-go first pillar state pension system. In both cases, the most affected financial institutions were foreign owned.

In 2014, the Hungarian state acquired MKB Bank[4] from its German owners. The German parent bank was unwilling to run the Hungarian subsidiary at a loss and sold it to the only serious buyer—the Hungarian state. The losses, however, were caused by various negative changes in the business environment initiated by the Hungarian government and by the process of reimbursing private foreign-exchange debtors. The achievement of 50% national ownership in the banking sector was heralded soon after. Later that year, FHB Bank was purchased by the Hungarian Post, increasing national ownership to more than 60% of bank assets.

Retail trade chains and other trading companies, firms in the telecommunications and energy sectors, as well as media were also harassed by disadvantageous selective regulations and sector-specific taxes and fees in Hungary. In order to save local business from the effect of the new taxes, specific selection rules were applied. In the case of a tax on broadcasting advertising, for example, a high-level turnover threshold was fixed so that the tax affected only one major foreign-owned medium.[5] More transactions and regulatory changes over a longer period of time were undertaken with the stated purpose of limiting utility costs. This promise of savings on utility costs was a major campaign tool in the 2010 and 2014 election campaigns. The government had already prohibited public utility price increases in 2010. Later, prices were set by government agencies at significantly lower levels than before, thus eliminating profits from this sector. This measure directly affected the profitability of private businesses. Limiting utility costs through price decreases caused companies to go into the red. Owners soon felt encouraged to sell their loss-producing assets. This process is regulatory taking: company revenues dry up because of unfavourable changes in market regulations or excessive taxes. Thus, many of the utility firms were sold to centralized or local public bodies. Some received quite generous compensation (for example, German RWE).[6]

The nationalized utility firms were in foreign ownership, and their regulatory takings heralded a third important consideration that seems to at least partly explain the unfriendly relationships with selected foreign companies. The Hungarian government repeatedly enacted market regulations and changed the tax system to take a bigger bite of cash revenues from large multinational firms and create more favourable conditions for owners of domestic capital. Nevertheless, this was targeted against certain types of companies: financial institutions, media firms, large retail chains, and telecom companies. Governmental communication explained their negative treatment by arguing that such companies do not contribute to the material (real economic) production platform of the Hungarian economy.

In Hungary, the left-wing Bajnai government declared the privatization process complete in 2008 (Hungarian Government 2009). This meant that substantial, effective state ownership remained in place. The statement itself also could be understood as potentially allowing nationalization. Indeed, this happened sporadically until 2010 and, on larger scale since then, under right-wing governments. In terms of asset volume, property renationalized after 2010 was smaller by one magnitude than privatized assets after 1990 (Mihályi 2015). Nevertheless, the change in the attitude toward state ownership has far-reaching impacts. The importance of the relationship has not declined since the 1990s when it was a most topical issue. Rapaczynski (1996) explained the complex role of the state in enforcing property rights, including the need for occasional nationalizations. A property-rights system's stability is best supported by a significant historical record of state forbearance from excessive and redistributive regulation as well as excessive encroachments.

Considering a list of renationalizations (Mihályi 2015, p. 17), the overall picture shows that between 2010 and 2014, 209 companies were affected, and the total value of the transactions was slightly over HUF1573 bn (about €5 bn). This amount included the sales price paid to the previous owners, increased share capital, and other commitments as well. The numbers and amounts seem to be very high, especially if we consider that the Hungarian government had already accumulated public debt in excess of the Maastricht criteria prior to the 2008–2009 crisis. However, as Mihályi (2015) explained, these transactions did not increase the gross state debt, since they represented a simple change in the asset structure—a kind of securities swap of more liquid assets. However, if we look at the list of transactions, we discover that the overwhelming majority of financial commitments stemmed from transactions in the energy and banking sectors (HUF1366 bn).

Among the reasons for renationalization, various political goals can be detected. The first outstanding transaction was the nationalization of the second pillar of the pension system at the turn of 2010/2011. The official explanation called for the security of accumulated pension funds to be taken out of the hands of private pension funds that failed to bring the expected returns (they "played with hazardous securities"). Account holders of private pension funds were called to withdraw their savings and channel them to the state pension system at the risk of losing their pension rights in the pay-as-you-go state pension system. The government used the "opting out" trick, meaning that those who wanted to keep their pensions untouched had to face the threat. Thus, in the end, 2.8 million account holders channelled their savings back into the state pension system at a value of approximately HUF3000 bn (€10 bn)—equivalent to 10% of GDP. Most observers believe that the "voluntary" nationalization of private pension funds was aimed at using the obtained assets for debt relief (which was, on the other hand, accumulated partly by the social security system).

In order to make a formal difference between favoured and punished firms, the Hungarian government signed strategic agreements with a number of foreign companies. The process started in the summer of 2012, when Hungary's macroeconomic situation worsened. GDP fell, and major business ventures were postponed. The sluggish business conduct of large firms could not be counterbalanced by supporting small and medium-sized enterprise activity. The Hungarian government decided to encourage the activity of selected multinational firms with declarations of partnership. Before September 2015, 60 such strategic agreements were signed, of which, 54 partners were foreign-owned companies. The partners were concentrated in three major manufacturing branches: the electronic, automotive, and pharmaceutical industries. According to Transparency International's calculations, the contracts signed by mid-2014 covered firms representing 18% of manufacturing employment and 40% of manufacturing exports—a significant share of Hungary's manufacturing base (Transparency International Hungary 2014).

Agreements were initiated mainly, but not exclusively, by the government. A set of conditions was applied to big multinational businesses: a five-year track record in Hungary; significant contribution to GDP production and exports; investments exceeding HUF5 bn; contribution to employment—at least 1000 employees; intention to create more jobs for skilled workers; participation in education; and at least 10% production input from local suppliers). The content of the agreements was rather uniform. Usually, intentions to co-operate in job creation, training and education, research and development, and the development of local supply networks were declared. No concrete measures of co-operation were included. Our previous analysis of FDI attraction policies pointed out that these areas used to be the main foci after 2004. Thus, the Hungarian government did nothing more in the strategic partnership agreements than reassure selected foreign firms about the possibility of the type of co-operation and support that had been normatively expanded to all business players before 2010.

7.5 Conclusion and Interpretation of the Research Results

What does the dual treatment of selected domestic firms and foreign-owned companies mean for Hungary's business model? In another paper, I argued that the arbitrary involvement of the state in ownership patterns of the Hungarian economy would bring important systemic risks (Szanyi 2016). Basic market economic institutions, such as the security of the private property regime and the rule of law, can be seriously undermined if the government does not consequently apply the law to its own transactions. The dual treatment of local and international business is another piece of policy practice in the same direction. It is a different concept of regulation that is in conflict with principles of competition policy. The ways in which winners and losers are picked may also matter. The decline of normative regulation and the preferences of selective measures will deliver the wrong message to economic agents—that their success will depend more on the development of their network capital than on their business activity. The danger of increasing corruption is also bound to the process. This may all strengthen the negative tendencies of the evolution of crony capitalism.

In my understanding, crony capitalism means a legally uncontrolled (badly controlled) interaction between a polity and business interests that works against the principles of free enterprise and fair competition. Policymakers and influential business people co-operate to create preferential treatment for friendly businesses in exchange for the material support of parties, politicians, and election campaigns. This type of co-operation is not unknown in developed economies, although a more-developed institutional background and the strong control of a civil society may limit the most harmful impacts of cronyism on institutions of the market economy. If the financial support of political parties is transparent and lobbying for industry (company) interests is institutionalized, crony capitalism is under social control. It does not mean, of course, that the markets are free of marginal interest enforcement. In cases where cronyism is not transparent and not controlled, it may lead to very high social losses and even illegal transactions. A major difference between most of the established market economies and most of the transition economies lies in the level of institutional and social control of polity-business interactions. Loose control in transition economies causes the investment and business climate to deteriorate, which is expressed in rather low rankings in competitiveness reports and high costs of financing.

State favouritism in Hungary, ranging from public procurement to market regulation, seriously contradicted normative regulation and violated the principle of equal treatment and EU laws of competition. Many major competition policy-related processes were launched in Brussels against the current Hungarian government. Levies on retail trade supervision and taxes on tobacco products were suspended, and grants for road construction were no longer transferred to Hungary due to ongoing competition policy procedure infractions. In the first two cases, tax policy measures were designed to favour a selected number of politically linked agents. Cases of public procurement were investigated because of unusually high prices. Observers also regarded road construction to be one of the main areas of patronage.

Selective advantages have been provided to clients, and, simultaneously, competitors of clients were frequently punished by unfavourable regulations. This is most clearly visible in the example of punishing multinational businesses using selective disadvantages (extra taxes, exclusive regulation). Meanwhile, other members of the same community were rewarded and included in the close circle of strategic partners of the Hungarian government. The simultaneous steps in opposite directions can be interpreted as a deliberate policy aimed at splitting the established business networks (those of foreign companies/multinational businesses). According to Schoenman's typology, this is a move toward narrow networks and the patronage state (business capture).

These cases illustrate a departure from the competition state. The concept of an illiberal state reduces the free market system and democratic institutions. The above cases, as well as the whole process of departure from Western values, have been conceptualized in Hungary and are, therefore, regarded by the Hungarian government as a sovereign decision to establish a new economic system. Populist followers of the Hungarian agenda can also be found in Poland. The PiS party openly declared its appreciation of the concept, declaring that, hopefully, Warsaw will be like Budapest. However, Polish observers believe that the concept of economic patriotism has already been introduced in Poland as well.

When comparing the fundamentals of the FDI-led development model and the current policy changes in Hungary, my assumption is that economic development accompanied by a loss of FDI cannot be run without an important decline of international competitiveness. I am not even sure whether the replacement or substitution of multinational business is technically possible at all, even in the long run. Even if it is, I do not think that such a change could be carried out without a significant drop in economic activity, income generation, and living standards. Therefore, such an undertaking is also hardly feasible politically. Thus, I evaluate increasing cronyism not as a fatal danger but rather as a factor that deteriorates economic performance due to less effort toward improving levels and quality of business activity.

Acknowledgments The paper was developed in the framework of research supported by the Hungarian National Research, Development and Innovation Office (Grant No. 112069) and by the Institute of Economic Research of Hitotsubashi University, Tokyo. The author expresses his special thanks for the kind comments and suggestions of Gábor Hunya and Sándor Richter as well as for the editorial assistance of Tammy Bicket.

Notes

1. A most striking action was the introduction of Lex MOL, an amendment of the commercial code that changed corporate governance regulations to help the Hungarian oil company repel the takeover ambitions of its Austrian competitor, ÖMW. The legal changes were passed in a rare agreement between the government and the opposition.
2. The other main source of investment financing was EU transfers. The share of Hungarian national sources was rather small.
3. Documents of various government officials' media communication on the ideological differentiation between "good, productive" and "bad, speculative" businesses were analysed by Mihályi (2015) and Transparency International Hungary (2014).
4. Magyar Külkereskedelmi Bank Rt: Hungarian Foreign Trade Bank Co.; until 2014, its owner was the Hungarian affiliate of Bayerische Landesbank.
5. A government communication explained the measure citing suspected tax evasion of the company. However, it was never explained why, if there was something illegal in RTL's taxation, this was not repaired by the responsible state institution, the tax office.
6. It is, of course, another question whether today's sales revenues are sufficiently high for the necessary investments. Observers state that public utility companies are still in an extremely bad financial situation and do not invest any more, which may threaten the quality of their services.

References

Antalóczy, K., Sass, M., & Szanyi, M. (2011). Policies for attracting foreign direct investment and enhancing its spillovers to endogenous firms: The case of Hungary. In E. Rugraff & M. W. Hansen (Eds.), *Multinational corporations and Local Firms in Emerging Economies* (pp. 181–210). Amsterdam: Amsterdam University Press.

Boycko, M., Shleifer, A., & Vishny, R. (1996). A theory of privatization. *Economic Journal, 106*, 309–319.

Clift, B., & Woll, C. (2012). Economic patriotism: Reinventing control over open markets. *Journal of European Public Policy, 19*, 307–323.

Drahokoupil, J. (2008). Who won the contest for a new property class? Structural transformation of elites in the Visegrád Four region. *Journal for East European Management Studies, 13*, 360–377.

Drahokoupil, J., Van Apeldorn, B., & Horn, L. (2008). Introduction: Towards a critical political economy of European governance. In J. Drahokoupil, B. Van Apeldorn, & L. Horn (Eds.), *Contradictions and limits of neoliberal European Governance: From Lisbon to Lisbon* (pp. 1–17). Basingstoke: Palgrave Macmillan.

Frydman, R., & Rapaczynski, A. (1994). *Privatization in Eastern Europe: Is the state withering away?* Budapest: Central European University Press.

Helleiner, E., & Pickel, A. (Eds.). (2005). *Economic nationalism in a globalizing world*. Ithaca: Cornell University Press.

Hungarian Government. (2009). *J/8582. jelentés az ÁPV Zrt. és jogelődei – mint a privatizáció lebonyolítására létrehozott célszervezetek – tevékenységéről és a teljes privatizációs folyamatról (1990–2007)* (Report No. 8582 about the activity of State Asset Holding Plc. and its predecessors – as special organizations to carry out privatization – and the complete privatization process, 1990–2007). Budapest.

Iwasaki, I., & Tokunaga, M. (2014). Macroeconomic impacts of FDI in transition economies: A meta-analysis. *World Development, 61*, 53–69.

Kalotay, K., & Sass, M. (2012, October 18). *Inward FDI in Hungary and its policy context*. Columbia FDI Profiles. Vale Columbia Center on Sustainable International Investment.

Laki, M. (2002). A nagyvállalkozók tulajdonszerzési esélyeiről a szocializmus után (About chances of obtaining property by entrepreneurs after socialism). *Közgazdasági Szemle, 49*, 45–58.

Laki, M., Szalai, J. (2013). *Tíz évvel később – a magyar nagyvállalkozók európai környezetben* (Ten years after: Hungarian entrepreneurs in European environment). Budapest: Közgazdasági Szemle Alapítvány.

Levy, J. (Ed.). (2006). *The state after statism: New state activities in the age of liberalization*. Oxford: Harvard University Press.

McDermott, G. A. (2002). *Embedded politics: Industrial networks and institutional change in post-communism*. Ann Arbor: University of Michigan Press.

Mihályi, P. (2015). *A privatizált vagyon visszaállamosítása Magyarországon 2010–2014* (Re-nationalization of privatized property in Hungary 2010–2014) (Discussion Paper No. 2015/7). Budapest: Institute of Economics, Centre for Economic and Regional Studies of the Hungarian Academy of Sciences.

Naczyk, M. (2014). *Budapest in Warsaw: Central European business elites and the rise of economic patriotism since the crisis.* Unpublished manuscript. Available at: http://papers.ssrn.com/sol3/papers.cfm?abstract_id=2550496

Nölke, A., & Vliegenhart, A. (2009). Enlarging the varieties of capitalism: The emergence of dependent market economies in East Central Europe. *World Politics, 61*, 670–702.

Rapaczynski, A. (1996). The roles of state property and the market in establishing property rights. *Journal of Economic Perspectives, 10*, 87–103.

Schoenman, R. (2014). *Networks and Institutions in Europe's Emerging Markets.* Cambridge: Cambridge University Press.

Stark, D. (1996). Recombinant property in East European capitalism. *American Journal of Sociology, 101*, 492–504.

Stark, D., & Bruszt, L. (1998). *Postsocialist pathways: Transforming politics and property in East Central Europe.* Cambridge: Cambridge University Press.

Stark, D., & Vedres, B. (2012). Political holes in the economy: The business network of partisan firms in Hungary. *American Sociological Review, 77*, 700–722.

Szanyi, M. (1996). Adaptive steps by Hungary's industries during the transition crisis. *Eastern European Economics, 34*, 59–77.

Szanyi, M. (2002). *Spillover effects and business linkages of foreign-owned firms in Hungary* (Working Paper No. 126). Budapest: Institute of World Economics, Centre for Economic and Regional Studies of the Hungarian Academy of Sciences.

Szanyi, M. (2016). The reversal of the privatization logic in Central European transition economies. *Acta Oeconomica, 66*, 33–55.

Szentes, T. (Ed.). (2005–2006). *Fejlődés, versenyképesség, globalizáció* (Development, competitiveness, globalization). Budapest: Akadémiai Kiadó.

Transparency International Hungary. (2014). *Lifting the lid on lobbying: Strategic partnership agreements in an uncertain business and regulatory environment* (National Report of Hungary). Budapest: Transparency International Hungary.

Yakovlev, A. (2006). The evolution of business-state interaction in Russia: From state capture to business capture? *Europe-Asia Studies, 58*, 1033–1056.

CHAPTER 8

Impact of Global Companies' Real Options Implementation on Their Hungarian Subsidiaries

Andrea Szalavetz

8.1 Introduction

Most contributions to the burgeoning scholarship on global companies' (GCs) responses to the global financial crisis of 2008–2011 rely on the conceptual framework of the real options (RO) theory (Christopher and Holweg 2011; Chung et al. 2010; Driouchi and Bennett 2011, 2012; Lee and Makhija 2009). RO theory refers to a portfolio of options that firms can use to calculate in the context of environmental uncertainty. The theory offers a framework of analysis that supports managerial decision-making with regard to investments and other strategic decisions.

Options that managers consider and evaluate are (1) commitment, (2) withdrawal, or (3) deferral. Accordingly, executives may opt for increased investment (they can buy up rivals, expand activity in existing subsidiaries, enter new markets, or invest in research and development—R&D); conversely, they may decide to withdraw from certain locations

A. Szalavetz (✉)
Institute of World Economics, Centre for Economic and Regional Studies, Hungarian Academy of Sciences, Budapest, Hungary

P. Havlik, I. Iwasaki (eds.), *Economics of European Crises and Emerging Markets*, DOI 10.1007/978-981-10-5233-0_8

or business areas, terminate joint ventures, scale down activities, or sell or close subsidiaries. The third option to consider is to adopt a wait-and-see attitude.[1]

Above and beyond considering and selecting from a portfolio of options, another advantage of the real options framework is its flexibility. The theory recognizes that investments are not once-and-for-all actions; hence, RO valuation and reasoning embody the possibility of sequencing, staging, and—more importantly—reversing commitments.

Most RO research has focused exclusively on headquarters (HQ) when investigating adjustments of GCs' investment commitments in response to fluctuations in the global, or, even more frequently, in the local host-country environment. The objective of these papers is to identify how RO implementation allows GCs to preserve strategic flexibility, reduce risks, and open new growth opportunities (Chung et al. 2013; Dikova et al. 2013; Lee 2013; Lee and Makhija 2009; Song et al. 2014).

In contrast, relatively little research has addressed the heterogeneous impact of global companies' RO implementation on their subsidiaries (Belderbos and Zhou 2009; Chung et al. 2010; Lee 2013; Maitland and Sammartino 2009; Song 2013). In the wording of Chung et al. (2010), it is "a general assumption that MNE subsidiaries are more or less the same because they belong to the same parent firm" (p. 501).

The global crisis of 2008 has, however, confronted researchers and practitioners with a highly complex and multifaceted real-world situation. In an era when turbulence in the overall business environment is coupled with rapid and disruptive technological development, when the spectacular expansion of some host country markets coincides with drastic contraction in some home countries, when stock markets are particularly vulnerable and bound to overreact to firms' selected announcements, GCs' flexible and staged approaches to both downside risk reduction and upside potential enhancement (Tong and Reuer 2007b) may yield a wide variety of outcomes for individual subsidiaries. Moreover, GCs' actual responses to the global crisis usually involved a combination of the possible options listed above, making the prediction of subsidiary-level effects even harder to fathom.

This chapter is intended to contribute to the RO literature from a subsidiary-focused perspective. Drawing on interviews carried out at GCs' manufacturing subsidiaries, we analyse the micromechanisms of actions undertaken by GCs to reconfigure their network organizations as a response to the crisis—as perceived by their subsidiaries.

More specifically, we investigate (1) the factors that determined the timing of investments/divestments, and (2) the role of organizational experimentation in preserving GC-level flexibility. The other research issue concerns the impact of organizational restructuring and resource reallocation on Hungarian subsidiaries.

Another purpose of this chapter is to contrast the empirical experience of the surveyed companies with the findings of the received literature. This will help us refine and possibly extend the literature on RO implementation in times of crisis.

The macroeconomic context of our investigations is Hungary—a small, open economy whose modernization and industrial upgrading has been driven mostly by the inflow of efficiency-seeking foreign direct investment (Csáki 2001; Szanyi 2001). The corporate context comprises subsidiaries that specialize in activities represented at the bottom of the smile curve of value-added in manufacturing.[2]

The rest of the chapter is structured as follows: Sect. 8.2 briefly summarizes the theoretical background; Sect. 8.3 presents the research method and the sample of the companies that we interviewed; Sect. 8.4 reviews the findings; and Sect. 8.5 provides conclusions and presents some limitations of our research.

8.2 Conceptual Framework

Our research is related to multiple literature streams, including those concerned with corporate restructuring (Bowman and Singh 1993), general post-crisis developments in global value chains (Cattaneo et al. 2010), the drivers of offshoring firms' location choices (Jensen and Pedersen 2011), subsidiary upgrading (Birkinshaw et al. 2005), and the application of RO theory in drafting business strategies (Reuer and Tong 2007).

Due to space limitations and the breadth of each of these streams of literature, our review will be limited to, first, crisis-related aspects of RO literature and, second, to literature that focuses on changes in the perspectives of GCs' Central and Eastern European subsidiaries after the global crisis.

The RO theory is concerned with firms' discretionary investment opportunities (in real assets) carried out under uncertainty (Trigeorgis 1996).[3] Obviously, most of the options investigated are related to growth and expansion, such as decisions on (1) market entry modes, (2) investment in R&D and in new technology, (3) the establishment of strategic partnerships and/or joint ventures, and (4) the transfer of assets and resources to subsidiaries (see the survey by Driouchi and Bennett 2011, 2012).

In contrast, crisis-related RO theorizing investigates the abandonment or deferral of investment plans, the reduction of resource commitments, and the reconfiguration and switching of assets and resources (Kogut 1985; Kumar 2005; Tong and Reuer 2007a). It is no surprise that, following the global crisis of 2008, the number of contributions focusing specifically on the application of RO theory in divestment decisions increased rapidly (Belderbos and Zhou 2009; Damaraju et al. 2015; Song et al. 2014; Zschoche 2015).

This latter research suggests that multinationality offers a portfolio of resource reconfiguration options, which ensures operational flexibility and reduces risks. Exercising these options, however, involves considerable costs (Barnett 2003; Maitland and Sammartino 2009). Zschoche (2015) warned that, in the short run, the benefits of disposing of unprofitable production locations will not necessarily outweigh the costs that arise from withdrawal. In turbulent environments, when the value of specific business units considered to be divested is not known, a wait-and-see attitude (deferral of the divestment) may be the rational reaction (Damaraju et al. 2015).

There are few subsidiary-focused research papers that distinguish among the perspectives of individual subsidiaries. One example is Belderbos and Zhou (2009), who investigated the factors that influence strategic decisions on foreign subsidiary divestment. They found that crisis-triggered resource reconfiguration leads to the relocation of activities from subsidiaries in high-cost, to ones in low-cost, locations. Export-oriented manufacturing subsidiaries are more likely to be divested if they share this role in the host country with other affiliates of the owner or if the macroeconomic conditions in the host country are similar to those in other host countries, i.e., with partner manufacturing subsidiaries of the same owner.

Chung et al. (2010) and Lee (2013) found that subsidiaries with a within-country-growth orientation turn out to be less valuable for HQ and, consequently, are more likely to be scaled down or closed than cross-country-oriented subsidiaries that contribute to GC-level operational flexibility.

Subsidiary fate is also influenced by a multitude of additional factors, such as behavioural factors in decision-making, specific attributes of the host country environment, the structure of GCs' existing portfolios of subsidiaries, and existing interdependencies among subprocesses across subsidiaries (Barnett 2003; Nachum and Song 2011). Furthermore, a subsidiary's fate is closely associated with the path dependency thesis emphasized in Adner and Levinthal (2004). These authors claimed that future investment opportunities are contingent upon prior investment commitments.[4]

As for the regional context of our investigations, Rugraff and Sass (2016a, 2016b) investigated the factors that determine GCs' reactions to the crisis (relocation or, conversely, counter-cyclical investments and acquisitions aimed at strengthening their market positions). Drawing on field interviews with Hungarian automotive suppliers, they found that size, structure, and network embeddedness influence GCs' strategic choices in turbulent times. They posited that the relocation of production to even lower-cost locations was not characteristic in the context of foreign-owned facilities operating in Hungary; a number of "keep factors" locked automotive investors into their Hungarian locations.

Zooming in on the Czech Republic and Slovakia, Pavlínek (2015) scrutinized the divestment of peripheral facilities. He found that there had been only a few divestments and plant closures in the automotive industries of these countries; however, local subsidiaries (as well as domestically owned suppliers) faced enormous pressures to improve efficiency and reduce costs. Filippov and Kalotay (2011) presented a comprehensive overview of GCs' responses to the crisis in the new EU member states. They found that responses were heterogeneous, including both contraction and expansion. Some subsidiaries in the new member states faced downsizing and partial closures; others benefited from the relocation of additional production and of advanced functions. This contributed to their functional upgrading.

Several other papers that examined GCs' organizational reactions to the crisis from the perspective of a host country or a peripheral subsidiary, in general, and in a Central and Eastern European (CEE) context, in particular, also emphasized the possibilities for upgrading opened up for local actors by the crisis-triggered restructuring of global value chains (GVCs) (Domański et al. 2013; Sass and Szalavetz 2013; Sturgeon and Kawakami 2011; van Tuijl 2014). Upgrading occurred partly as a consequence of owners' pressure on subsidiaries to reduce costs and improve efficiency (Pavlínek 2015) and partly as a result of the increasing delegation of more advanced functions to local subsidiaries (Sass and Szalavetz 2013).

However, according to Schuh's (2012) persuasive arguments, scenarios suggesting that the successful upgrading of products, processes, and functions will contribute to the CEE-based subsidiaries' upgraded position within GVCs (e.g., that they might become regional headquarters) are less likely after the crisis. Lead firms would rather reconsider the organizational model they adopted for CEE countries; they no longer consider the region as a homogeneous bloc. Instead, they increasingly differentiate among CEE countries, assessing them according to the opportunities they (i.e., the individual countries and the given subsidiaries) can offer. This argument is reiterated by Szent-Iványi and Vigvári (2012), who scrutinized the evolution of CEE countries' potential to benefit from FDI by constructing a composite indicator of countries' spillover potential. These authors found substantial cross-country differences and argued that GCs should, therefore, clearly diversify their investment strategies toward the CEE region, rather than treating the countries as a homogenous group.

8.3 Research Method and Sample

Since the objective of this chapter is to open the black box of organizational processes and study them as they unfold over time, exploratory research based on multiple case studies was considered the most appropriate method of investigation (Doz 2011; Eisenhardt 1989). An interview guide containing predominantly open-ended questions (see Annex) allowed interviewees to provide rich descriptions of complex, multifaceted processes—to speak about the real-world phenomena of crisis-driven organizational transformation and its impact on the surveyed manufacturing subsidiaries. The interviews, 60–90 minutes in length, were conducted between September and November 2015. Interviewed managers were, in most cases ($N = 11$), CEOs of Hungarian subsidiaries; in two cases, divisional leaders were interviewed. To preserve anonymity, neither corporate names nor main products will be specified.

In the process of sample selection, we applied a purposeful sampling method (Patton 1990). Our aim was to select information-rich cases—companies whose insights draw on a multiplicity of experiences, i.e., companies whose cases promise observations about issues of central importance to our research. For this purpose, we selected large companies—local manufacturing subsidiaries of GCs that are important global actors in their industries (Table 8.1). At the time of the interviews, these companies had been operating in Hungary for at least a decade.

Table 8.1 Summary of surveyed companies

No.	*Industry*	*HQ location*	*Interviewee*	*No.*	*Industry*	*HQ location*	*Interviewee*
1	E	SE	CEO	8	E	USA	Divisional leader
2	M	DK	CEO	9	E	USA	CEO
3	A	DE	CEO	10	M	DE	CEO
4	E	DE	CEO	11	AE	USA & DE	CEO
5	A	USA	CEO	12	AE	DE	CEO
6	M	USA	Divisional leader	13	AE	DE	CEO
7	M	DE	CEO of the carved-out and sold division				

Note: *A* automotive; *E* electronics; *AE* automotive electronics; *M* machinery; *SE* Sweden; *DK* Denmark; *DE* Germany; *CEO* chief executive officer; *HQ* headquarters

Source: Author's compilation

Altogether, our sample consists of 13 manufacturing subsidiaries of American, Danish, German, and Swedish GCs operating in the automotive (2), automotive electronics (3), electronics (4), and machinery (4) industries. On average, these companies had been operating in Hungary for more than 20 years at the time of the interviews. They exhibited strong upgrading performances, in terms of both products and processes. Moreover, a number of advanced functions have been moved to the local facilities, including R&D (nine companies have R&D departments), process engineering and testing, software development, procurement, repair, logistics, and distribution.

The surveyed GCs had an average of 99,700 employees in 2014 (four companies had less than 10,000 employees, and six GCs had more than 100,000 employees). The Hungarian subsidiaries averaged 1920 employees in 2014. The average global turnover was €24.1 billion in 2014.[5] As for the surveyed Hungarian subsidiaries, the average net sales amounted to €608.6 million. The importance of the surveyed Hungarian subsidiaries, considered in terms of their contribution to their parent companies' total production and/or total revenues, is heterogeneous; some are listed among the largest production facilities of their mother companies, contributing to 15–23% of the total turnover, while others account for a mere 0.2% of total sales. The surveyed Hungarian companies are highly export oriented; the average share of exports in total sales amounts to 82.8%.[6]

When selecting the sample, we immediately faced the problem of respondent bias. In line with global developments with respect to the average tenure and turnover of executives (average tenure shows a continuous decline, and CEO turnover increases—Schloetzer et al. 2015), also in Hungary, it was difficult to find large local subsidiaries with interviewed managers who had been in the same managerial position during the crisis years. In our sample, only six managers of the 13 would fulfil this requirement. Not all the interviewed managers had been with the same firm seven or eight years prior to the interview; only 11 of 13 had remained within the same company. Interestingly, the two "newcomer CEOs" worked previously (during the crisis years) at another firm in our sample. Nevertheless, all interviewed managers confirmed that they had sufficient information about firm-specific developments during and after the crisis years to assist us. Moreover, we believe that the quality of the respondents compensates for their occasional lack of personal experience in the given position.

The first couple of questions were intended to set the context and collect information about the multiplicity of crisis-driven organizational transformation processes that affected the organization of the surveyed firms' value chains. The core part of our questions investigated the mechanism by which organizational transformation was decided and implemented (e.g., the factors that determined the timing of investments/divestments, the factors that shaped the valuation of options, and the impact of organizational restructuring and resource reallocation on the mandates and responsibilities of the Hungarian subsidiaries).

In line with the framework proposed by Doz (2011), we ensured internal validity through three measures. First, we tried to control for factors that may distort the causality of the arguments. The restructuring of GVCs, including developments such as network consolidation, the establishment of shared services centers (SSCs), relocations, divestments, and outsourcing, may be the outcome of "normal" organic development, or these developments may be a response to the crisis. In an effort to distinguish between the outcomes of organic evolution and organizational changes prompted by perceived environmental turbulence, we repeatedly asked our interviewees to confirm whether the specific organizational transformation action they recounted was a reaction to the crisis.

Second, we applied a constant comparative method in which each case helps to confirm or reject the insights emerging from previous cases

(Glaser and Strauss 1967). Third, we relied on both primary and secondary information sources and triangulated the findings to maximize reliability. In addition to interview information, we collected secondary data about both the interviewed subsidiary and its parent company, such as annual reports, corporate information, press releases, newspaper articles, balance sheets, and notes pertaining to the financial statement.

Construct validity was ensured through systematic cross-case analysis, which allowed us to look at the identified commonalities from multiple angles (Yin 2003). This facilitated analytical generalization, while cross-case analysis helped identify the contingent limitations of our research method.

Cross-case analysis was assisted by a predetermined technique of making case study notes and dedicating some time at the end of each interview to reviewing the chief findings, and asking interviewees to identify additional issues that they perceived to be relevant and important that were missing from the interview. External validity (Gibbert et al. 2008) was also enhanced by sending the draft paper to the interviewed managers for approval and feedback. The question we particularly emphasized in the covering letter that accompanied the draft paper was whether the interviewed managers considered the general statements formulated as key findings of the interviews to adequately generalize the issues raised by them and/or by their peer interviewees. Focused feedback helped us improve analytical rigour, and, at the same time, it enhanced the cross-sectional validity of the arguments.

8.4 Findings

8.4.1 Timing of RO Implementation, as Perceived by the Hungarian Subsidiaries

Inquiring about the micro-mechanisms of real options implementation, we asked executives to provide details about crisis-driven changes within the organization of their GC owner. The first conspicuous commonality of the answers was that it was difficult to establish an unambiguous direct association between organizational changes and the crisis.

On the one hand, relocation and divestment actions had already been frequent before the crisis, while decisions to expand in new areas and acquire competitors or actors in adjacent technological fields were made with seemingly non-abating frequency during and after the crisis as well.

> *I really cannot tell whether these consecutive relocation actions were driven by the crisis or they would have been implemented anyway. We have been experimenting with organizational simplification actions for a while. The crisis may have accelerated and intensified these reconfiguration moves.* (Case No. 2)

On the other hand, the majority of managers interviewed maintained that organizational reconfiguration decisions presumably driven by the crisis have been implemented with relatively long time lags after the crisis. This calls into question the direct association of organizational transformation with the adverse turn in the business cycle.

Delays in divestment were sometimes caused by experimentation with alternative solutions, such as the merger of subsidiaries, merger of business areas, creation of spinoffs, reclassification of business divisions, and changes in the reporting structure.

> *There were so many changes before arriving at the present organizational setup! It would be quite difficult to recall all the changes we have experienced in the past couple of years. Even our name [that of the Hungarian subsidiary] changed several times, as well as our reporting structure. And finally, after a number of organizational changes, seven years after the crisis, our business segment was carved out from the equity of our parent company and sold to a financial investor. Whether this action, or any of the previous rearrangements, can be associated with the crisis or not, that's a good question.* (Case No. 7)

Another reason for the time lag in GCs' responses to the crisis is the consideration of the stock market's expected reaction. Accordingly, the successful disposal of a business segment requires its restructuring first. Consequently, disposal transactions are preceded by investments in retrenchment and turnaround. HQs concentrated operations to improve capacity utilization and profitability, stabilize revenues, and increase operating cash. These reorganization actions continued for several years before they culminated in the disposal of the given segment.

Therefore, subsidiary executives found it difficult to interpret these developments and assess whether the seemingly straightforward signs of "commitment" reflect a systematic and proactive medium-term organizational strategy *culminating* in a successful disposal transaction or a reactive organizational experimentation. In this latter case, the disposal of the segment can be interpreted as the failure of previous strategic steps.

Peripheral subsidiaries in low-cost regions first experienced mainly the benefits of corporate reorganization (additional tasks have been relocated, responsibilities increased, and investments implemented). Consequently, the ultimate decision about the disposal of the given segment often came as a shock for them. The accounts of informants in two firms illustrate this exasperation:

> *I think it was a strategic mistake to give up that manufacturing site and sell it. What a waste of resources! Our owner kept investing in that facility; it was expanded with relocated activities, capital investment soared, accompanied by considerable intangible investment. Additional blue collar workers and new executives were hired. Within a relatively short time frame, crisis years' unsatisfactory key performance indicators started to improve. Last year, the given facility was even publicly praised as one of the top performers within the organization. Everybody was astonished when our owner's decision was announced.* (Case No. 7)

> *Although I was really surprised at that time, I must acknowledge that our owner chose a good exit strategy. What we discerned during the crisis was only that the global HQ managed business difficulties with extraordinary success through capacity alignments, relocations, streamlining, and occasional closure of operations in advanced economies. Now I realize that in this process, our owner recognized that the consolidation of financial performance indicators is a necessary but insufficient condition of survival. If you try to compete with stand-alone products or product families in the automotive industry, you will be out; you have to offer integrated solutions. This recognition prompted our owner to make a fundamental decision: he sold the firm [i.e., the global company] to another automotive company that is specialized in complementary products and technologies.* (Case No. 5)

Altogether, the often-perceived lack of a direct association between the crisis and the organizational restructuring actions of HQs and, in particular, their action lag, i.e., the long period between the cyclical downturn and fundamental organizational restructuring steps, suggests that deferral was a frequently selected strategic option among the surveyed companies.

8.4.2 RO Implementation: Experimentation and Reversibility

Another finding that crystallized from the accounts of our informants was that parent companies' organizational realignment actions—however strategic they are—can often be reversed or easily modified. Organizational reconfiguration is considered experimental, and flexibility is deliberately incorporated in the design of actions. The subsequent paragraphs provide some illustrations.

The first example is the case of a subsidiary where functional upgrading, more specifically, gaining responsibility for the procurement function, was followed by the loss of this mandate. Already before the crisis, the subsidiary had assumed ever-greater responsibilities with respect to core activity-related procurement. During and after the crisis, the subsidiary kept increasing its procurement responsibilities. It became entrusted with scanning the regional market for new suppliers. It hired supplier relationship management experts, performed supplier audits, designed and implemented supplier development programmes, and was responsible for the localization of selected inputs. However, at one point in time, several years after the crisis, it lost its procurement mandate because HQ decided to centralize procurement activities in a group purchasing department to be located in Switzerland.

Another subsidiary also gained a regional procurement mandate and did its best to develop (enhance the knowledge intensity of) this support function. It accumulated knowledge about the specifics of regional partner subsidiaries' activities and procurement needs. It managed to efficiently organize a regionally integrated procurement system, together with the related logistics and other support activities. Later, however—again, years after the crisis—HQ decided to decentralize procurement. Thus, the interviewed subsidiary lost its regional mandate, and the partner subsidiaries in the region assumed responsibility for operational procurement themselves.

In a third case, local manufacturing operations were discontinued in 2007, i.e., already before the crisis, and the Hungarian subsidiary became a pure R&D facility—a center of excellence within the group. In 2013, the owner decided to restart manufacturing activities in Hungary in a new, greenfield facility. Production expanded rapidly; in 2016, a second greenfield manufacturing facility was under construction in Hungary.

The accounts of two informants illustrate the turbulence local subsidiaries occasionally experienced as a result of their parent companies' experimentation with the organizational structure.

> *During the crisis year, we became entrusted with a number of group-level procurement tasks. Later, however, these were partly recentralized to Germany. Nevertheless, I don't think the organizational position of procurement has stabilized. It is true—problems and inefficiencies emerged after the relocation of procurement to Hungary. However, recentralization did not solve these problems, since similar inefficiencies were experienced also in Germany. You know, an organizational transformation step will not yield the expected results if you*

realign one single function. Functions consist of a number of interrelated activities, and functions themselves are interrelated. If you centralize only one function in an isolated manner without realigning the whole organizational architecture, a number of new problems will emerge. And indeed, they did. (Case No. 3)

We have gained responsibility for the production of a newly developed sophisticated product. Since the launching of a new product requires the development department experts' quasi-continuous support, i.e., the joint work of product developers, design engineers, process engineers, technicians, and assemblers, the relocated processes turned out to be excessively costly (German experts had to spend long months in Hungary). Moreover, quality problems were numerous. Finally, HQ decided to backshore the given production activity to Germany. Although the factory in Germany experienced similar problems, it was decided that scale-up development will be finalized in Germany. When production gets standardized, it will probably be relocated again, but this time not to Hungary, rather to the rapidly growing Romanian subsidiary of HQ. (Case No. 12)

According to the managers interviewed, parent companies consider these actions neither as sunk investments nor as failures, but rather as signs of organizational flexibility that ensure efficiency gains. Several managers interviewed mentioned that scheduled organizational reviews took place every (second) year; hence, reorganization and experimentation with new organizational setups were normal.

8.4.3 RO Implementation: Impact on the Hungarian Subsidiaries

Overall, the interviewed managers considered the outcome of their HQs' reconfiguration of the global organization beneficial for the subsidiary. Crisis-driven organizational realignment reinforced subsidiaries' ongoing organic upgrading processes. A crisis often prompted the owners to relocate additional production activities from high-cost subsidiaries, among others from newly acquired competitors, to the relatively low-cost Hungarian location. Moreover, the recognized synergy effects of locating production-related support tasks to production sites prompted the owners to locate development and testing activities in Hungary also, i.e., activities that would support the newly located production activities.

Consequently, the most frequent outcome of RO implementation by GCs was the increase of their local commitment (see Table 8.2, regarding the composition of RO outcomes from the perspective of the surveyed firms).

Table 8.2 Summary of real options implemented at the companies in the sample

No.	*C*	*W*	*D*	*Examples*
1	X	X		(C) Launching of programmes that improve efficiency and cut costs (intangible investments) and frequent organizational changes; (C+W) Concentration of selected activities in Hungary and the relocation of other activities away from Hungary
2	X	X		(C) Relocation of new production lines to Hungary, the establishment of SSCs in Hungary, and the location of selected production-related R&D activities to Hungary; (W) Relocation of selected support activities to other subsidiaries, the creation of SSCs (outside Hungary), and the relocation of support activities there
3	X	X		(C) Relocation of production to Hungary; (C) Relocation of R&D activities to Hungary; (C+W) Organizational experimentation: the relocation of several support activities to Hungary and the backshoring of selected activities; (W) Global centralization of selected support activities and the loss of the related mandates of the Hungarian subsidiary
4	X	X	X	(C) Relocation of logistics and the warehousing of other technical activities from Germany to Hungary, the establishment of an R&D facility in Hungary, production relocation, and the expansion of local R&D; (C+W) During and immediately after the crisis: substantial investment in and expansion of a new division that had been established before the crisis and withdrawal from that division years after the crisis; (W) Relocation of selected high-volume, standard activities from Hungary to the Romanian subsidiary; (W) Loss of regional procurement mandate: decentralization of regional procurement
5	X	X	X	(C) Investments to improve efficiency and stabilize revenues and the location of new activities to Hungary; (W) Closure of one of the Hungarian facilities but consolidation of and additional investments in the other facility; (D)Takeover of the GC by a competitor
6	X	X		(C) Investments to improve efficiency and reduce costs; (C+W) Frequent organizational changes: the location of new production and support activities in Hungary, investment in the expansion of locally performed support activities, the establishment of a new center of excellence, relocation (away from Hungary), and the backshoring of selected production activities
7	X	X	X	(C) Production relocation from HQ's Swedish subsidiary to Hungary; (W) Equity carve-out and sale of the subsidiary but new support tasks (new responsibilities) under the new owner

(*continued*)

Table 8.2 (continued)

No.	*C*	*W*	*D*	*Examples*
8	X	X		(C+W) Continuous changes in the product mix, the location of new production to Hungary, the relocation of selected activities to even lower-cost subsidiaries (e.g., Ukraine), and reshoring from China to Hungary
9	X	X	X	(W) Downsizing and changing the reporting structure of production; (C) Expansion of services activities and new responsibilities in the field of IT related to the support of major organizational transformation
10	X			(C) Production relocations, capacity expansion, the location of a new SSC to Hungary, and the location of support activities to Hungary
11	X			(C) Capacity expansion, production relocation to Hungary, the location of production-related support activities, and substantial tangible and intangible investments
12	X	X		(C+W) Production relocation to and from Hungary, the expansion of R&D activities in one facility but the loss of the R&D mandate at the other Hungarian facility, and the restructuring of production activity at one facility (shift to higher-volume but lower unit value-added production)
13	X		X	(C) Expansion of local R&D activity and greenfield investments many years after the crisis: the establishment of manufacturing facilities and the location of new production activities in Hungary

Note: *C* commitment; *W* withdrawal; *D* deferral

Source: Author's compilation

Increased commitment was manifested in (1) capacity expansion and product upgrading; (2) tangible and intangible investments in process upgrading and efficiency increases; and/or (3) functional upgrading of subsidiaries driven by HQs' delegation of additional tasks and responsibilities.

Although the synergy effect of co-locating production and advanced support processes was recognized well before the crisis, nevertheless, these moves became more frequent after the crisis years. These are some typical answers to a question about the impact of HQs' crisis-driven consolidation moves on the Hungarian subsidiary:

> *The development of the Hungarian location has been going on quite rapidly through consecutive production relocation decisions. New production sites have been added to the original one; now we have four factories in Hungary. We host some production-related research activities as well, and the volume of R&D activities keeps expanding. Upgrading took a new qualitative turn with the location of various SSCs to Hungary. Over time, a finance and an information*

> *technology SSC were located to Hungary and a regional sales and distribution center that is responsible also for repair and service activities. As I see it, the next functional consolidation step will be in the field of human resource (HR) management; we are competing now for the possibility of hosting an SSC in HR.* (Case No. 2)

> *One positive impact of the crisis (positive for us) was the relocation of R&D activities; our HQ decided to locate a number of R&D tasks to us and to India.* (Case No. 3)

> *Alongside a considerably upgraded product mix, we gained responsibility for corporate-wide accounting tasks, for testing and programming (writing software embedded in the production machinery), and for selected operational procurement tasks. Additionally, we have a patent engineering team working for the parent company.* (Case No. 10)

Not even the occasional disposal actions (e.g., the sale of the business division) resulted in the closure of the surveyed subsidiaries; ownership changes often represented new opportunities within the new owners' organization.

> *Having taken our company over, the new owner could expand its portfolio with our products and, thus, offer even more integrated solutions to its customers.* (Case No. 7)

In another case, the weight of the subsidiary increased considerably within the organizational structure of its new owner, as compared to its importance in the previous organization. Before the ownership change, the interviewed subsidiary was a simple manufacturing facility, one of its owner's several manufacturing sites in Hungary. Equity carve-out (the sale of the business division) necessitated investment in separating the given company's information system from its previous owner's system and integrating the subsidiary in its new owner's system. Consequently, new IT experts were hired (transferred from the previous owner's organization), and they undertook these knowledge-intensive development tasks. Similarly, sales specialists and procurement officers were transferred from the previous owner's organization. Altogether, the activity mix of the subsidiary became much more diversified under its new owner than previously.

Nevertheless, we also identified adverse developments from the subsidiaries' perspective, i.e., examples of HQ opting for withdrawal. In one case, the takeover of a competitor indirectly resulted in the downgrading of the Hungarian subsidiary. One of the R&D centers of the acquired competitor was in Romania, and HQ decided to consolidate R&D activities in its Romanian subsidiary. This brought an end to the period of gradual, R&D-based upgrading of the Hungarian subsidiary; R&D activities in the Hungarian location have been phased out.

Relative downgrading was driven in some cases by the shifting composition of global demand. The new market imperative (Coe and Yeung 2015, p. 101) was mentioned by almost all of our informants as a trigger for strategy transformation. The flip side of the coin was a relative degradation of the importance of Europe and of the Central European facilities, as perceived by our informants. Here is what some of them said:

> *While rationalization moves addressed mainly our owner's European operations, buzzwords in other regions were different, for example, "expansion of the global footprint" and "next frontiers of growth".* (Case No. 9)

> *Relatively well-capitalized when the crisis erupted, our owner took over one of our major competitors that had been hit hard by the crisis. Several executives of that company have been kept following the takeover, and they received key positions. The new executives brought a new orientation; we have increasingly turned toward the global markets. This implied, however, diminished attention to Europe, at least in relative terms. In our case, what I notice is that our owner pays somewhat less attention to us; HQ is less willing to consider our initiatives.* (Case No. 4)

> *Why not Hungary for the location of the new global IT-development facility? You know what our global strategic officer would ask himself before making a location decision? He would ask: "Where are our most important customers located?" As you know, there are tremendous opportunities in Southeast Asia; that's what influences the location decision of new corporate functional centers.* (Case No. 1)

In summary, the factors that determined the ultimate outcomes of organizational restructuring and resource reallocation for the Hungarian subsidiaries were rather heterogeneous. Moreover, some of the effects became evident with such a long time lag (deferral was a frequently chosen option) so that the direct association of subsidiary-level developments with the crisis was not considered straightforward. As detailed in Table 8.2, GCs' responses frequently involved a combination of possible options; hence, the balance (the ultimate outcome) of HQs' strategic actions proved difficult to predict.

8.5 Conclusions

The surveyed empirical evidence indicates that the complexity of the business environment shaping the valuation of options has increased considerably. Our first finding is that in the volatile economic environment of the crisis years, flexibility was regarded of utmost importance when deciding on organizational reconfiguration actions. Flexibility was ensured through a variety of techniques, including staged investment and divestment, the avoidance of hasty decisions (deferral of decisions that may destroy options), and deliberate organizational experimentation.

The flip side of the coin is that the impact of managerial decision-making on subsidiaries has become even harder to predict, irrespective of the fact that some of the observed subsidiary-level developments have supported the received literature on the determinants of the impact of HQs' RO implementation on subsidiaries.

The surveyed evidence supports, in particular, the importance of host country attributes (wage level) for subsidiary survival. In line with the literature (Barnett 2003; Nachum and Song 2011), the structure of the owners' existing portfolios of subsidiaries and interdependencies among activities have also proved to be important explanatory factors of subsidiaries' benefiting from the crisis-driven concentration and consolidation of value-chain activities (consider the location of advanced support functions near production that had been relocated from high-wage countries).

As for the role of path dependency influencing subsidiary fate (Adner and Levinthal 2004), our findings are ambiguous. In several instances, prior commitment was considered to be an important explanatory factor of subsequent developments during and after the crisis. However, as outlined earlier, parent companies' decisions often proved reversible. RO implementation necessitated substantial organizational learning that was driven and facilitated by a process of systematic organizational experimentation. Consequently, some of subsidiaries' previously gained mandates were sometimes lost as a result of HQs' new strategic direction.

Notwithstanding occasional turbulence, on balance, the surveyed Hungarian subsidiaries have benefited from their owners' cost-cutting and restructuring actions. Production activities relocated from owners' facilities in advanced economies led to capacity expansion and product upgrading. The location of advanced support activities to the expanding local production facilities contributed to subsidiaries' functional upgrading. In this respect, path dependency, i.e., the volume of existing, committed assets in the Hungarian subsidiaries, proved an important motive in shaping HQs' subsequent investment decisions.

Altogether, the experiences of the surveyed subsidiaries are consistent with the well-known commitment–flexibility trade-off (as surveyed in Driouchi and Bennett 2012) that makes predictions based on RO theorizing so difficult for subsidiaries.

This research has a number of limitations. One limitation is sample selection bias; large, global companies may weather the crisis more easily than family-owned internationalized ventures with a couple of low-cost production facilities. Crisis-driven adjustment and reorganization steps, as well as reliance on counter-cyclical strategies, may significantly differ across various size categories.

Another limitation is our reliance on subsidiary managers' subjective perceptions. However, since the purpose of our research was to explore the micromechanisms of RO implementation, reliance on local executives' accounts, i.e., on their perceptions of these developments, is not a problem. At the same time, these perceptions affirm that, in today's global environment, even the RO framework—however sophisticated it is as compared to conventional financial analysis methods, such as net present value or discounted cash-flow-based reasoning—seems indecisive, as the drivers of RO implementation are so complex and multifaceted.

Acknowledgments The author thanks Tammy Bicket for providing editorial assistance. I am indebted to the participants of the Vienna workshop for providing helpful comments regarding the previous version of this chapter.

Annex: Interview Protocol

1. Please describe the changes the global financial crisis of 2008–2011 induced in your parent company's global organization. (Consolidation/rationalization of the value chain—relocations, offshoring/outsourcing, closing down or sale of selected subsidiaries; OR expansion—establishment of new subsidiaries and acquisition of competitors).
2. How did the owner schedule his organizational restructuring actions? Which factors influenced the timing of implementation?
3. Did the above-described organizational transformations have an impact on the activities/position of the Hungarian subsidiary? Please specify.
4. Did the crisis-driven reconfiguration of the owner's organizational structure create any upgrading opportunities for the Hungarian

subsidiary (in terms of new production tasks and new functions, such as R&D, procurement, etc.), or did it rather provoke a loss of previous mandates in specific functions? Please specify.

5. Are you aware of any crisis-driven changes in the development of partner subsidiaries in the region? Did these changes have an impact on the mandates of the Hungarian subsidiary?
6. Do you perceive any other changes in the organizational configuration, in management practices, or in the business model over the past five to seven years that occurred as consequences of the crisis?
7. How do you assess the alignment of the overall organizational strategy with the changes in the global/regional business environment?

Notes

1. The portfolio of real-world options is, of course, much more variegated—and not only at times of crisis. For example, firms may consider relocating or outsourcing selected activities, or, conversely, increasing vertical integration. Although not mentioning the RO theory explicitly, some papers address one or two of these options: see, e.g., Kinkel (2012) on the production-relocation and backshoring implications of the global crisis, Fisch and Zschoche (2012) on the withdrawal from and closure of foreign production locations, or Knudsen and Foss (2015) on changes in the vertical integration of core activities as a response to a crisis.
2. Mudambi (2008) used the metaphor of *smile curve economics* following Shih (1996), to describe the relation between global value chain specialization (i.e., specialization in specific activities along the value chain) and value-added. The curve depicts the distribution of value-added at each stage of the chain. It makes it obvious that production activities, represented at the bottom of the smile curve, generate much less value-added than do pre- and post-production types of service activities.
3. Over time, the application domains of RO theory have expanded considerably, and have included internalization and network options for GC management, the choice of governance modes and options related to the management of GCs' international operations, and options concerning diversification and resource reallocation (Driouchi and Bennett 2012).
4. Indeed, according to some critiques of the RO logic, the issue of path dependence is not sufficiently considered in the RO reasoning (Adner and Levinthal 2004; Barnett 2003; Driouchi and Bennett 2012).
5. This average masks large differences. Four companies had net sales below €1 billion. The turnover of three companies ranged between €1 billion and €10 billion; five companies accounted for net sales between €10 billion and €100 billion, and the revenues of one GC exceeded €100 billion.

6. In reality, the share of exports is even higher, since, in some cases, a substantial share of "domestic sales" is delivered to an independent legal entity partner subsidiary of the same GC in Hungary or to an independent legal entity distribution center of the headquarters (located in Hungary). These products will, presumably, be exported as well; however, exports are accounted for by the given intermediary entity and not by the company in the sample.

References

Adner, R., & Levinthal, D. A. (2004). What is not a real option: Considering boundaries for the application of RO to business strategy. *Academy of Management Review, 29*, 74–85.

Barnett, M. L. (2003). Falling off the fence? A realistic appraisal of a real options approach to corporate strategy. *Journal of Management Inquiry, 12*, 185–196.

Belderbos, R., & Zou, J. (2009). Real options and foreign affiliate divestments: A portfolio perspective. *Journal of International Business Studies, 40*, 600–620.

Birkinshaw, J., Hood, N., & Young, S. (2005). Subsidiary entrepreneurship, internal and external competitive forces, and subsidiary performance. *International Business Review, 14*, 227–248.

Bowman, E. H., & Singh, H. (1993). Corporate restructuring: Reconfiguring the firm. *Strategic Management Journal, 14*(S1), 5–14.

Cattaneo, O., Gereffi, G., & Staritz, C. (Eds.). (2010). *Global value chains in a postcrisis world: A development perspective*. Washington, DC: World Bank.

Christopher, M., & Holweg, M. (2011). "Supply chain 2.0": Managing supply chains in the era of turbulence. *International Journal of Physical Distribution & Logistics Management, 41*, 63–82.

Chung, C. C., Lee, S. H., Beamish, P. W., & Isobe, T. (2010). Subsidiary expansion/contraction during times of economic crisis. *Journal of International Business Studies, 41*, 500–516.

Chung, C. C., Lee, S. H., Beamish, P. W., Southam, C., & Nam, D. D. (2013). Pitting real options theory against risk diversification theory: International diversification and joint ownership control in economic crisis. *Journal of World Business, 48*, 122–136.

Coe, N. M., & Yeung, H. W. C. (2015). *Global production networks: Theorizing economic development in an interconnected world*. Oxford: Oxford University Press.

Csáki, G. (2001). The inflow of foreign direct investment into Hungary. In G. Csáki & G. Karsai (Eds.), *From Transition to Integration: Macroeconomic Development in Hungary 1990–2002* (pp. 226–261). New York: Columbia University Press.

Damaraju, N. L., Barney, J. B., & Makhija, A. K. (2015). Real options in divestment alternatives. *Strategic Management Journal, 36*, 728–744.

Dikova, D., Smeets, R., Garretsen, H., & Van Ees, H. (2013). Immediate responses to financial crises: A focus on US MNE subsidiaries. *International Business Review, 22*, 202–215.

Domański, B., Guzik, R., Gwosdz, K., & Dej, M. (2013). The crisis and beyond: The dynamics and restructuring of automotive industry in Poland. *International Journal of Automotive Technology and Management, 13*, 151–166.

Doz, Y. (2011). Qualitative research for international business. *Journal of International Business Studies, 42*, 582–590.

Driouchi, T., & Bennett, D. (2011). RO in multinational decision-making: Managerial awareness and risk implications. *Journal of World Business, 46*, 205–219.

Driouchi, T., & Bennett, D. J. (2012). Real options in management and organizational strategy: A review of decision-making and performance implications. *International Journal of Management Reviews, 14*, 39–62.

Eisenhardt, K. M. (1989). Building theories from case study research. *Academy of Management Review, 14*, 532–550.

Filippov, S., & Kalotay, K. (2011). Global crisis and activities of multinational enterprises in new EU member states. *International Journal of Emerging Markets, 6*, 304–328.

Fisch, J. H., & Zschoche, M. (2012). The effect of operational flexibility on decisions to withdraw from foreign production locations. *International Business Review, 21*, 806–816.

Gibbert, M., Ruigrok, W., & Wicki, B. (2008). Research notes and commentaries what passes as a rigorous case study. *Strategic Management Journal, 29*, 1465–1474.

Glaser, B. G., & Strauss, A. (1967). *The discovery of grounded theory: Strategies for qualitative research*. New York: Aldine Publishing Co.

Jensen, P. D. Ø., & Pedersen, T. (2011). The economic geography of offshoring: The fit between activities and local context. *Journal of Management Studies, 48*, 352–372.

Kinkel, S. (2012). Trends in production relocation and backshoring activities: Changing patterns in the course of the global economic crisis. *International Journal of Operations & Production Management, 32*, 696–720.

Knudsen, E. S., & Foss, K. (2015). The effect of recessions on firms' boundaries. *Industrial and Corporate Change, 24*, 1081–1108.

Kogut, B. (1985). Designing global strategies: Profiting from operational flexibility. *Sloan Management Review, 27*, 27–38.

Kumar, S. (2005). The value from acquiring and divesting a joint venture: A real options approach. *Strategic Management Journal, 26*, 321–331.

Lee, A. P. J. Y. (2013). Dual-option subsidiaries and exit decisions during times of economic crisis. *Management International Review, 53*, 555–577.

Lee, S. H., & Makhija, M. (2009). Flexibility in internationalization: Is it valuable during an economic crisis? *Strategic Management Journal, 30*, 537–555.

Maitland, E., & Sammartino, A. (2009). Subsidiaries in motion: Assessing the impact of sunk versus flexible assets. In J. L. C. Cheng, E. Maitland, & S. Nicholas (Eds.), *Managing subsidiary dynamics: Headquarters role, capability development, and china strategy, Advances in international management, No. 22* (pp. 55–83). Bingley: Emerald Group Publishing.

Mudambi, R. (2008). Location, control and innovation in knowledge-intensive industries. *Journal of Economic Geography, 8*, 699–725.

Nachum, L., & Song, S. (2011). The MNE as a portfolio: Interdependencies in MNE growth trajectory. *Journal of International Business Studies, 42*, 381–405.

Patton, M. Q. (1990). *Qualitative evaluation and research methods.* Newbury Park: SAGE Publications.

Pavlínek, P. (2015). The impact of the 2008–2009 crisis on the automotive industry: Global trends and firm-level effects in Central Europe. *European Urban and Regional Studies, 22*, 20–40.

Reuer, J. J., & Tong, T. W. (Eds.). (2007). *Real options theory* (Advances in strategic management, Vol. 24). Greenwich, CT: Elsevier/JAI Press.

Rugraff, E., & Sass, M. (2016a). Voting for staying: Why didn't the foreign-owned automotive component suppliers relocate their activity from Hungary to lower-wage countries as a response to the economic crisis? *Post-Communist Economies, 28*, 16–33.

Rugraff, E., & Sass, M. (2016b). How did the automotive component suppliers cope with the economic crisis in Hungary? *Europe-Asia Studies, 68*, 1396–1420.

Sass, M., & Szalavetz, A. (2013). Crisis and upgrading: The case of the Hungarian automotive and electronics sectors. *Europe-Asia Studies, 65*, 489–507.

Schloetzer, J. D., Tonello, M., & Aguilar, M. (2015). *CEO succession practices: 2015 edition* (Research Rep No. 1575-15-RR). New York: The Conference Board.

Schuh, A. (2012). Strategy review for Central and Eastern Europe: Strategic responses of foreign multinational corporations to the recent economic and financial crisis. *Journal of East-West Business, 18*, 185–207.

Shih, S. (1996). *Me-too is not my style: Challenge difficulties, break through bottlenecks, create values.* Taipei: The Acer Foundation.

Song, S. (2013). FDI structure, investment specificity, and multinationality value under host market uncertainty. *Management International Review, 53*, 795–817.

Song, S., Makhija, M., & Lee, S. H. (2014). Within-country growth options versus across-country switching options in foreign direct investment. *Global Strategy Journal, 4*, 127–142.

Sturgeon, T. J., & Kawakami, M. (2011). Global value chains in the electronics industry: Characteristics, crisis, and upgrading opportunities for firms from developing countries. *International Journal of Technological Learning, Innovation and Development, 4*, 120–147.

Szanyi, M. (2001). Privatization and greenfield FDI in the economic restructuring of Hungary. *Transnational Corporations, 10*, 25–38.

Szent-Iványi, B., & Vigvári, G. (2012). Spillovers from foreign direct investment in Central and Eastern Europe: An index for measuring a country's potential to benefit from technology spillovers. *Society and Economy, 34*, 51–72.

Tong, T. W., & Reuer, J. J. (2007a). Real options in multinational corporations: Organizational challenges and risk implications. *Journal of International Business Studies, 38*, 213–230.

Tong, T. W., & Reuer, J. J. (2007b). Real options in strategic management. In J. J. Reuer & T. W. Tong (Eds.), *Real options theory* (Advances in strategic management, Vol. 24, pp. 3–28). Greenwich, CT: Elsevier/JAI Press.

Trigeorgis, L. (1996). *Real options: Managerial flexibility and strategy in resource allocation*. Cambridge, MA: MIT Press.

van Tuijl, E. (2014). Car makers and upgrading: Renault in Romania. *Journal of Business Strategy, 35*, 13–18.

Yin, R. K. (2003). *Case study research: Design and methods* (Vol. 5). California: Thousaend Oaks.

Zschoche, M. (2015). Performance effects of divesting foreign production affiliates: A network perspective. *Long Range Planning, 49*, 196–206.

PART IV

Poland

CHAPTER 9

Potential Macroeconomic Effects of the Trade Collapse Due to Economic and Political Crises: The Case of Poland

Jan Hagemejer

9.1 Introduction

The political and economic relations between the European Union (EU) and Russia have worsened substantially since 2013. This decline was triggered by events in Ukraine involving the overthrow of the government in light of the disagreement in Ukrainian society regarding the direction of trade integration in the form of Association Agreements with the EU and the Eurasian Union, the economic union of major economies of the former USSR, including Russia, Belarus, and Kazakhstan. This resulted in a military escalation between Ukraine and Russia and, subsequently, the annexation of Crimea by the Russian Federation and military conflict in Donbass.

In March 2014, the European Council agreed on a set of sanctions against Russia as a way of condemning the annexation of Crimea. These initial sanctions included travel bans and the freezing of major Russian officials' assets. The second wave of sanctions was introduced in July 2014 and strengthened in September 2014. However, even this second wave of sanctions was only partially trade related. They mainly targeted the

J. Hagemejer (✉)
Faculty of Economic Sciences, University of Warsaw, Warsaw, Poland

P. Havlik, I. Iwasaki (eds.), *Economics of European Crises and Emerging Markets*, DOI 10.1007/978-981-10-5233-0_9

sectoral co-operation between Russia and the EU and included a ban on the purchase or sales of the bonds of Russian banks, energy companies, and defence companies and the provision of loans to those companies. Direct trade restrictions were mainly aimed at military imports and exports and trade of dual-use goods and energy-related equipment and services. Similar sanctions were imposed by the United States, Canada, Switzerland, Norway, and Australia. The goods covered by the EU sanctions are mainly products of the metal industry, machinery and equipment, and motor vehicles, and they do not contribute in a large part to the overall exports in those sectors.[1] Gross and Mustilli (2015) claim that the effects of those sanctions are, in fact, negligible.

The Russia's response to the EU sanctions, besides a travel ban on certain high-profile US officials, involved a very specific trade ban on agricultural and food products originating in the United States, the EU, Norway, Canada, and Australia. The list of products covers most of the EU exports of agri-food products to Russia. As we will see later in the chapter, while the economic significance of those banned goods is more pronounced than the reciprocal sanctions by the EU, it is still relatively mild. However, it does involve just one sector of the economy, and in economies where the food sector is an important part of overall exports, the impact of the sanctions is larger. These economies include Poland and the other new member states (NMS) of the European Union.[2]

The direct effects of the Russian ban on EU products are difficult to track. The period under consideration is also a period of falling resource prices, including coal, gas, and oil, a major source of Russian gross domestic product (GDP), which had an obvious negative effect on Russia's imports from the EU. While the specific products affected by the embargo of exports to Russia contribute around €5.2 billion or 17% in 2013, the direct macroeconomic impacts at the EU level amount to a 0.12% fall of total extra EU exports (Kutlina-Dimitrova 2015). The analysis by Christen et al. (2015) leads to similar conclusions.

Given the fact that some computable general equilibrium-based analyses of the effects of the crisis in Russian-EU economic relations are available, we take the opportunity to provide some more stylized results. We do not intend to perform a detailed analysis of the effects of the Russian trade ban and the EU embargo. However, we are interested in the types of trade-related mechanisms that take place in the event of a sudden substantial trade collapse. In that vein, we analyse two contrasting simulation scenarios, one in which one trading partner introduces a ban on a selected sector—in this case, the food sector—and we compare the reactions of the Polish economy and others to a much more profound trade ban where countries cease trading on a much larger scale, encompassing all non-resource sectors. We show that even in that drastic simulation scenario, the effects on the EU economies, and Poland in particular, are very small as compared to those in Russia.

The contrasting results for Poland and Russia partially stem from very different trade and production structures within the EU. First, trade between Poland and Russia (and, similarly, between the EU and Russia) is much more inter-industry than intra-industry (some calculations can be found in Gusev 2007). On the other hand, Polish trade with the EU is increasingly intra-industry and, therefore, adjusting the geographical structure following a trade disruption is easier, i.e., imports of a particular good are procured from different sources, and exports go to several destinations. Russia's trade is much more specialized, and so is its economy. Adjusting to a disruption of imports leads to a painful reallocation of resources to industries where Russia has no comparative advantage. Moreover, Poland is much more involved in global value chains than Russia, which dampens the adverse effects of trade disruption, i.e., non-oil trade with Russia is not essential to the production possibilities of Polish firms.[3]

One must keep in mind, however, that even the comprehensive trade collapse that we model does not include trade of natural resources. There are several reasons for that. First, this would require a completely different way of modelling the energy sector. Second, trade in oil and gas between the EU and Russia is essential to the functioning of all of the involved economies, and a ban on trade in resources would not be politically feasible. Third, one cannot really think of a model that could, in fact, accommodate such a dramatic structural change.

This chapter is structured as follows. Section 9.2 briefly covers the evolution of the trade structure of Poland and the rest of the EU with Russia, with a special focus on the agri-food sectors. Section 9.3 provides a description of the model and database. Section 9.4 covers the simulation scenarios, and Sect. 9.5 briefly summarizes the results. The last section concludes.

9.2 Russia's Importance to the Trade of Poland and Other EU Countries

Russia is an important trading partner for the EU-15, in both exports and imports. According to the Polish Central Statistical Office (GUS 2015), as far as exports are concerned, the countries that had been, in relative terms, most dependent on Russian demand were, naturally, the Baltic States: Lithuania (where exports to Russia were more than 13% of total exports), followed by Latvia and Estonia. Russia's share of Polish exports amounted to roughly 5%. On average, EU-15 countries had considerably lower shares of exports than did those of the NMS. Besides the Scandinavian countries (particularly Finland), in Germany, shares of exports to Russia amounted to over 3%, which was higher than the EU-15 average. In terms of the importance of exports to Russia relative to the size of the economy, the pattern is similar. In the case of Poland, exports to Russia relative to GDP amounted to roughly 2.5%.

While the uneven spread of export relations with Russia is at least partly explained by distance and, more importantly, historical considerations (such as being a part of either the USSR or the Soviet bloc), there are visible differences in sectoral involvement. Most of all, the food sector (agriculture and food processing combined) stands out in this comparison. Here, exports to Russia are much more polarized across country groups. As far as Poland is concerned, exports to Russia covered at least 6% of the total food exports in 2013, while being closer to 8% in the other NMS countries.

The falling prices of oil, gas, and other natural resources have negatively affected economic activity in Russia, which, in turn, triggered falling demand for exports. As those events occurred roughly at the same time as the conflict in Ukraine and the ban on selected EU products, it is impossible to disentangle the effects of the different factors by looking at the trade data alone. One can see, however, the evident fall in EU exports to Russia in 2014 and 2015. In the case of Poland and the NMS countries, it meant a cut in exports to Russia by almost half in 2015, relative to 2013 (over 2 percentage points). Relative to the initial share, the fall in other EU countries was similar; however, in absolute terms, it was naturally most prominent in Germany, which is also Russia's largest trading partner in the EU-15 (Fig. 9.1).

The effects of the Russian ban on the EU products are most apparent in the food sector. As the embargo covers entire sections of the HS classification in that sector, the fall in trade is substantial and concentrated in Poland and other NMS countries. In the case of Poland, trade of food products was cut by over two-thirds, while in the other NMS countries, by half. In both cases, the cumulative fall in trade from 2013 to 2015 was approximately 3% of the overall export of agri-food products.

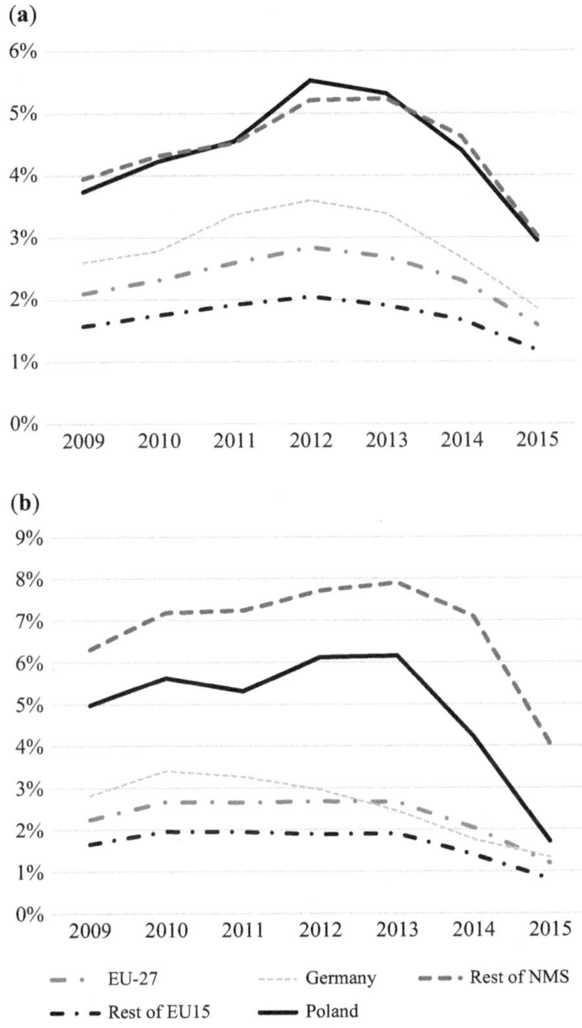

Fig. 9.1 The evolution of Russia's share of exports by source countries/groups. (**a**) Total merchandise exports. (**b**) Agri-food exports
Source: UN COMTRADE

In 2013, from the official merchandise trade statistics, almost 50% of overall Russian exports went to the EU. Of that amount, Poland and Germany each imported around 5%. However, most of Russia's exports to the EU are natural resources and energy products, in particular, oil and gas. Excluding natural resources, the EU takes less than 20% of Russia's overall exports. In that respect, Ukraine is also an important Russian export destination, taking 10% of exports overall (Fig. 9.2).

9.3 Model and Data

The model used in this study is a standard GTAP (Global Trade Analysis Project) model—a multiregion, multisector, CGE model widely applied in trade policy analysis. As with every CGE model, GTAP is a theoretical description of an economy, in this case, the global economy. It models the maximization processes taking place in the economy: utility of consumers, profits of producers subject to budget and resource constraints, and accounting relationships; it describes all of the physical and financial flows between all economic agents, according to the double accounting principle.

The GTAP model assumes the existence of a so-called regional household that makes all of the spending decisions that take place within the economy of a given region.[4] This entity allocates expenditure to private consumption, the government, or savings. It derives its income from ownership and the sale of primary factors of production—capital, labour (skilled and unskilled), land, and natural resources. This concept has very convenient characteristics. The utility function governing the division of expenditure is, in fact, a social utility function that can be used to analyse changes in economic policy.

The structure of preference of the regional household is based on the multiple nested utility function. According to this function, the division of expenditure is made at different levels of aggregation. In the case of the GTAP model, on the top level or the top nest, the household makes a decision concerning the allocation of expenditure between private consumption, government consumption, and savings. The allocation is made according to the Cobb-Douglas utility function. Government consumption expenditure is further allocated into domestic and imported goods, according to the constant elasticity of substitution (CES) function. Private consumption expenditure is governed according to constant difference of elasticities (CDE) preferences to account for the non-homotheticity of consumer demands. The imported goods are differentiated according to the Armington aggregation, using a CES function.

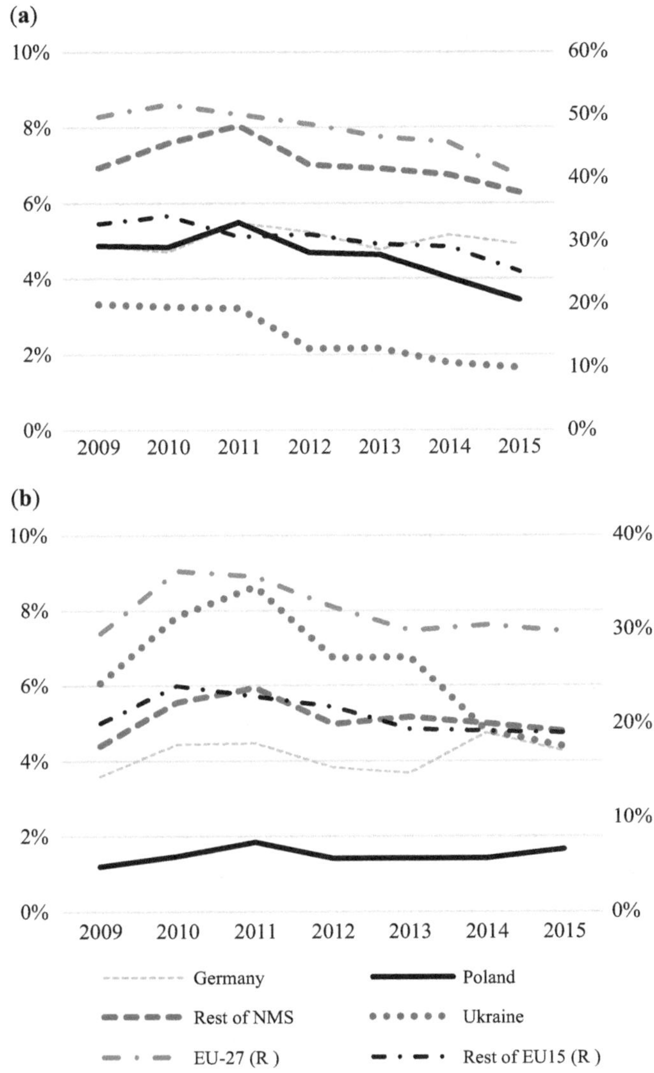

Fig. 9.2 Evolution of shares of Russian exports by countries/groups. (**a**) Including oil. (**b**) Excluding oil
Note: R: Right axis; None: Left axis
Source: UN COMTRADE

Firms produce using primary factors purchased from the regional household and intermediates. The sources of primary factors are purely domestic; it is assumed that the factors are strictly immobile internationally and mobile within a region (with the exception of land and natural resources). Intermediate goods can be either domestically produced or imported.

The factor demands derived from the production function allocate expenditure into primary factors and intermediates. The demand for these two broadly defined aggregates is Leontief. In its basic version, the model does not allow substitution between primary factors and intermediate goods. After assigning the shares of costs into broad, top-level aggregates, the further allocation of factors is governed by a more general CES function that allows substitution. Intermediates are differentiated by country of origin using a CES aggregate.

The GTAP database is specifically designed for use in a computable general equilibrium simulation. It is ready to use with the GTAP model. It is constructed using the input-output data of individual countries, macroeconomic data, and data on international trade obtained from different sources, both country-specific and international. In its most disaggregated form, the latest database, version 9, contains information about 140 regions (countries and subsets of countries).

The database contains information on 57 sectors in all of the regions. These data include information on the production volume, domestic and international sales, intermediate use, and primary factor use. Data also contain information about bilateral trade between countries in both goods and services and on taxes, tariffs, and subsidies. Finally, it covers data on transport costs and the international flow of transport services. Version 9 of the database uses 2011 as the reference year.

9.4 Simulation Scenarios

We consider two simulations scenarios. In both, we introduce a shock to trading barriers. These shocks in the GTAP model are imposed on the *ams* parameter. This corresponds to the concept of the iceberg transport cost. "Shocks to ams(i,r,s) represent the negative of the rate of decay on imports of commodity or service *i* from region *r* imported by region *s*. When ams(i,r,s) is shocked by 20%, then 20% more of the product becomes available to domestic consumers—given the same level of exports from the source country. In order to ensure that producers still receive the same revenue on their sales, effective import prices (pms) fall by 20%" (Hertel et al. 2001). In our simulations, we shock the ams downwards, so that the effective prices of products go up, and less of the good exported is delivered to the ultimate destination. We introduce the shock to ams by a so-called closure swap, i.e., we target a certain level of exports, and the ams parameter will adjust endogenously to reach that target level.

The first scenario, AF (agri-food), is an asymmetric scenario where Russia bans all agri-food exports from the EU, Ukraine, and the United States. There are no retaliatory shocks on the part of the EU, i.e., the trade barriers on EU imports remain unaffected. This scenario resembles the factual scenario, i.e., the Russian ban covered most EU agri-food exports, and the EU sanctions were either in areas other than international trade or they were almost negligible for the EU and Russia, as far as trade is concerned (as they covered far less than 1% of exports of the affected machinery and transport equipment sectors).

The second scenario, NO (non-oil), is a comprehensive bilateral trade ban between all EU members, Russia, Ukraine, and the United States. It covers all non-resource sectors, including the service sectors. The exclusion covers mining, gas and energy supplies, and the petroleum and coal refining sectors. This scenario has a long-run version, LR, where comparative statics under fixed capital stocks are complemented with a quasi-long-run scenario, where the capital stocks change at the same rate as GDP, resembling the steady state of a dynamic growth model.

9.5 Simulation Results

The macroeconomic effects of the AF scenario are negligible for all countries except Russia, where the drop in real GDP amounts to 0.5% of GDP. The welfare effects, measured by the equivalent variation in the percentage of GDP, are roughly the same. The trade frictions in Russian imports cause a slight increase in its terms of trade: due to the fall in effective import demand, the prices of domestic goods and Russian exports go up relative to the prices of imports, at the same time, dampening the welfare effect and leading to a deterioration in terms of trade between EU countries. Ukraine stands out with a large deterioration in terms of trade, which emphasizes the interrelations between Russia and the Ukraine.

The across-the-board NO and NO LR scenarios bring many more macroeconomic adjustments. As expected, the largest changes in the EU countries appear in Poland and the rest of the NMS countries, where the GDP drops by 0.2% and 0.3%, respectively. The welfare effects in the EU are amplified by a light deterioration of the terms of trade, amounting to 0.4% and 0.6% of GDP for Poland and the other NMS countries, respectively. Both Russia and Ukraine suffer large drops of GDP in the order of more than 4% and 2%, respectively, and sizeable negative welfare consequences that are greatly amplified by the sizeable deterioration in terms of trade (Table 9.1).

Large differences in the initial bilateral trading shares are reflected in changes in overall exports and imports. After all adjustments in production, imports, and exports, Poland's overall exports and imports are not largely affected in the AF scenario, which is similar to the effects in other EU countries, while Russian exports are. The explanation is quite simple. The banned products exported to Russia can be sold in other countries after price adjustments due to relative changes in demand. At the same time, most of the Polish and EU imports are not very source-source specific as long as they are not produced in global value chains or they are not natural resources. Therefore, if the ban excludes natural resources, given the existing supply-demand linkages, missing goods in Poland and the EU can be replaced by imports from other countries. However, in Russia, where trade with the EU is based to a larger extent on comparative advantages in the Heckscher-Ohlin sense, imports from the EU must be

Table 9.1 Simulated GDP and welfare changes

	Real GDP			*Equivalent variation (% of GDP)*			*Terms of trade*		
	AF	*NO*	*NO LR*	*AF*	*NO*	*NO LR*	*AF*	*NO*	*NO LR*
Poland	0.0	−0.2	−0.2	0.0	−0.4	−0.4	−0.1	−0.4	−0.4
Rest of NMS	0.0	−0.3	−0.3	0.0	−0.6	−0.6	−0.1	−0.3	−0.4
Germany	0.0	−0.1	−0.1	0.0	−0.2	−0.2	−0.0	−0.2	−0.3
Rest of EU-15	0.0	−0.1	−0.1	0.0	−0.1	−0.1	−0.0	−0.1	−0.1
USA	0.0	0.0	0.0	0.0	0.0	0.0	−0.0	0.0	−0.1
Rest of Europe	0.0	0.0	0.0	0.0	0.2	0.1	0.1	0.3	0.4
Russia	−0.5	−4.0	−4.1	−0.5	−4.5	−4.5	0.2	−2.5	−0.4
Ukraine	0.0	−2.4	−1.5	−0.5	−3.6	−7.0	−0.9	−7.8	−3.7
Rest of former USSR	0.0	0.0	0.1	0.0	0.2	0.2	0.1	0.8	0.5
Rest of America	0.0	0.0	0.0	0.0	0.0	0.0	0.1	0.2	0.1
Asia	0.0	0.0	0.0	0.0	0.1	0.1	0.0	0.4	0.3
Rest of the world	0.0	0.0	0.0	0.0	0.0	0.0	0.0	−0.0	0.1

Source: Author's own simulations

Table 9.2 Simulated import and export changes

	Exports			*Imports*		
	AF	*NO*	*NO LR*	*AF*	*NO*	*NO LR*
Poland	0.0	−0.7	−0.7	−0.1	−1.0	−1.1
Rest of NMS	0.1	−0.3	−0.5	0.0	−0.9	−0.9
Germany	0.0	−0.5	−0.5	0.0	−0.7	−0.8
Rest of EU-15	0.0	−0.5	−0.3	0.0	−0.3	−0.4
USA	0.0	−1.1	−0.4	0.0	−0.1	−0.4
Rest of Europe	0.0	0.3	0.6	0.2	1.2	1.0
Russia	−0.8	−5.4	−13.3	−0.7	−31.2	−19.0
Ukraine	1.8	20.9	−3.3	−1.2	−22.3	−7.2
Rest of former USSR	0.1	1.0	1.4	0.3	2.9	2.0
Rest of America	0.0	−0.4	0.2	0.1	0.6	0.3
Asia	0.0	−0.3	0.3	0.0	0.8	0.6
Rest of the world	0.0	−0.1	0.2	0.1	0.4	0.2

Source: Author's own simulations

replaced by means of the reallocation of resources away from its export sectors. Therefore, Russia's total exports and imports drop by slightly less than 1% (Table 9.2).

The two remaining scenarios show a much larger response of both imports and exports of Poland and the NMS countries in the order of 0.5–1%, with a slightly smaller adjustment in trade by the rest of the EU and Germany. In Russia, the drop in imports amounts to more than 30% and, in exports, by slightly more than 5% (the effect on exports is dampened by the large share of resources in exports and also by a small increase in their exports due to changes in relative prices).

We analyse the geographical structure of the changes in Polish trade in more detail in Table 9.3. The table shows the decomposition of the overall change in percentage terms into parts that are due to changes in trade with the respective trade partner. One can observe that the negative shock to Polish exports to Russia, which leads to an overall drop in total exports by 4.5%, is dampened by the substantial increase of exports to other trading partners, most of all Germany and the rest of the EU-15, followed by the other NMS countries and other trade partners. Similar adjustments can be observed in imports. The elimination of all the non-resource imports from Russia leads to a drop in trade by 1.5%; however, this is dampened by a positive reaction of imports from other EU countries.

Table 9.3 Decomposition of trade changes by partner country—Poland, NO scenario

	Overall	*Rest of NMS*	*DE*	*Rest of EU-15*	*USA*	*Rest of Europe*	*Russia*	*Ukraine*	*Rest of former USSR*	*Rest of USA*	*Asia*	*Rest of the world*
Exports	−0.7	0.5	1.1	1.5	0.2	0.1	−4.5	−0.2	0.0	0.1	0.4	0.1
Imports	−1.0	0.3	0.4	0.1	−0.1	−0.1	−1.5	0.5	0.0	−0.1	−0.6	0.0

Source: Author's own simulations

The sectoral reaction of the Polish economy is shown in Table 9.4. One can observe that in the AF scenario, naturally, the sector that is directly affected is the food sector, where exports drop by almost 5% and, at the same time, imports (mostly of intermediate goods) drop by 0.8%. This leads to a substantial decrease in output of roughly 1%. However, due to the reallocation of resources, both output and all other exports increase, and the change in exports is spread quite evenly across all other sectors, including the most important Polish export sectors. The most important increase in output is found in the electrical equipment, machinery, and metal sectors.

The NO and NO LR scenarios bring an across-the-board reduction in exports, except in selected sectors, such as petrochemicals and metals.

Table 9.4 Changes in exports, imports, and output—Poland

	Exports			*Imports*			*Output*		
	AF	*NO*	*NO LR*	*AF*	*NO*	*NO LR*	*AF*	*NO*	*NO LR*
Agriculture and food	−4.8	−2.8	−3.0	−0.8	−1.2	−1.3	−1.1	−0.6	−0.7
Mining	0.3	−0.8	0.0	0.0	0.7	0.4	0.1	0.1	0.5
Textiles and apparel	0.8	−0.4	−1.1	0.0	−1.1	−1.1	0.4	0.5	0.1
Wood, paper, publishing	0.6	−0.9	−1.1	−0.2	−1.6	−1.7	0.3	0.0	−0.1
Petrochemical	0.1	1.2	0.6	−0.1	−0.1	−0.2	0.0	0.3	0.1
Chemical nec	0.5	−1.7	−2.1	−0.1	−1.0	−1.0	0.3	0.1	−0.1
Minerals	0.3	−5.8	−1.9	−0.2	−1.4	−1.3	0.1	−0.9	−0.2
Metals and metal products	0.8	3.8	3.8	0.1	−0.4	−0.5	0.5	2.3	2.3
Transport equipment	0.5	−1.2	−1.2	0.0	−1.2	−1.1	0.3	−0.3	−0.4
Electrical equipment	0.7	0.4	−0.1	0.1	−0.8	−0.7	0.6	0.9	0.5
Machinery nec	0.7	−2.0	−1.3	−0.1	−1.1	−0.8	0.5	−0.4	−0.1
Manufacturing nec	0.7	−3.7	−3.9	−0.2	−2.0	−1.7	0.2	−0.3	−0.4
Utilities and energy	0.3	3.2	3.0	−0.4	−9.7	−10.0	0.1	1.8	1.7
Construction	0.5	−6.4	−6.7	−0.3	−6.7	−7.0	0.0	−0.3	−0.2
Services	0.3	0.5	0.2	−0.2	−1.7	−1.5	0.0	0.1	0.0
Non-market services	0.4	2.0	2.4	−0.2	−1.3	−1.3	0.0	−0.2	−0.2

Source: Author's own simulations

These sectors are largely dependent on the use of resources, and they enjoy access to lower prices (due to low economic activity in Russia) and increased imports of those resources from Russia (mining); together with the energy sector, they increase output substantially. Due to a different structure of the relative price change, the output and exports of the food industry go down by less than in the AF scenario.

In Russia (Table 9.5), the drop in imports and exports in the non-oil scenario is substantial. However, due to the specialization of the Russian economy in sectors not directly affected by the collapse of trade, the output reaction is very diverse. The output of many sectors goes up in

Table 9.5 Changes in exports, imports, and output—Russia

	Exports			*Imports*			*Output*		
	AF	*NO*	*NO LR*	*AF*	*NO*	*NO LR*	*AF*	*NO*	*NO LR*
Agriculture and food	−10.5	1.4	−21.5	−25.5	−37.2	−30.1	−21.5	7.3	3.0
Mining	0.0	6.5	3.0	−0.4	−1.8	−2.9	−0.2	3.9	0.9
Textiles and apparel	−3.4	−38.9	−59.4	0.2	−18.7	−10.8	−1.4	19.4	6.0
Wood, paper, publishing	−3.8	−13.9	−36.4	1.7	−58.7	−51.1	−1.4	13.8	8.3
Petrochemical	−0.1	6.6	2.0	0.0	0.5	−0.6	−0.2	2.5	−0.1
Chemical nec	−1.1	−50.3	−58.7	0.1	−43.7	−39.9	−0.7	8.6	2.1
Minerals	−2.7	−49.4	−60.4	0.7	−52.5	−40.0	−0.2	−9.6	3.0
Metals and metal products	−1.7	−24.5	−47.4	0.6	−47.9	−36.7	−1.0	2.0	−5.9
Transport equipment	−2.0	−35.3	−51.8	0.2	−33.0	−20.7	−1.0	21.5	17.4
Electrical equipment	−3.4	−35.7	−59.4	0.1	−22.6	−6.4	−1.4	26.0	16.4
Machinery nec	−3.0	−14.0	−45.7	0.7	−54.2	−36.3	−0.8	19.8	22.9
Manufacturing nec	−2.8	−33.4	−58.8	1.0	−43.3	−30.0	−0.5	5.4	0.5
Utilities and energy	−1.1	−43.5	−54.1	0.1	−27.9	−20.5	−0.3	−1.5	−3.0
Construction	−1.3	−35.6	−50.2	0.7	−66.6	−51.4	0.0	−18.6	−1.1
Services	−1.2	−41.3	−50.8	0.3	−62.9	−57.8	−0.3	−0.8	−1.2
Non-market services	−1.5	41.3	8.1	0.4	−20.4	−5.4	−0.4	−1.0	−2.2

Source: Author's own simulations

order to make up for the loss of imports. Notable exceptions include the construction and mineral sectors, as well as the energy sector. While the fall in the former is mainly related to decreased investment activity, the latter is caused by a shift of resources to import-substituting industries.

All changes in sectoral output and the resulting changes in demand for factors of production lead to substantial changes in real factor earnings. Due to the large concentration of food products in Russian imports, the factor that is most negatively affected in all economies of the EU, especially Poland and the NMS countries, is land where real rents go down by 1.8 and 1.4%, respectively. Capital wages and labour fall less than a half of that factor and are somewhat similar across those factors. Due to increased production of both resource-related sectors, the rent from natural resources goes up by more than 2%. In Russia, while the increase in the rent from natural resources is substantial, the reallocation of the economy toward the substitution of imports leads to a large decrease in the wages of both labour and capital and a slight increase in land rents.

The decomposition of the overall change in the GDP for the NO scenario is presented in Table 9.6. In Poland, the major driver of the change in GDP is the drop of consumption demand, followed by a drop in investment demand. Due to a more pronounced fall in imports than in exports, the contribution of the change of net exports to GDP is, in fact, positive. In Russia, reduced access to imports of investment goods leads to a very large drop in investment demand of roughly 5% of GDP, followed by a drop in consumption demand. In the case of Russia, the positive contribution of net exports to GDP amounts to over 4% of GDP (Table 9.7).

9.6 Conclusions

Increased trading barriers lead to a deterioration of the welfare of affected partner countries. While this is a trivial conclusion found in many economics textbooks, developments in the world economy over the past few years may bring about a reversal of some of the trade liberalization that has occurred over the last 60+ years around the world and after 1989 in the economies of Central and Eastern Europe.

Taking the recent Russian ban on EU products in the aftermath of the political developments surrounding the conflict in Ukraine and the EU sanctions on Russia, we show what kind of effects one can expect from a ban like this or a larger, across-the-board trade collapse. We have shown that, while the macroeconomic and welfare results of the original ban

Table 9.6 Changes in real-factor earnings—NO scenario

	Poland	*Rest of NMS*	*Germany*	*Rest of EU-15*	*USA*	*Rest of Europe*	*Russia*	*Ukraine*	*Rest of former USSR*	*Rest of America*	*Asia*	*Rest of the world*
Land	−1.8	−1.4	−1.1	−0.8	0.0	1.3	0.3	0.9	1.4	0.4	0.0	0.1
Unskilled labour	−0.5	−0.6	−0.3	−0.2	0.0	0.3	−4.4	−5.1	0.9	0.1	0.1	0.1
Skilled labour	−0.5	−0.7	−0.3	−0.2	−0.1	0.3	−6.4	−5.7	0.6	0.0	0.1	0.1
Capital	−0.5	−0.7	−0.2	−0.2	0.0	0.2	−5.9	−4.8	0.5	0.0	0.1	0.0
Natural Resources	2.3	2.3	1.8	1.0	0.1	−1.6	1.5	28.9	−4.5	−1.0	−1.6	−0.8

Source: Author's own simulations

Table 9.7 Decomposition of GDP change—NO scenario

	Poland	*Rest of NMS*	*Germany*	*Rest of EU-15*	*USA*	*Rest of Europe*	*Russia*	*Ukraine*	*Rest of former USSR*	*Rest of America*	*Asia*	*Rest of the world*
$\frac{DC}{GDP}$	−0.3	−0.4	−0.1	−0.1	0.0	0.1	−2.9	−7.3	0.1	0.0	0.1	0.0
$\frac{DI}{GDP}$	−0.1	−0.3	0.0	0.1	0.1	0.2	−5.3	−18.5	0.4	0.2	0.3	0.2
$\frac{DG}{GDP}$	0.0	−0.1	0.0	0.0	0.0	0.0	−0.2	−1.1	0.0	0.0	0.0	0.0
$\frac{DNX}{GDP}$	0.2	0.5	0.1	−0.1	−0.1	−0.3	4.4	24.5	−0.6	−0.2	−0.4	−0.2
$\frac{DGDP}{GDP}$	−0.2	−0.3	−0.1	−0.1	0.0	0.0	−4.0	−2.4	−0.1	0.0	0.0	0.0

Source: Author's own simulations

were not very large in the aggregate, a full-fledged trade ban indeed has far-reaching consequences. The size and distribution of the effects across the trading partners stem from two asymmetries: asymmetry in the size of the affected economies and asymmetry of the structures of the affected economies.

The EU is a major destination for Russia's exports. Fifty per cent of Russian exports go to the EU-27. At the same time, roughly 5% of EU exports go to Russia. Therefore, this alone will account for a large difference in the macroeconomic and welfare losses between the EU and Russia.

A large part of Russia's exports to the EU is natural resource-based. Moreover, unlike trade among the EU members, Russia's trade with the EU is very inter-industry and based on a Heckscher-Ohlin type of comparative advantages, i.e., Russia exports natural resources and imports a large share of its consumer goods and investment goods from the EU. Therefore, a ban on imports from the EU will cause the reallocation of resources in the Russian economy toward goods where it does not have a comparative advantage. On the other hand, Polish and EU exports are much more diversified, both product-wise and geographically. The ban on their exports will, therefore, be accommodated more easily.

However, asymmetries exist within the EU as well. All of the scenarios expect Poland and the NMS to be the most adversely affected economies in the EU. Due to a large share of food in the exports of Poland and NMS countries, the drop in the food sector's overall exports is the most substantial in all scenarios.

Such asymmetry leads to large changes in real-factor relative earnings. While natural resource rents go up, the prices of capital and labour fall. However, the most profound negative impact on welfare comes from the large drop in land rents. Such an effect can adversely affect a large share of the population and trigger some effects in the political economy.

One has to keep in mind that even the most severe shock to trade with Russia does not harm Poland or other EU countries significantly in a macroeconomic sense. The effect on Russia is much larger, and the potential socio-economic effects are also stronger. One has to remember, however, that the presented simulation excluded natural resources from the trade collapse. Disruptions of trade in natural resources are probably several orders of magnitude larger, and the consequences could be unpredictable, in both the macroeconomic and political senses.

Acknowledgments I would like to thank the participants of the Hitotsubashi University and wiiw workshop in Vienna for their valuable comments on earlier versions of this research, and Tammy Bicket for her editorial assistance. The remaining mistakes are my sole responsibility.

Notes

1. These are the author's own calculations based on Comtrade data. The EU-27 share of banned goods was 0.03% of the total metal product exports in 2013, 0.1% of machinery and equipment, and 0.03% of motor vehicles. One must note, however, that this does not take into account trade of purely military-purpose goods, where trade data are confidential.
2. The list of products can be found, for example, at this site: http://www.eurofoodlaw.com/policy/trade/list-of-products-banned-by-russia-with-custom-codes-102084.htm, which also includes links to the original Kremlin press releases.
3. See, for example, OECD analysis at: http://www.oecd.org/sti/ind/GVCs%20-%20RUSSIAN%20FEDERATION.pdf
4. This section follows Herte and Tsigas (1997).

References

Christen, E., Fritz, Z., & Streicher, G. (2015). *Effects of the EU-Russia economic sanctions on value added and employment in the European Union and Switzerland* (WIFO Study). Vienna: Austrian Institute of Economic Research.

Gros, D., & Mustilli, F. (2015). *The economic impact of sanctions against Russia: Much ado about very little* (CEPS Commentary). Brussels: Centre for European Policy Studies.

GUS. (2015). Powiązania gospodarki polskiej z Rosją, Ukrainą i Białorusią – wybrane aspekty. Information note, Glowny Urzad Statystyczny. http://stat.gov.pl/download/gfx/portalinformacyjny/pl/defaultaktualnosci/5732/5/1/1/powiazania_gospodarki_polskiej_z_rosja_ukraina_i_bialorusia_wybrane_aspekty.pdf

Gusev, M. S. (2007). Russia's intra-industry trade in international exchange: Major trends and growth potential. *Studies on Russian Economic Development, 18*, 196–205.

Hertel, T., & Tsigas, M. E. (1997). Structure of GTAP. In T. W. Hertel (Ed.), *Global trade analysis: Modeling and applications* (pp. 13–73). Cambridge University Press: Cambridge.

Hertel, T., McDougall, R., & Itakura, K. (2001). *GTAP model version 6.0* (GTAP Resource No. 576). West Lafayette: Center for Global Trade Analysis, Department of Agricultural Economics, Purdue University. Available at: https://www.gtap.agecon.purdue.edu/resources/res_display.asp?RecordID=576

Kutlina-Dimitrova, Z. (2015). *The economic impact of the Russian import ban: A CGE analysis* (European Commission Chief Economist Note No. 3). Brussels: European Commission.

CHAPTER 10

Upstreamness of Employment and Global Financial Crisis in Poland: The Role of Position in Global Value Chains

Jan Hagemejer and Joanna Tyrowicz

10.1 Introduction

Towards the end of the twentieth century, growing international trade brought about the processes of production fragmentation across borders within the value chain (Hummels et al. 2001). However, as documented by Fally (2011), fragmentation itself remained roughly constant until the end of the 1990s. Improvements in communication technologies allowed for substantial innovations in management: a final product is almost never produced in a single location, and the number of production stages has increased substantially since 2000 (Baldwin 2011; Baldwin and Venables 2013; Baldwin and Evenett 2015). As a result, globalization brought not only more trade in goods, but also more increased managerial and technological know-how. Many countries were able to industrialize much faster by joining global value chains rather than by building their own (Baldwin and Robert-Nicoud 2014).

J. Hagemejer (✉)
Faculty of Economic Science, University of Warsaw, Warsaw, Poland

J. Tyrowicz
Faculty of Economic Science, University of Warsaw, Warsaw, Poland

FAME|GRAPE, Warsaw, Poland

P. Havlik, I. Iwasaki (eds.), *Economics of European Crises and Emerging Markets*, DOI 10.1007/978-981-10-5233-0_10

Also, in advanced countries, the higher fragmentation of production improves long-run export performance (Guerrieri and Caffarelli 2012). Danninger and Joutz (2008) found that the fragmentation of production chains was a key determinant of Germany's improved export performance. Bas and Strauss-Kahn (2015) analysed firm-level data of French exporters and concluded that an increase in the set of imported input varieties significantly increased the number of exported varieties. These findings are all consistent with the underlying theory: firms that can fragment their production stages and/or delocalize tasks because of lower communication and co-ordination costs benefit from lower production costs and increase their efficiency and international competitiveness—hence, their export performance (Baldwin 2011).

Against this general background of global adjustments in trade and production structures that enhance the strength of economic links between countries, the global financial crisis has marked an unprecedented collapse of trade. For the first four quarters after the collapse of Lehman Brothers (2008Q1–2009Q1), world trade fell by about 15% in real terms, i.e., roughly four times as much as the fall in global GDP. The fall was concentrated especially among major global traders; however, it affected virtually all countries of the world and all types of products. After reviewing substantial literature in the field, Bems et al. (2013) argued that the main driver of this exceptional fall in global trade was the collapse in aggregate expenditure, concentrated in trade-intensive durable goods. The second wave of decline, which deepened the collapse of trade after the initial shock, was the adjusting of inventories and negative shocks to the credit supply—relevant particularly for global value chains without integrated ownership.

Despite the relatively short time since the event, the literature has focused substantial attention on the consequences of the great trade collapse in the context of global value chains. In 2010, The World Bank published a book analysing changes in the global value chains in the aftermath of the global financial crisis. The focus of the analysis was on the reallocation of production processes between countries. Milberg and Winkler (2010) argued that the asymmetrical recovery of trade volumes led to the consolidation of global value chains, with the effects of consolidation more prevalent in buyer-led chains. Some sectors experienced substantial consolidation of global value chains (Sturgeon and Kawakami 2010), while, in others, there was substantial reshuffling of production stages between countries (Sturgeon and Biesebroeck 2010).

As suggested by Bems et al. (2013), the so-called bullwhip effect played an important role. This effect involved and amplified reactions in inventories to adverse shocks in demand, and it is felt substantially more strongly by firms from intermediate industries (Altomonte et al. 2012) with a faster rebound in output and production within ownership chains than for firms operating at arm's length from the buyers. Zavacka (2012) showed that the volatility in demand for intermediate goods has sometimes been too substantial for the trade link to survive, often leading to a permanent collapse in the production of a given intermediate product.

Despite an immediate relationship between the collapse of trade and employment, much less research has, thus far, analysed this particular aspect of economic adjustment during various periods of the crisis. Sinha (2010) found that sectors in developing countries that were more globally linked often resorted to suppressing wages and increasing the extent of informality to accommodate these amplified shocks. Hurst et al. (2010) demonstrated that, in Asia, these adjustments were disproportionately concentrated among temporary and migrant workers. These analyses focused on developing countries and, thus, may be less informative about the path of adjustment in advanced and catching-up transition economies. Timmer et al. (2010) showed that advanced economies are increasingly specializing within the global value chains in activities carried out by high-skilled workers, which is likely to mitigate employment effects. On the other hand, a large share of internationalization in the catching-up transition economies consisted of processing trade. While this helped to maintain a relatively high share of employment and value-added in the manufacturing sector, during times of global financial crisis, it might have had acute consequences for employment.

Our analysis aims to address this empirical relationship between upstreamness and employment. On the one hand, one should expect from this theory that higher upstreamness is associated with higher demand for labour and more resistance to adverse product demand shocks. On the other hand, it is likely that the distance from the final demand may affect upstream firms non-linearly. Hence, it could be the case that events such as the great trade collapse spur negative employment shocks: directly and by amplifying the result on inventories associated with the bullwhip effect. Following the recent methodological contribution by Antràs et al. (2012), we use the measures of upstreamness for Poland and other countries in Central and Eastern Europe as computed by Hagemejer and Ghodsi (2016). Using firm-level data, we estimate the overall effect of upstreamness on labour demand and its features. We also analyse specific adjustments over the course of the global financial crisis, with a special emphasis on the possibly diversified positions in the global value chains. We present comparative evidence for other countries of Central and Eastern Europe (CEE) as well.

We find that the transition economies of CEE do not exhibit strong bullwhip effects. While demand for labour changed in the period of the global financial crisis, this change was only affected to some extent by position in the global value chain, and only in a few selected cases, foreign-owned firms responded differently from domestic firms in terms of employment.

Our study is structured as follows. In the next section, we describe the data and identification strategy. After a descriptive analysis of overall trends in upstreamness, we move to an econometric analysis of various measures of employment. We analyse the effects as well as (net) job creation and destruction during the time of the recent global financial crisis and outside this period.

10.2 Data and Empirical Strategy

This study uses firm-level data from the Bureau van Dijk, also known as the Amadeus database, widely used in firm-level trade literature (e.g., Altomonte et al. 2013; Egger et al. 2015; Bloom et al. 2016). These data are distributed throughout multiple editions, with each edition covering up to 10 years of firms' histories. Clearly, not every firm in a given edition of the Amadeus data has existed for 10 years. Effectively, the median duration of a panel for most countries in Amadeus is about 4–6 years. When combined, subsequent editions of Amadeus may yield longer firm-level panels. In this study, we combined editions from 2004, 2008, 2010, and 2012, thus obtaining nominal data coverage from 1997 to 2011. However, availability for the countries of interest was low in the 1990s and increased only gradually; therefore, the bulk of the data came from 2000 to 2011. Thanks to harmonizing the identifiers across different revisions of Amadeus, we are able to track individual firms over time.

The number of firms in each edition of Amadeus depends on the year and the country. Those from recent years have far more comprehensive data than those from earlier, and there are more records for larger than for smaller countries. For example, in total, a 2014 edition of Amadeus is comprised of data on 18.3 million firms from 44 countries; however, a 2004 edition is comprised of data on only 6.8 million firms and from only 38 countries.

Amadeus data usually comes from national information providers and are based on registry courts. Hence, data coverage by size differs between countries, as does the availability of relevant economic information. We followed the procedure of Kalemli-Ozcan et al. (2015). After removing the incorrect and missing information, the final database contains information from balance sheets and income statements, particularly employment, the investment rate, output, and cost of employment, together with the NACE codes of the main activity (revision 1 and revision 2, where applicable). In addition, the data identify foreign ownership.

We merged the resulting firm-level database with sector-level measures computed on the basis of the World Input-Output Database (WIOD) rev. 2013 for the same period (see Timmer et al. 2015 as well as Dietzenbacher et al. 2013). Data were merged using the WIOD aggregation of NACE rev. 1 (two-digit categories) and required matching of NACE rev. 1 and NACE rev. 2 codes for post-2008 Amadeus data. Table 10.1 shows the overall final sample size and gives descriptive statistics for Poland, in particular, and CEE economies overall. Despite well-known shortcomings of Amadeus data, the final sample remains large and appears to replicate the main features of these economies in terms of production structure as well as firm size distributions.

10.3 Trends in Internationalization

The process of opening up the former socialist economies in CEE that has been ongoing since the beginning of the 1990s manifested itself in the increased importance of international trade, as well as the increased participation of foreign capital in the ownership of enterprises (Fig. 10.1). In most of the analysed countries, roughly 5–15% of firms in the Amadeus database are foreign owned. However, the foreign firms in all analysed economies generated more than 20% of the value-added of all enterprises in the Amadeus database.

Ownership integration is not the only mode of internationalization in the region. The exports' share of output increased significantly, as did the imports' share of costs (Fig. 10.2). By 2011, the latter variable amounted to roughly 12% of the value of the gross output in most CEE economies. Although intermediates constituted a large part of exports already in 1997, this share continued to grow in the 2000s. The upstreamness of exports (the distance from the final demand) also increased over time, both due to the overall increase of fragmentation in world w the greater

Table 10.1 Summary statistics

Variable	*N*	*Mean*	*Median*	*S.D.*	*N*	*Mean*	*Median*	*S.D.*
	Poland—full sample				*NMS—full sample*			
Employment	87,398	177.8	70.0	745.4	1,334,832	62.7	12.0	442.9
Employment growth	87,398	0.0	0.0	0.3	1,334,832	0.0	0.0	0.4
Job creation	87,398	0.0	0.0	0.2	1,334,832	−0.1	0.0	0.3
Job destruction	87,398	0.1	0.0	0.2	1,334,832	0.1	0.0	0.3
Unit labour cost	87,381	0.2	0.1	3.1	1,334,471	0.2	0.1	1.4
Value-added	87,398	20070.5	6942.0	85261.2	1,334,832	4987.3	572.0	41753.6
Investment rate	87,398	0.3	0.0	1.4	1,334,832	0.4	0.0	2.4
Intermediate imports/output	87,398	0.1	0.1	0.1	1,334,832	0.1	0.1	0.1
1/Upstreamness	87,398	0.5	0.4	0.1	1,334,832	0.5	0.5	0.1
Export share	87,398	0.2	0.1	0.2	1,334,832	0.2	0.2	0.2
Intermediate exports/exports	87,398	0.1	0.0	0.1	1,334,832	0.1	0.1	0.1

Variable	*N*	*Mean*	*Median*	*S.D.*	*N*	*Mean*	*Median*	*S.D.*
	Poland—manufacturing				*NMS—manufacturing*			
Employment	26,879	205.1	108.0	339.2	298,819	116.9	31.0	338.3
Employment growth	26,879	0.0	0.0	0.2	298,819	0.0	0.0	0.4
Job creation	26,879	0.0	0.0	0.1	298,819	−0.1	0.0	0.3
Job destruction	26,879	0.1	0.0	0.2	298,819	0.1	0.0	0.3
Unit labour cost	26,877	0.2	0.1	0.1	298,787	0.2	0.2	0.9
Value-added	26,879	22565.6	7830.0	66411.9	298,819	7481.9	957.0	51997.6
Investment rate	26,879	0.2	0.0	1.7	298,819	0.3	0.0	1.7
Intermediate imports/ output	26,879	0.2	0.2	0.1	298,819	0.2	0.2	0.1
1/Upstreamness	26,879	0.5	0.4	0.1	298,819	0.5	0.4	0.2
Export share	26,879	0.5	0.5	0.2	298,819	0.4	0.4	0.3
Intermediate exports/ exports	26,879	0.3	0.3	0.1	298,819	0.2	0.2	0.2

Note: Foreign firms are defined by any foreign ownership as coded in the originally reported ownership data. Sample not weighed. Data: Amadeus

Source: Authors' calculations

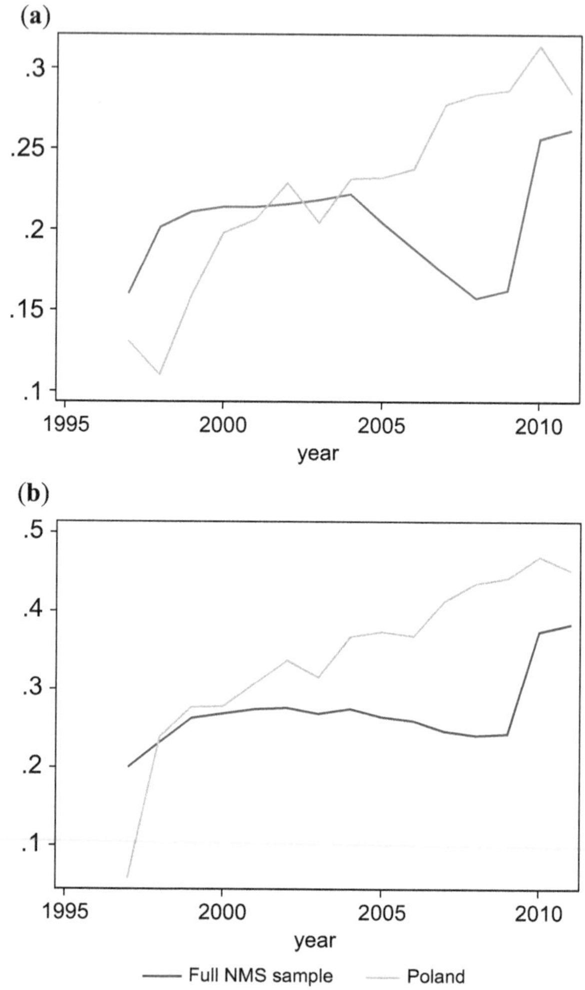

Fig. 10.1 Percentage of foreign firms to total employment: all firms and manufacturing. (**a**) Full sample. (**b**) Manufacturing

Note: Foreign firms defined by any foreign ownership as coded in the originally reported ownership data. Non-weighted average. Data: Amadeus

Source: Authors' illustration

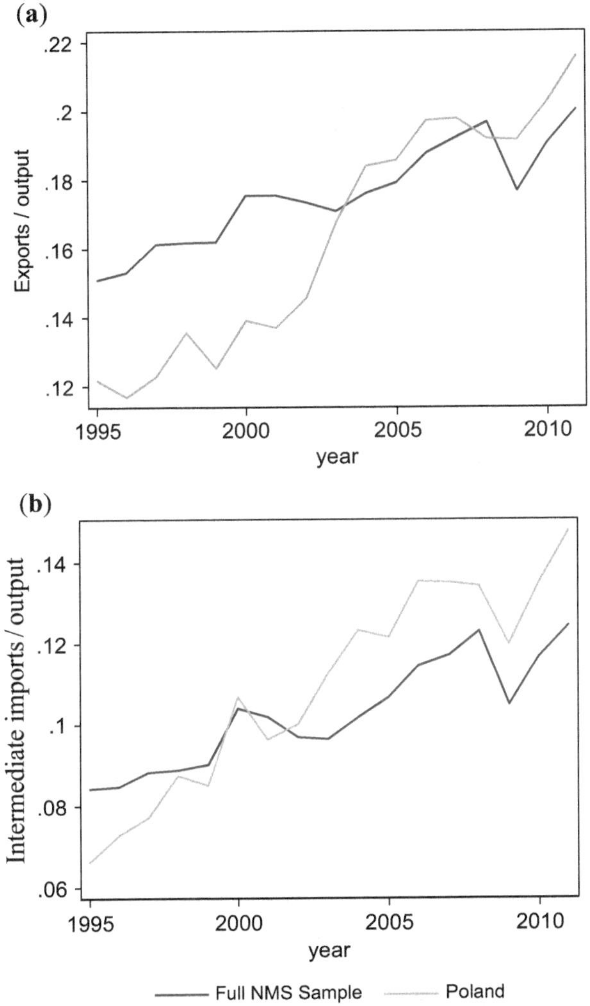

Fig. 10.2 Openness indicators. (**a**) Share of exports in output. (**b**) Share of intermediate imports in output

Notes: Calculations based on the WIOD. Note that the NMS indicators are computed at the regional level and are not averaged across countries

Source: Authors' illustration

wspecialization of CEE economies in intermediate goods. Hagemejer (2015) reported that vertical specialization, as defined by Wang et al. (2013), has increased and, by 2011, reached as much as 40% in the Czech Republic and Hungary. In Poland for example, vertical specialization increased from 15% to almost 30%.

The employment share of internationalized firms (either by foreign ownership or by foreign sales) continued to increase over the entire analysed period, as seen in Fig. 10.1. While the growth rate was not monotonous, it appears to have increasingly driven the employment dynamics in the analysed countries. For Poland, evidence from other studies shows that this increase was not only pronounced but also accompanied by a compensation policy of systematic and relatively high wage growth. NBP (2015) demonstrates that although foreign firms are only 10% of 9+ enterprises, they account for more than 20% of employment and more than 60% of payroll growth.

10.4 Empirical Strategy

Our measure of upstreamness is drawn directly from Antràs et al. (2012, 2013). We use the measures computed by Hagemejer and Ghodsi (2016). They have used the World Input-Output Database for 1997–2012 to compute global position at the sector level for all countries in the sample (Timmer et al. 2015). The definition by Antràs et al. (2012) is as follows:

$$u_i = 1 \cdot \frac{X_i}{Y_i} + 2 \cdot \frac{\Sigma_{ij}^{N} z_{ij} X_j}{Y_i} + 3 \cdot \frac{\Sigma_{k=1}^{N} \Sigma_{ij}^{N} z_{ij} z_{jk} X_i}{Y_i} + \cdots, \quad (10.1)$$

where Y_i is the gross output of sector i, and X_i is the final demand for goods from sector i, where z_{ij} is the input-output coefficient of the intermediate use of goods from sector i used in the production of sector j. Therefore, the measure weighs the contribution of production at each stage: (1) if output is used in the final demand, (2) if output is used in the production of goods that are subsequently used in the final demand, (3) if output is used in the production of goods that are used further in the production of intermediate goods that are then used in satisfying the final demand, and so on. This measure is, by construction, bounded below by 1 (for details and a comparative overview of CEE economies, see Hagemejer and Ghodsi 2016). In our regressions, we use the inverse of upstreamness.

This measure is between 0 and 1, where 1 means very downstream and 0 very upstream.

We estimate a labour demand function. We are not particularly interested in the determination of the level of employment; our dependent variable is the growth of employment at the firm level. All regressions control for the growth rate of output at the firm level, the investment rate, and changes in labour costs.

First, we analyse the relationship between the level of employment and the inverse of upstreamness. Naturally, the coefficients here may be flawed by endogeneity. However, unless any given firm has a globally dominant position, the upstreamness of the sector is not likely to be directly influenced by firm-level decisions, at least not contemporaneously. We also cluster standard errors at the sector level to avoid inflating the statistical significance. Despite these precautions, this specification does not favour direct causal interpretations, as we are well aware. Moreover, our equations account for changes in employment as well as (net) job creation (JC) and job destruction (JD). Given innate first differences, these specifications are free of the bias that would stem from firm-specific, time-invariant, unobservable heterogeneity.

In all regressions, we are particularly interested in the potentially specific character of the nexus between position in global value chains and employment decisions. Hence, in addition to the employment measure, we also introduce an interaction between this variable and a dummy for the global financial crisis, which takes the value of 1 in the years 2008 and 2009 and equals 0 otherwise.

In addition to controlling for upstreamness, we also include other indicators of globalization. First, we include sector-level exports as a share of total output. While engaging in exports is clearly a firm-level decision, this indicator captures changes in foreign demand and allows us to control for exposure to foreign demand shocks. Second, we also control for foreign ownership. Relying on the identification of ownership in the Amadeus data, we code the firm as being foreign owned if it has any share of foreign ownership. In the analysed period, Amadeus does not report actual shares of ownership, only the existence of some non-domestic legal or physical entity among owners or shareholders. Hence, this measure is likely to overstate foreign ownership; thus, the estimated coefficient is likely to be somewhat lower. Third, given the growing relevance of the processing trade, we also control for intermediate imports. Fourth, in order to control for the involvement of exports in global value chains, we include the sectoral share of intermediate goods in exports. All of the above variables are computed using the WIOD database.

Our employment growth regressions are estimated by ordinary least squares (OLS). Job creation and job destruction regressions are estimated using a Tobit model, due to a natural truncation of those variables. One must also keep in mind that job destruction is measured as an employment growth rate truncated below zero, i.e., an increase in the JD variable means lower job destruction. In other words, the interpretation of a positive coefficient in both job creation and job destruction equations is that an increase in the variable under consideration leads to higher employment growth, other things being equal.

10.5 Results

We first present the results for Poland—the largest economy of the CEE region. Subsequently, we test to what extent the conclusions for Poland are, in fact, universal for the region. Results of the baseline set of regressions are presented in Table 10.2. Naturally, the overall growth rate of employment, the rate of job creation (JC), and the (negative of the) rate of job destruction (JD) are negatively related to changes in unit labour costs and are positively related to changes in output. Investment often replaces capital with labour, which has a negative effect on employment. This is a general tendency, observed also in other countries of the region.

Globalization seems to affect job creation and job destruction rates in different ways: while export shares are negatively related to job creation, job destruction is slower in export-oriented sectors. A similar pattern is seen in a sector's involvement in importing intermediate goods. One can also see that the share of intermediate exports in overall exports is positively related to the job creation rate.

Analysing the role of global value chains and how they intertwine with global crises as exemplified by the recent financial crisis reveals that few patterns previously identified in developing economies are also present in in CEE countries. In the interest of brevity, we report the results for Poland in Table 10.2; estimates of the coefficients of interest are also presented in Fig. 10.3 for all analysed countries.[1] Naturally, the global financial crisis was associated with less job creation and, to some extent, more job destruction. Firm-level growth of employment was lower by roughly 4 percentage points in Poland during the 2009–2010 period. It also appears that the point estimate is somewhat higher for job creation

Table 10.2 Estimating labour demand in Poland

Variables	*All firms*				*Manufacturing*			
	Level	*Growth*	*JC*	*JD*	*Level*	*Growth*	*JC*	*JD*
	[1]	*[2]*	*[3]*	*[4]*	*[5]*	*[6]*	*[7]*	*[8]*
	AREG	*AREG*	*TOBIT*	*TOBIT*	*AREG*	*AREG*	*TOBIT*	*TOBIT*
Labour cost	−0.65***	−0.49***	−0.71***	−0.63***	−0.78***	−0.48***	−0.71***	−0.56***
	(0.05)	(0.02)	(0.00)	(0.01)	(0.07)	(0.03)	(0.01)	(0.01)
Output	0.77***	0.34***	0.52***	0.47***	0.80***	0.36***	0.57***	0.44***
	(0.03)	(0.02)	(0.00)	(0.01)	(0.01)	(0.02)	(0.01)	(0.01)
Investment rate	−0.20***	0.06***	0.11***	0.07***	−0.28***	0.07***	0.13***	0.09***
	(0.05)	(0.00)	(0.00)	(0.01)	(0.03)	(0.01)	(0.01)	(0.01)
1/Upstreamness (1/U)	1.91**	−0.44***	0.18*	−1.96***	0.05	−0.03**	−0.09***	−0.02
	(0.73)	(0.07)	(0.10)	(0.10)	(0.03)	(0.01)	(0.03)	(0.03)
Intermediate inputs/outputs	−2.64***	0.21**	−0.61***	2.52***	−1.50***	0.12	−0.45***	1.49***
	(0.73)	(0.10)	(0.13)	(0.13)	(0.49)	(0.12)	(0.15)	(0.14)
Intermediate exports/exports	0.12	0.32**	0.91***	−0.19	0.03	0.21*	0.57***	−0.11
	(0.52)	(0.12)	(0.14)	(0.14)	(0.55)	(0.11)	(0.14)	(0.14)
Export share of sales	−0.34	−0.19**	−0.60***	0.26***	−0.37	−0.09	−0.38***	0.38***
	(0.34)	(0.07)	(0.09)	(0.09)	(0.32)	(0.05)	(0.08)	(0.08)
Global financial crisis (GFC)	0.16*	−0.04***	−0.11***	−0.06***	0.05	−0.03**	−0.09***	−0.02
	(0.08)	(0.01)	(0.02)	(0.02)	(0.03)	(0.01)	(0.03)	(0.03)

(continued)

Table 10.2 (continued)

Variables	*All firms*				*Manufacturing*			
	Level	*Growth*	*JC*	*JD*	*Level*	*Growth*	*JC*	*JD*
	[1]	*[2]*	*[3]*	*[4]*	*[5]*	*[6]*	*[7]*	*[8]*
	AREG	*AREG*	*TOBIT*	*TOBIT*	*AREG*	*AREG*	*TOBIT*	*TOBIT*
Foreign ownership (FO)	−0.02	0.00	0.04	0.05**	−0.07	0.05	0.15**	−0.06
	(0.18)	(0.01)	(0.02)	(0.02)	(0.08)	(0.03)	(0.07)	(0.06)
GFC # 1/U	−0.37**	0.06***	0.19***	0.06*	−0.31***	0.01	0.06**	−0.00
	(0.14)	(0.02)	(0.04)	(0.04)	(0.06)	(0.02)	(0.02)	(0.03)
FO # 1/U	−0.08	0.02	0.02	−0.00	0.43**	0.01	−0.05	0.08
	(0.33)	(0.03)	(0.05)	(0.05)	(0.16)	(0.03)	(0.05)	(0.06)
GFC # FO	−0.08	0.00	0.01	−0.07	0.08	−0.01	−0.01	−0.07
	(0.10)	(0.03)	(0.05)	(0.05)	(0.08)	(0.04)	(0.06)	(0.06)
GFC # FO # 1/U	0.36*	−0.03	−0.02	0.01	−0.04	−0.02	−0.00	0.04
	(0.21)	(0.06)	(0.10)	(0.10)	(0.18)	(0.08)	(0.13)	(0.13)
No. of observations	87,406	87,398	87,398	87,398	26,879	26,879	26,879	26,879
R-squared	0.72	0.43			0.73	0.42		

Note: Constant included but not reported; all linear specifications with firm-level fixed effects with standard errors clustered at the sector level; Tobit models estimated with standard errors clustered at the sector level. Specifications in columns [1] and [4] in logs; the remainder of the table in first differences (except for investment rate, because it is measured as flow). Standard errors reported in parentheses, ***$p < 0.01$, **$p < 0.05$, *$p < 0.1$

Source: Authors' estimation

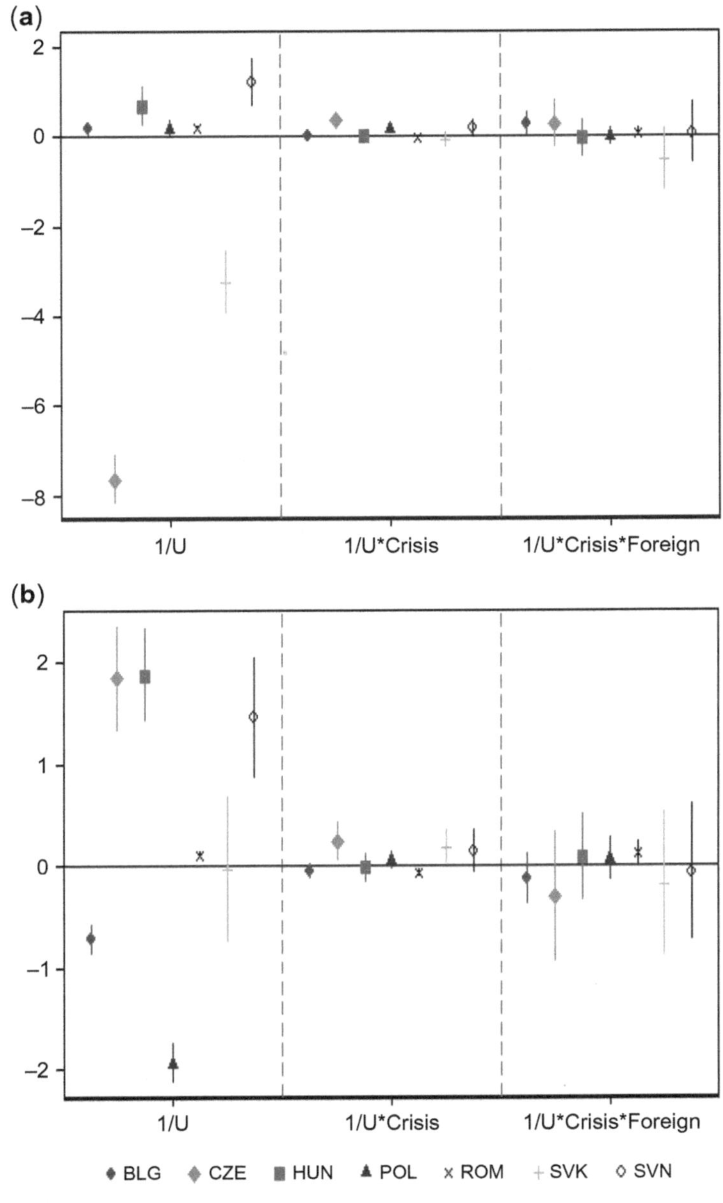

Fig. 10.3 Estimated elasticity for job creation and job destruction across countries. (**a**) Job creation. (**b**) Job destruction

Note: Estimates analogous to columns (3) and (4) in Table 10.2, obtained separately for the reported countries in the sample. Detailed logs available upon request. Data: Amadeus

Source: Authors' illustration

than for job destruction. Hence, while the global financial crisis has triggered some recession-type cleansing effects, even in countries that did not experience recession, such as Poland, it seems that employment effects mostly concerned a freeze on job creation. Regressions for the other six New Member States (NMS) of the European Union (Bulgaria, Czech Republic, Hungary, Poland, Romania, Slovakia, and Slovenia) show a great deal of heterogeneity in job creation and job destruction behaviours during the crisis years. In most of the analysed economies (except Slovenia), the job creation response was much larger than that of Poland. The highest employment reaction to the crisis was found in Romania and Slovakia.

Overall employment growth is dependent on the sector's position in the production chain (faster employment growth occurs further away from the final demand), it seems mostly to be driven by differences in job destruction rates. In manufacturing, faster employment growth occurred further away from the final demand. This effect is mostly due to differences in job creation rates along the production chain, as to the job destruction regressions the 1/U variable is not statistically significant and, therefore, evidence of the bullwhip effect is limited. At the same time, foreign ownership is, in general, related to less job destruction and (in manufacturing) more job creation.

During the global financial crisis, upstreamness mattered to levels and changes in labour demand. The coefficient of the interaction between 1/U and the global financial crisis dummy is positive for job creation, indicating faster job creation and less job destruction closer to the final demand. This effect is also visible, albeit smaller, for job creation in manufacturing. These effects do not seem to be affected by foreign ownership, both as far as the financial crisis effect is concerned as well as in the case of interaction with the 1/U.

These patterns are far from universal in the region, as depicted by the dispersion of estimates in both panels of Fig. 10.3. While the patterns of job creation were somewhat similar across all countries (although the size of the effect varied considerably), job destruction patterns were very heterogeneous. Unlike in Poland, in the Czech Republic, Hungary, and Slovenia, job destruction was milder closer to the final demand. As far as the behaviour of job destruction during the global financial crisis along the value chain is concerned, the effects of lower job destruction closer to the final demand were also visible in the Czech Republic, Slovakia, and Slovenia. In all of the countries of the region, the role of foreign ownership in global value chains departs from what was suggested in earlier literature as related to developing countries. In fact, foreign-owned firms typically behaved no differently than domestic firms.

10.6 Conclusions

In the aftermath of the global financial crisis, substantial literature has emerged analysing the role of global value in spreading the crisis across countries. Through reduced downstream demand in advanced economies, amplified by overshooting in inventory decisions (the so-called bullwhip effect), the global financial crisis disproportionately and strongly impacted labour markets in developing economies. This chapter analyses this process for the CEE economies. Being closely integrated with many advanced market economies, these countries are interesting cases to study.

We focused on labour demand and found that the reaction to the global financial crisis was heterogeneous. While involvement in global value chains, in general, and upstreamness, in particular, matter for employment levels as well as job creation and job destruction in net terms, there appears to be substantial dispersion across countries as to how these processes influence employment decisions. In particular, we saw limited evidence of the bullwhip effect.

Our study comes with a few caveats. First, while the Amadeus data set is the largest directly comparable firm-level data set for these countries, sample sizes differ substantially across countries, thus making it hazardous to extend the external validity of the estimates obtained to the whole economy. Second, our study does not control for the direction of trade. Since the Central and Eastern European countries analysed in this study are closely integrated with industrialized EU economies, especially with Germany, it is possible that the shock was smaller than in the case of developing economies, as studied in earlier research—indeed, the economic downturn in Germany was short lived and shallow, relative to other industrialized economies. Finally, these countries are characterized by relatively sound demand for their own production, which means that adverse external shocks, if short lived, may to some extent be mitigated by domestic consumption.

Acknowledgments We would like to thank Peter Szewczyk and Lucas van der Velde for their wonderful research assistance. Work on this project was facilitated by the Suntory Foundation and by earlier research by Jan Hagemejer on the role of global value chains (grant from the National Science Center, UMO-2013/09/D/HS4/01519). The authors would like to thank the participants of Hitotsubashi University and the wiiw workshop in Vienna for their valuable comments on earlier versions of this research. The remaining mistakes are the sole responsibility of the authors.

Notes

1. Detailed logs are available upon request.

References

Altomonte, C., Aquilante, T., Békés, G., & Ottaviano, G. I. (2013). Internationalization and innovation of firms: Evidence and policy. *Economic Policy, 28*, 663–700.

Altomonte, C., di Mauro, F., Ottaviano, G.I.P., Rungi, A., & Vicard, V. (2012). *Global value chains during the great trade collapse: A bullwhip effect?* (European Central Bank Working Paper No. 1412).

Antràs, P., Chor, D., Fally, T., & Hillberry, R. (2012). Measuring the upstreamness of production and trade flows. *American Economic Review, 102*, 412–416.

Baldwin, R. (2011). *Trade and industrialization after globalization's second unbundling: How building and joining a supply chain are different and why it matters* (NBER Working Paper Series No. 17716). National Bureau of Economic Research.

Baldwin, R. E., & Evenett, S. (2015). Value creation and trade in 21st century manufacturing. *Journal of Regional Science, 55*, 31–50.

Baldwin, R., & Robert-Nicoud, F. (2014). Trade-in-goods and trade-in-tasks: An integrating framework. *Journal of International Economics, 92*, 51–62.

Baldwin, R., & Venables, A. J. (2013). Spiders and snakes: Offshoring and agglomeration in the global economy. *Journal of International Economics, 90*, 245–254.

Bas, M., & Strauss-Kahn, V. (2015). Input-trade liberalization, export prices and quality upgrading. *Journal of International Economics, 95*(2), 250–262.

Bems, R., Johnson, R. C., & Yi, K. M. (2013). The great trade collapse. *Annual Review of Economics, 5*, 375–400.

Bloom, N., Draca, M., & Van Reenen, J. (2016). Trade induced technical change? The impact of Chinese imports on innovation, IT and productivity. *Review of Economic Studies, 83*, 87–117.

Danninger, S., & Joutz, F. (2008). What explains Germany's rebounding export market share? *CESifo Economic Studies, 54*, 681–714.

Dietzenbacher, E., Los, B., Stehrer, R., Timmer, M., & De Vries, G. (2013). The construction of world input–output tables in the WIOD project. *Economic Systems Research, 25*, 71–98.

Egger, P. H., Erhardt, K., & Lassmann, A. (2015). Productivity and R&D as drivers of exports and domestic sales: Semi-parametric evidence from French firm-level data. *The World Economy, 38*, 1115–1129.

Fally, T. (2011). *On the fragmentation of production in the US.* Mimeograph. Available at: http://www.etsg.org/ETSG2011/Papers/Fally.pdf

Guerrieri, P., & Caffarelli, V. F. (2012). Trade openness and international fragmentation of production in the European Union: The new divide? *Review of International Economics, 20*, 535–551.

Hagemejer, J. (2015). *Productivity spillovers in the GVC: The case of Poland and the new EU member states* (Working Papers No. 2015-42). Warsaw: Faculty of Economic Science, University of Warsaw.

Hagemejer, J., & Ghodsi, M. (2016). *Up or down the value chain? The comparative analysis of the GVC position of the economies of the new EU member states* (Working Paper No. 2016-23). Warsaw: Faculty of Economic Science, University of Warsaw.

Hummels, D., Ishii, J., & Yi, K. M. (2001). The nature and growth of vertical specialization in world trade. *Journal of International Economics, 54*, 75–96.

Hurst, R., Buttle, M., & Sandars, J. (2010). The impact of the global economic slowdown on the value chain labor markets in Asia. In A. Bauer (Ed.), *Poverty and sustainable development in Asia: Impacts and responses to the global economic crisis* (pp. 113–130). Mandaluyong City: Asian Development Bank.

Kalemli-Ozcan, S., Sorensen, B., Villegas-Sanchez, C., Volosovych, V., & Yesiltas, S. (2015). *How to construct nationally representative firm level data from the ORBIS global database* (Working Paper No. 21558). Cambridge, MA: National Bureau of Economic Research.

Milberg, W., & Winkler, G. (2010). *Trade crisis and recovery: Restructuring global value chains* (Policy Research Working Paper No. 5294). Washington, DC: World Bank.

NBP (National Bank of Poland). (2015). *Quarterly labor market review*. Warsaw: NBP.

Sinha, A. (2010). Global meltdown and informality: An economy-wide analysis for India—Policy research brief. In A. Bauer (Ed.), *Poverty and sustainable development in Asia: Impacts and responses to the global economic crisis* (pp. 131–140). Mandaluyong City: Asian Development Bank.

Sturgeon, T., & Kawakami, M. (2010). *Global value chains in the electronics industry: Was the crisis a window of opportunity for developing country* (Policy Research Working Paper No. 5417). Washington, DC: World Bank.

Sturgeon, T., & Van Biesebroeck, J. (2010). *Effects of the crisis on the automotive industry in developing countries: A global value chain perspective* (Policy Research Working Paper No. 5330). Washington, DC: World Bank.

Timmer, M. P., Inklaar, R., O'Mahony, M., & van Ark, B. (2010). *Economic growth in Europe: A comparative industry perspective.* Cambridge, MA: Cambridge University Press.

Timmer, M. P., Dietzenbacher, E., Los, B., Stehrer, R., & Vries, G. J. (2015). An illustrated user guide to the world input–output database: The case of global automotive production. *Review of International Economics, 23*, 575–605.

Wang, Z., Wei, S. J., & Zhu, K. (2013). *Quantifying international production sharing at the bilateral and sector levels* (Working Paper No. 19677). Cambridge, MA: National Bureau of Economic Research.

Zavacka, V. (2012). *The bullwhip effect and the great trade collapse* (Working Paper No. 148). London: European Bank for Reconstruction and Development.

PART V

The Russian Federation

CHAPTER 11

Political Response to the Crisis: The Case of Russia

Natalia Akindinova, Andrey Chernyavskiy, Nikolay Kondrashov, and Andrei Yakovlev

11.1 Introduction

Having emerged from the transformational crisis of the 1990s with a nearly halved gross domestic product (GDP), Russia embarked on a course of economic growth in the 2000s. In the period from 1999 to 2008, the Russian economy was growing at an annual rate of 6.9%. This was consistent with the performance of rapidly developing countries (such as China and India). However, during the global financial crisis, Russia showed a considerably greater decline than did other countries (−7.8% in 2009). After the biannual period of restoration (2010–2011), in 2012–2014, the pace of Russian economic growth slowed to an annual 1.8%—i.e., a pace typical of slowly growing developed economies. Later, in 2015,

N. Akindinova (✉) • A. Chernyavskiy • N. Kondrashov
Development Center, National Research University—Higher School of Economics, Moscow, Russia

A. Yakovlev
Institute for Industrial and Market Studies, National Research University—Higher School of Economics, Moscow, Russia

P. Havlik, I. Iwasaki (eds.), *Economics of European Crises and Emerging Markets*, DOI 10.1007/978-981-10-5233-0_11

GDP dropped and continued decreasing in 2016. For 2016–2017, Russian GDP will be close to the 2008 level. Why are the dynamics of Russian economic development so unstable and so different from both developed and developing countries?

In this chapter, we show that dominant groups within the ruling elite were not ready to restrain their own ambitions or to take into account broader interests. These political constraints, combined with a lack of a shared vision for the future, led to the inability of Russian elites to formulate an adequate response to new global challenges discovered during the 2008–2009 crisis.

Our analysis is based on the limited access order (LAO) framework of North et al. (2009, 2013). According to this concept, violence has been and remains an important factor in economic development; however, in the overwhelming majority of countries, the state does not hold a monopoly on violence.[1] In reality, the potential for violence is distributed among influential groups within the elite, who can use violence to capture the incomes and property of other social groups. Such a scenario (observed many times in history) kills incentives for economic development, as investments lose all sense because the yields of investment may be expropriated at any moment.

An alternative to this destructive scenario is the attainment of "non-aggression" agreements between key elite groups disposing of the potential for violence. However, compliance with the agreements by these groups is justified only if they get regular access to rent sources. This rent is generated by artificially created access barriers to economic and political activity—and this is precisely why North et al. (2009, 2013) define this form of organization as a LAO.

According to this approach, the sustainability of a LAO largely depends on the measure with which the ruling coalition, when faced with new challenges, finds itself capable of reaching new rent distribution agreements and, later, ensuring their compliance. Historically, the successful overcoming of crises within the LAO framework has usually involved the inclusion of new elite groups in the ruling coalition and the lowering of access barriers to economic and political activity for other social groups.[2]

Notwithstanding democratic and market reforms, according to the terminology of North et al. (2009, 2013), contemporary Russia undoubtedly falls into the category of a LAO. After the sociopolitical shocks of the early 1990s, triggered by the collapse of the Soviet Union and resulting in the establishment of the Russian Federation as an independent state, the composition of the ruling coalition has remained extremely narrow for 20 years. Starting from the presidential elections of 1996, the ruling coalition consisted of three elite groups: oligarchic businesses disposing of political connections, an upper-level federal bureaucracy, and top-level officers of security services and police (the so-called *siloviki*).

The resource base for the Russian LAO in the 1990s mainly included the proceeds of privatization and profits from gambling with price distortions between the domestic and external markets inherited from the planned economy. In the growing world economy of the 2000s, super profits from the export of oil and gas became the main source of rent. Monopolization of control over the sources of this rent allowed the ruling coalition to tackle internal political problems by the "purchase of loyalty" of wide social groups, coercion of opponents, and clever use of mass media. Such a system, with poorly functioning feedback mechanisms, ensured sociopolitical stability but at the same time limited opportunities for economic development. As a result, the narrow structure of the ruling coalition led to the accumulation of economic and social tensions. The solution to this problem was postponed due to the ruling elites' reluctance to curb their ambitions and consider the interests of other elite groups, including successful medium-sized businesses, regional bureaucracies, and public sector elites.

Section 11.2 gives an overview of the main stages of the previous development of the Russian political and economic system—the 1990s model (an attempt to create a liberal market democracy) and the state-led capitalism model of the 2000s. Section 11.3 analyses the role of the 2008–2009 economic crisis and the 2011 political crisis in transforming the state-led capitalism model and the transition, starting in 2012, to ideological opposition of the West within the framework of the besieged fortress model. Sections 11.4 and 11.5 review the specifics of the current political and economic crisis as a consequence of the choice made in 2012 in favour of the besieged fortress model and explain the impossibility of persisting in the present course due to much stricter budget constraints. Section 11.6 describes the main intersections and possible development paths of political changes for creating conditions for transitioning to a new model of economic development. The final section provides a conclusion.

11.2 Previous Developments: Attempt to Construct Liberal Democracy in the 1990s and State-Led Capitalism in the 2000s

From the viewpoint of North et al. (2009, 2013), the Soviet Union had a specific form of LAO that could not cope with external competition and whose elites turned out to be incapable of transforming its economic and social governance model. The collapse of the Soviet planned economy and political system resulted in the radical destruction of access barriers to economic and political activity. The introduction of democratic institutions, the liberalization of prices and foreign trade, and privatization created conditions for the emergence of new social groups. In the 1990s, Russia tried to introduce liberal market democracy.

We can define the following key features of this time period:

- a dilution of the sources of rent the Soviet LAO used to rely upon (in the form of the accumulation of financial resources in the state budget and their further redistribution);
- the weakening of government institutions that ensure conflict resolution and restrict violence in the economy and society as well as a declining capacity to collect taxes;
- the privatization of the levers of power by the new influential elites disposing of economic or political resources, such as businesses (oligarchs), criminal groups, and regional administrative elites.[3]

By the mid-1990s, the weakness of the government and its inability to oppose influential interest groups (Blasi et al. 1997) had created "partial reform traps", in the terms of Hellman (1998), and led to massive state capture (Hellman et al. 2003). All of this resulted in a much deeper transformational decline in Russia than in other transitional economies of Eastern Europe (almost 50% of GDP) and stabilization only by 1996–1997.

An economy generating practically no added value (Gaddy and Ickes 1998) could not become the basis for a sustainable new LAO. Within this context, the 1998 financial crisis can be regarded as a natural, logical conclusion of this period. Budgetary problems and the growing debt in the second half of the 1990s were reasons for the default in August 1998 and the severe crisis; in 1998, the ruble was devalued four times, inflation reached 84%, and GDP fell 5.3%.

Oligarchs occupying dominant positions in the ruling coalition after the 1996 elections had to acknowledge that an excessively weak state posed risks to themselves and had to agree to dialogue regarding a new vector of national development. The ultimate consequence of this dialogue was a reform programme in the spheres of the economy and state governance (known as the Gref programme) that has largely accounted for the positive economic and social dynamics of the beginning and mid-2000s.

However, further development showed that each contracting party considered the existing balance of forces temporary and proceeded from the assumption that it would later gain the upper hand during a confrontation of forces (Yakovlev 2006). Mikhail Khodorkovsky's arrest led to a change in the balance of forces within the ruling coalition.[4] The victory of the senior bureaucracy and the *siloviki* in this conflict resulted in a final reorientation toward the model of state-led capitalism, according to Lane (2008).

Key features of this state-led capitalism were:

- economic growth based on the dramatic hike in world oil prices accompanied by an inflow of direct foreign investment and the termination of capital flight;
- using part of the oil and gas rent to benefit non-primary economic sectors and meet social needs (development of state corporations similar to South Korean chaebols and tacit social agreement with the logic of increased incomes in exchange for loyalty).

Hence, it can be assumed that a new LAO had formed in Russia by the mid-2000s that relied on the distribution of oil and gas rent and a certain vision for the future of the logic of state-led capitalism shared by the elites and not rejected by wider social groups. This result created an impression of long-term sociopolitical stability and also became a factor in the stormy inflow of investment in Russia in 2006–2007. However, further developments exposed the serious inner instability of the over-centralized hierarchical model of economic and social management created in Russia in the 2000s.

11.3 Reaction to the 2008–2009 Crisis and Attempts to Transform the State-Led Capitalism Model

Russia's ruling elite (as well as the majority of the national population) was not ready for the 2008–2009 global crisis that seriously affected Russia. When the crisis occurred, the ruling elite tried to mitigate its consequences at the expense of the Central Bank reserves (managed depreciation) and the budget (expensive anti-crisis programme). Contrary to the Western approach of supporting firms without rescuing their owners, Russia was more active in its attempts to rescue owners.

Yet the main distinction of the Russian reaction to the crisis was the broad support of the population (Simachev et al. 2009; Malle 2013). By all appearances, this focus can be attributed to the elite's desire to maintain sociopolitical stability.[5]

The social component of the anti-crisis programme included significant changes to the Russian pension system. These changes included the valorization of pensions[6] and the introduction of social supplements to pensions to guarantee pensioners' standards of living. As a result of the adjustments and reforms, the average size of retirement pensions grew 40% by the end of 2010.

These measures improved the material status of millions of pensioners but at the same time brought about a significant increase in social spending from the budget. In 2009, over 50% of the Reserve Fund was spent on covering the deficit, and during 2009–2010, more than 80% was spent. This has seriously undermined the financial position of a ruling coalition accustomed to counting on sovereign funds as a security deposit to ensure greater discretion.

New public social obligations made budget constraints tougher for the ruling elite. As a result, the government tried to compensate for higher social expenses by raising the tax burden on businesses. The payroll tax rate was raised from 26% in 2010 to 34% in 2011, including an increase in payments to the pension fund from 20% to 26%.

As a response, business moved into the shadow sector, and the payroll tax contributions received were 10% below the estimate. The Russian authorities later admitted that the drastic rise in the payroll tax rates was a mistake. In 2012, the payroll tax rate was reduced to 30%. Therefore, this time, businesses refused to shoulder part of the ruling elite's expenses used in support of social stability.

The state of public finance was also strongly impacted by a change in military spending, particularly by the adoption in 2010 of a state armament programme for 2011–2020, with total funding exceeding 20 trillion rubles (Cooper 2016). The position of law enforcement was already being strengthened before the 2008–2009 crisis and was connected to the beginning of tensions between Russia and the West (Karaganov 2007; Malle 2016; Yakovlev 2016) and ambitions of Russian leadership to make Russia again a superpower in international politics.

As a result, the distribution of budgetary expenses has changed significantly (see Fig. 11.1). The power block's share increased at the cost of a reduction of the shares of the federal bureaucracy controlling the

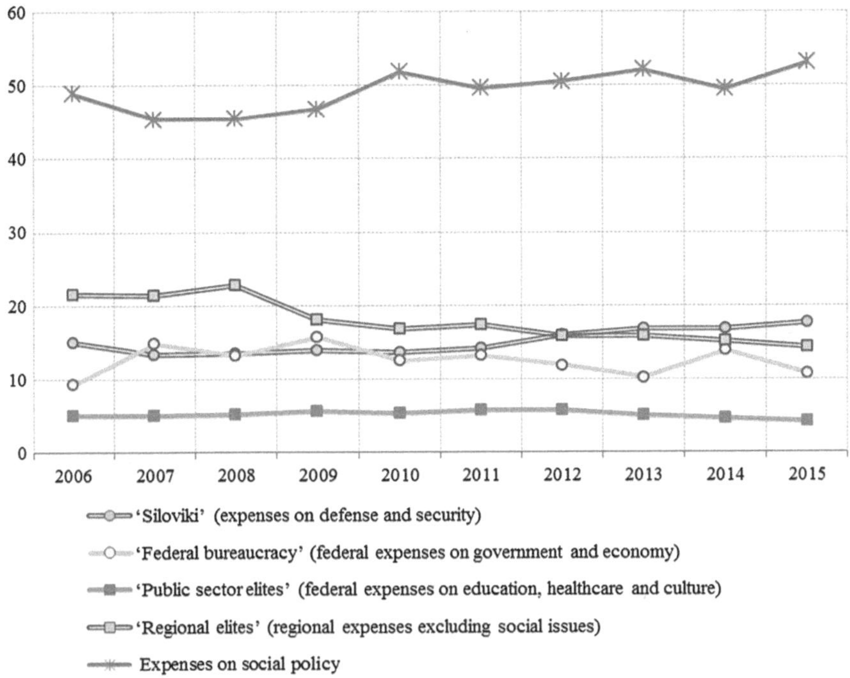

Fig. 11.1 Share of budget system expenses under the control of various elite groups as compared with social policy expenses in 2006–2015 (%)
Source: Russian Finance Ministry. Authors' estimates

compensation of public servants and distribution of subsidies and budget investments in the economy. Other affected groups include the regional elites, who started receiving comparatively fewer transfers, and public sector elites, who were confronted by restrictions in the funding of universities and medical institutions at the federal level.

The decisions made in 2009–2010 had far-reaching implications. Consolidated expenses of the public finance system increased from 34% of GDP in 2007–2008 to 38% of GDP in 2010, which created serious problems in subsequent years. As a result, the balancing of budget income and expenses in the wake of the crisis was achieved only with oil prices in excess of $100 per barrel. This, inter alia, prevented the accumulation of sufficient resources during the period of high oil prices for mitigating the crisis phenomena in 2014–2016.

On the whole, the 2008–2009 crisis demonstrated the fragility of the governance model of the 2000s due to its dependence on the regular high inflow of oil revenue. The realization of this fact compelled the Russian authorities to attempt strategic solutions (Malle 2012). In particular, we mention the article *Go Russia!*, by Dmitry Medvedev, published in September 2009.[7] It contained a sufficiently sober evaluation of the key problems of economic and social development and focused on stimulating innovation. At the same time, Medvedev's article reaffirmed Russia's striving for integration with the international community and stated the need to improve the efficiency of government machinery. This later aspect was manifested in that period by the adoption of the Anti-Corruption Law[8] and the radical reform of the Ministry of the Interior.[9]

In the economic sphere, the strategic reaction to the crisis also included resumed dialogue with businesses—mainly with the Business Russia association, which represented the interests of successful medium-sized companies. This dialogue resulted in amendments to the criminal code prohibiting the arrest of entrepreneurs at the investigative stage, the introduction in 2010 of the federal-level Regulatory Impact Assessment (RIA), and the creation in 2011 of the Agency for Strategic Initiatives (ASI)[10] and, later, the National Entrepreneurial Initiative (NEI) for improving the investment climate, aimed at radically increasing Russia's Doing Business rating.[11]

The attempt to formulate an economic development model was undertaken in the most systemic form in 2011 (Strategy-2020). Approximately 1000 experts took part in this work initiated by Vladimir Putin. Strategy-2020 contained detailed insight into a wide spectrum of problems, including the macroeconomy, social policy, infrastructure development, and improving government efficiency.[12] On the whole, Strategy-2020 was oriented toward a liberal economic policy. At the same time, as former finance minister Alexei Kudrin mentioned afterwards, the mistake of Strategy-2020 was the exclusion of foreign policy, security, and law enforcement issues from the discussion agenda. As a result, in changing international and internal political situations, elite groups representing those spheres started promoting a radically new vision of Russia's economic and social development, which can be characterized as a besieged fortress model.

11.4 Conservative Pivot in Domestic and Foreign Policy, Its Causes and Impact on Economic Development

As stressed in Yakovlev (2014), in the post-crisis period, a general consolidation of conservative nationalist-oriented groups among the Russian elite was related to a number of circumstances. First, budget constraints were visibly toughened in 2009 and in the following years, which forced the Kremlin to attempt to curb losses due to corruption. This fight resulted in a substantial rise in the influence of security and law enforcement agencies (or *siloviki*).

Second, the crisis of 2008–2009 and the related uncertainty of economic policies led to heavy capital outflow from Russia. The government responded to this outflow directly with an attempt to carry out stronger prosecution of entrepreneurs for tax evasion and use of offshore networks.

Third, political protests against electoral fraud in 2011–2012 in Moscow and other large cities played a substantial role in consolidating the positions of the *siloviki*. The consequences of the Arab Spring and, especially, developments in Egypt and Libya, caused the ruling elite in Russia to see these trends as a personal threat to themselves. Criminal cases were initiated against the most active representatives of political opposition. In 2012, Russia's Foreign Agent law was enacted to substantially limit the activities of non-governmental organizations (NGOs),[13] and, in the spring of 2013, the Public Prosecutor's Office launched a campaign to expose "foreign agents".

Such shifts in political life were accompanied by the development of an ideological basis for the "mobilization scenario" (Laruelle 2015). In this context, the activity of the Izborsk Club, which was established in September 2012, deserves attention.[14] The main propositions of the club's manifesto, published in January 2013, included accelerated development of the military–industrial complex, positioning of the public sector as the core of the national economy, and a requirement to renew and cleanse the national elite.[15] The experts of the Izborsk Club believed that all of these measures were predetermined by an intensified geopolitical struggle for control over resources and the threat of a Third World War, which could be initiated by the global financial oligarchy based in the United States. These shifts in domestic and foreign policy had a number of serious economic policy implications.

First, political considerations such as "opposition to the disruptive influence of the West" became increasingly dominant over long-term economic development objectives. Within this besieged fortress model, the role of the economy started boiling down to providing resources for maintaining political power in the hands of the incumbent elite.

Second, the logic of "vertical of power," or the over-centralized governance system formed in the 2000s, engendered in the senior bureaucratic elite an illusion of the total manageability of economic processes. This was manifested especially vividly in May 2012 with the issuance of a series of President Putin's decrees (the so-called May Decrees) formalizing his election promises to different social groups. The most expensive part of the decrees envisaged pay raises for doctors, teachers, and other workers in the social sphere that constituted the social base of support for the political regime. However, the target did not match the available funding. In 2013–2014, only about 30%, and in 2015 around 17%, of additional expenses for fulfilling the decrees were funded from the federal budget. This situation caused increases in the deficits and debts of regional budgets. Another negative impact of the decrees was the disruption of the traditional distribution of the budget authority, according to which, commitments made at the federal level were supposed to be funded from the same level. The adopted decisions infringed on the rights of the regional elites, i.e., according to the terminology of North et al. (2009, 2013), restricting their access to sources of rent.

Top leaders' continued insistence on their own enrichment despite the deteriorating economic situation in 2013–2014 created improper motivations for officials, and business started identifying these contradictions in incentives in public administration as indications of pursued policy's inadequacy and threat to macroeconomic stability.

Along with decrees on salary increases, measures for improving the business climate were boosted during that period. The position of Business Ombudsman was created in the presidential administration, and amnesty plans for persons convicted of economic crimes were announced (Yakovlev 2014). Russia successfully improved its Doing Business rating, based on an evaluation of the quality of formal procedures accompanying entrepreneurial activity. Russia managed to move from 120th place in 2011 to 51st place in 2016, although in a number of sensitive parameters, such as dealing with construction permits (119th place) and trading across borders (170th place), it remained an outsider.

Fig. 11.2 Stock indices dynamics
Source: Bloomberg

Notwithstanding the measures taken and the improved Doing Business rating, investment activity began to decline over that period. The circumstances associated with Vladimir Putin's return for a third presidential term were, on the whole, negatively assessed by the market. Despite rapid restoration and record-high oil prices, the Russian Trade System (RTS) index has been steadily demonstrating negative dynamics since mid-2011 (see Fig. 11.2).

The stagnation of investments, as well as invariably high levels of capital flight during that period, reflected investors' growing mistrust of the pursued policy, a lack of vision for the future, and, ultimately, the economy's inability to convert record-breaking oil and gas revenues into development resources. In 2013, economic growth slowed to 1.3%, which marked the beginning of Russia's lagging behind in global economic dynamics.

11.5 Deadlocks of the Besieged Fortress Model

Fading economic growth against the background of high oil prices at the end of 2012 and in 2013, as well as accumulating budget problems, led to a lowered rating of the current authorities. Under these circumstances, the task of maintaining a high rating required non-economic tools capable of ensuring the loyalty of the population consolidated around the leader. Such tools included further restrictions on the media and civil activity with the purpose of mobilizing political supporters and suppressing political opponents. This resulted in the destruction of already weak traditional feedback channels.

In addition to restrictive measures, "image-boosting" projects designed to encourage the population blended well with the objective of political mobilization. The Olympic Games in Sochi in 2014 were the central event of this sort. The political crisis that broke out in Ukraine at the same time generated an extremely negative reaction by the Russian leadership, who were fearful of a possible replication or similar scenario in Moscow. Nevertheless, Russian leaders managed to take control of the situation very quickly, successfully discrediting the Ukrainian revolution in the eyes of the population via the media, annexing the Crimea, and, later, supporting the separatist movement in Donbass. This made it possible to switch the agenda's focus from economics to politics for a long time and to strengthen the basis for patriotic mobilization in an atmosphere of the inevitable negative reaction of the West and increasing domestic economic problems.

In 2014–2015, Russia's growing international isolation in connection with the conflict in Ukraine and the exchange of sanctions with Western countries, falling oil prices, and the subsequent devaluation of the ruble combined with the aforementioned systemic flaws of the economic model.

Restrictions on access to foreign financing imposed in 2014 dealt a particularly strong blow to the interests of oligarchic businesses, as well as to the top management of companies and banks with public stakes, which were major borrowers of resources in the global financial market (Connolly 2016). The credit resources available to the economy by the onset of 2016 had been reduced by $217.5 billion, as compared to mid-2014.

The tumble of oil prices in 2014 and the volatility that followed led to losses for oil and gas companies and to the decline of financial reserves under the control of the ruling coalition (see Fig. 11.3). The volume of Russian exports was diminished by $158 billion in 2015 and continued falling in 2016.

A balance of payments crisis resulted in a 60% decline in the ruble's effective nominal rate from June 2014 to December 2015. The central bank's tight monetary policy and the restriction of the inflation adjustment of budgetary payments to the population helped avoid spiralling inflation, but only at the cost of suppressing domestic demand. Devaluation made it possible to compensate for part of large companies' losses in the oil and gas sector

Fig. 11.3 Average monthly Urals oil price dynamics, $ per barrel
Source: Reuters

and to mitigate the problem of replenishing the budget that confronted the elites. Nevertheless, the transition in 2014–2015 to double-digit inflation rates contributed, along with other factors, to the shrinking of household incomes in real terms in 2015–2016.

Another pro-inflation factor was Russia's embargo on the food supply from Europe and the United States, which increased the consumer price index by approximately 1.5%. Nevertheless, the decision to impose a food embargo was accepted by the population due to patriotic mobilization.

The shocks of 2014 resulted in a 2.8% curtailment of the economy in 2015 and a 0.2% curtailment in 2016. The productive sector's reaction to the crisis was more moderate than in 2008–2009 due to the previous stagnation. Nevertheless, all big market sectors demonstrated negative dynamics in 2015 except agriculture (+3.0%), the food industry (+2%), extractive industries (+0.4%), and the chemical industry (+6.3%) (see Table 11.1).

The positions of agricultural manufacturers were strengthened as a result of both new market opportunities and a new source of rent generated by the imposed food embargo. It should be mentioned that in the 2014–2015 season, Russia supplied to the global market a record-setting 31.7 million tons of grain and became the world's third largest exporter of wheat. In the chemical industry, the cheapening of the ruble also made it possible to build up physical quantities of produce for export.[16] Unlike in the agricultural sector, these opportunities are of a market nature and

Table 11.1 Dynamics of GDP and its elements by expenditure and value added

Indicators	*Growth, %*			
	2009	*2015*	*2016*	*2015–2016*
GDP	−7.8	−2.8	−0.2	−3.0
By expenditure				
Final consumption expenditure	−3.9	−8.1	−3.8	−11.6
Household final consumption expenditure	−5.1	−9.8	−5.0	−14.3
Gross capital formation	−41.0	−13.0	3.3	−10.1
Gross fixed capital formation	−14.4	−9.4	−1.4	−10.7
Exports	−4.7	3.7	2.3	6.1
Imports	−30.4	−25.5	−5.0	−29.2
By value-added				
Agriculture, hunting, forestry, fishing	1.6	2.9	3.2	6.2
Industry	−9.8	−2.2	1.0	−1.1
Mining and quarrying	−2.4	0.4	0.2	0.6
Manufacturing	−14.6	−4.1	1.4	−2.8
Electricity, gas, and water supply	−4.7	−1.2	2.4	1.2
Construction	−14.7	−4.9	−4.3	−9.0
Wholesale, retail trade	−5.8	−8.1	−3.6	−11.4
Hotels and restaurants	−14.9	−4.5	−3.5	−7.8
Transport, storage, and communications	−8.6	−0.9	0.4	−0.5
Financial intermediation	1.5	−6.0	2.3	−3.8
Real estate, renting, and business services	−4.5	−0.5	0.9	0.4
Public administration and defense	−0.1	3.0	0.0	3.0
Education	−1.4	0.2	0.1	0.4
Health	−0.2	0.2	−2.0	−1.8
Other community, social, and personal services; activities of private households as employers	−20.0	0.4	−0.1	0.3
Net indirect taxes	−14.0	−6.6	−0.1	−6.8

Source: ROSSTAT as of February 2017. Authors' calculations

do not depend on political decisions. In 2016, invigoration was also registered in some engineering industries and in clothing and footwear manufacturing.

At the microlevel, the situation in all economic sectors was characterized by escalating competition, the ousting of inefficient companies, and the adaptation of those remaining to decreased demand. Successful medium-sized businesses had the highest adaptation potential, as they learned during the period of "state capitalism" to exist in a competitive environment without state support, although they feared an increased tax burden and toughening regulations.

The distinctive feature of the 2014–2016 crisis was the decrease in final consumption by households that was crucial to the formation of the negative dynamics of GDP growth, whereas during the 2008–2009 crisis, external demand and capital formation suffered especially severely. Because of a lack of budget reserves during the 2015–2016 anti-crisis, policy was focused more on achieving macroeconomic stability than on supporting consumer demand, unlike the previous crisis. The ruling coalition's striving to retain reserves even under crisis conditions and to avert the escalation of debt was consistent with the principles of responsible budgetary policy, although it was probably motivated more by besieged fortress logic than by the aspiration to create conditions for resuming economic growth. The refusal to support the population was rather demonstrative[17] and was accompanied by the formation of a new law-enforcement entity (the National Guard) intended to maintain internal security. With the exhaustion of "Crimea euphoria" and conflict with the West shifting to a low-grade phase, the ruling elites started demonstrating readiness for the violent suppression of possible social protests in addition to individual independent organizations and political activists.

Compression of budgetary resources not only had a negative impact on living standards, but also led to the strengthening of the inter-elite struggle and became a challenge for public sector elites. In an attempt to resist cuts in budgetary financing, in part by lobbying for tax increases, they are compelled to simultaneously seek ways to optimize their activity. As a matter of fact, some of them (e.g., university managers) have already gained experience working in a competitive environment and developing paid services, which enables them to gain income increases even under the conditions of a shrinking market.

Considering Russia's remoteness from the technological border and its lagging behind the champions of economic growth, its potential in this respect is huge. However, in 2016, the Russian elite still lacked a common vision regarding ways to unlock this potential. This problem is rather typical for medium-income countries and is connected to the fragmentation of elite and non-elite groups and their inability to form a coalition in support of modernization (Doner and Schneider 2016). In Russia's case, the groups of emerging elites (regional elites, successful medium-sized businesses, and public-sector elites) were divided according to their positions with respect to budgetary problems and the increased tax burden. Another feature specific to Russia was the severe ideological split within the elite caused by many elite groups' nostalgia for the role of a superpower that had been played by the Soviet Union for several decades.

11.6 Who Can Facilitate Crisis Recovery, and How?

Political considerations (predominantly short-term ones) absolutely predominated over economic arguments in the decision-making process during the period of the besieged fortress model. For example, in an interview in March 2015, First Deputy Minister of Finance Tatyana Nesterenko said that "the Ministry of Finance was not asked in advance about the possible cost of the decision on accession of the Crimea".[18] The comments of leading entrepreneurs on the results of Vladimir Putin's closed-door meeting with representatives of big business in the Kremlin on December 24, 2015, were also quite characteristic. Three months after the meeting, participants said anonymously that "the President was speaking about geopolitics, touching upon Ukraine and Turkey, and political delicacy of the situation". The problems of individual companies were not mentioned, however, and "only one person spoke during the meeting—the President".[19]

However, we believe that the drop in oil prices at the beginning of 2016 to a level below $30 per barrel brought Vladimir Putin and his closest associates to understand the inevitability of changes in economic policy—despite the ruling elite's reluctance to change anything. In particular, it became obvious that if the current policy persisted against the backdrop of such oil prices, all reserves would be exhausted within 1–1.5 years. A subsequent increase in oil prices to $50–60 has somewhat improved the current budget situation but did not remove the basic problems that caused the economic crisis.

Notwithstanding, the main contents of the discussion still centre around standard debates between the followers of Milton Friedman (reduce state interference in the economy) and John Keynes (intervene to stimulate economic growth), whereas the principal problem for the economy consists of the political restrictions of the LAO that exist in Russia.

The first liberal camp is still pursuing the general goal of building an open and liberal economy. This model is expected to be based on private businesses (including foreign companies) as the main driver of the economy. It also assumes that business will attract investment resources, including those from global financial markets. The main drawback of this approach is that Russia has already seen several attempts at building this type of economy, which ultimately were not fully implemented. Actually, the reasons such attempts failed are quite clear—the poor quality of institutions (almost all public institutions) and the low level of trust in the government's economic policy among both businesses and the population. It is difficult to expect that any fresh attempt at building a liberal market would lead to positive results without radical changes in these spheres. There are even more crucial difficulties for the liberal camp's suggestions, stemming from the fact that the world has drastically changed since 2014. The accession of Crimea and the military conflict in the Eastern part of Ukraine have strongly impacted relations between Russia and other developed countries, resulting in passing the so-called point of no return. Even if the West was to lift all sanctions tomorrow (which seems hardly possible), informal barriers to accessing European capital and technologies for Russian companies will remain, simply because the West now perceives Russia as a potential enemy. This situation will remain unchangeable for many years.

The authors of the programme developed by the Stolypin Club seem to realize these challenges and are concentrating on a model of catch-up growth. As examples, they point to the experience of countries in Southeast Asia (China, South Korea, and Taiwan). These economies are characterized by a strong governmental role, the stimulation of investments via the issuance of credit, etc. At the same time, however, such suggestions do not take into account these countries' previous development as closed economies for long periods. During those extended periods of time, they worked actively to become successful exporters and evaluated the activities of their national companies in terms of their success in international markets. At the same time, these economies had protective import tariffs, and their national markets were simply closed to foreigners. There were also serious restrictions on the currency exchange market, whereby national companies were not allowed to buy and sell foreign currency freely. In other words, in order to succeed with the Stolypin Club's development programme, it is important to set up strict measures of currency exchange control and to close the financial market to foreign players. However, the programme itself lacks these measures. We also do not think that such measures would be supported by representatives of successful medium-sized businesses that are members of the association *Delovaya Rossiya* (Business Russia), which is closely associated with the Stolypin Club.

The Stolypin Club programme also has its own fundamental shortcomings. Historical experience shows that the quality of bureaucracy has been the main prerequisite for catch-up growth measures to be successful. Even the most successful Southeast Asian states have faced corruption-related problems. Indeed, we should make clear that corruption in general is common to countries that follow the path of state capitalism. However, in those countries, public officials seek rent not in the form of a share of the budget (the way it happens in Russia) but rather in the form of a share of the surplus. This can be close to Shleifer and Vishny's (1993) approach, which distinguishes corruption by theft from corruption without theft, in which the latter model hurts a country's economy and society much less than the former one.

The experiences of Southeast Asian countries also prove that corruption without theft may be combined with successful economic development stimulated by the government. However, a corruption-with-theft model remains dominant in Russia. That is why questions about the quality of the state and the role of public officials are so crucial. However, none of the programmes mentioned above address these questions.

What are the alternatives to these programmes? To answer this question, we should go back to the concept of LAOs (North et al. 2009, 2013). The ruling coalition within the current LAO has no incentive to change anything unless the elite faces strong pressure. Such pressure can be internal, in the event of the exhaustion of existing sources of rent and its insufficiency to soothe social tension and maintain the government staff's proper capacity. Pressure on the ruling coalition can also be external if the given LAO faces strong international competition. Recently, Russia has been confronted with both tendencies.

Experiences with the transformations of other LAOs in similar crisis situations show two possible scenarios in this context. The first one envisages the radical dismantlement of the former LAO, including changing the composition of the elites. Examples of this option include Iran's Islamic Revolution in 1979 and Egypt's course after the Arab Spring and before the 2013 military coup. The second scenario is a peaceful transformation of the regime based on agreement between the ruling coalition and other elite groups. Additional examples of this sort include Spain after Franco's death, Chile at the end of Pinochet's rule, and South Korea at the end of General Chun Doo-hwan's rule. In all cases, the pact between the elites ensured broader participation of new elite groups in political and economic activity with simultaneous guarantees to old elites. Using the terms of North and his co-authors, this led in fact to "access extension", with the simultaneous formation of mechanisms of collective political control over violence. However, the regimes did not automatically transform into open access orders—the processes merely signalled a maturing of the LAO and its greater sustainability (at the expense of an actual extension of the ruling coalition).

In view of the facts above, we believe that, in Russia, the political rather than the economic agenda will play the prime role in overcoming the current crisis, although only economic programmes are being discussed so far. However, at the moment, this political agenda does not involve the democratization that Russian elites associate with risks of slipping into chaos but rather the attainment of consensus between key groups of old and new elites concerning the vision for the future and possible paths of national development. This vision for the future may be developed only in the course of publicly discussing different ideas and approaches. It would be fruitful to involve representatives of all influential interest groups in such discussions.

11.7 Conclusions

Following the period of strong economic growth in the 2000s, Russia experienced a deep recession during the crisis of 2008–2009, which, after a brief period of recovery, was succeeded by stagnation and a new crisis in 2014–2016. In this chapter, we try to explain the instability of Russian economic growth as the unpreparedness of the dominant groups within the ruling elite to restrain their own ambitions and consider the interests of other players. Our analysis is based on the LAO framework formulated by North et al. (2009, 2013).

The main stages of the Russian political and economic systems' previous development were the 1990s model, which attempted to create a liberal market democracy, and the state-led capitalism model of the 2000s. The ruling coalition that developed in Russia during that period consisted of three elite groups: the federal bureaucracy, representatives of the military-security establishment (the so-called *siloviki*), and oligarchs (politically connected large businesses). In the first stage, the political influence of the oligarchs had grown. In the 2000s, the federal bureaucracy and the *siloviki* had their revenge. New elite groups also evolved within that system, including the regional bureaucracy, successful medium-sized businesses, and public sector elites; however, in the existing LAO, they could not accumulate sufficient resources to influence the political and economic agenda.

The 2008–2009 economic crisis and the 2011 political crisis played key roles in the transformation of the Russian state-led capitalism model and its transition, starting in 2012, to ideological opposition to the West within the framework of the besieged fortress model. The growth of social and military expenses characteristic of that period can be explained as a consequence of the political restrictions of the current model of governance. We showed that the economic crisis of 2014–2015 was a consequence of the choice made in 2012 in favour of the besieged fortress model. However, this model became increasingly unsustainable, due to much tighter budget constraints.

The consolidation of nationalistically minded Russian elites during that period was manifested in the attempt to curb corruption within their own environment, in the struggle against the export of capital by big businesses (deoffshorization), and in the tough response to the election protests of 2011–2012. The adoption of a set of laws restricting political and civil activity has led to the sacrifice of economic development objectives to the political goals of retaining power. Moreover, the ruling elite had the illusion that the economic processes were totally manageable, as expressed in Vladimir Putin's series of "May Decrees", which set unjustified and financially unsecured goals. The economy's change to the besieged fortress model culminated in an investment crisis.

Starting in 2014, Russia's growing international isolation due to the exchange of sanctions with the West after the Ukraine crisis, the impact of sliding oil prices, and the devaluation of the ruble have aggravated the already existing economic problems stemming from the besieged fortress model. Shrinking opportunities for access to foreign financing dealt a blow first and foremost to the interests of oligarchic businesses. Falling oil prices entailed losses for representatives of the primary industry and reduced the financial resources at the disposal of the federal elite. At the same time, the positions of manufacturers in the agro-industrial complex have been strengthened, due to the appearance of a new source of rent, following the imposition of the Russian food embargo. Opportunities for business development opened by devaluation in the chemical and some other sectors were, to a considerable extent, of a market nature. The situation at the microlevel in all sectors of the economy was characterized by growing competition in conditions of protracted scale-down of demand. Under such circumstances, successful medium-sized businesses gained an advantage, as they had development experience in a competitive environment during the period of state-led capitalism. Freezing budget expenditures and curtailing social programmes are fraught with risks of inequality and the deterioration of the population's living conditions; however, at the same time, they increase the significance of paid service development and work in a competitive environment for elites in the public sector.

Finally, we discussed conditions for transition to a new model of economic development. According to the LAO framework (North et al. 2009, 2013), the ruling coalition becomes motivated to change the existing social order only by encountering external or internal pressure. Russia has encountered such pressure in recent years. The quest for a successful economic model capable of bringing Russia to a trajectory of sustainable growth should take into account the political realities of Russia's growing international isolation and, at the same time, aim to align the interests not only of the three "old" elite groups but also to extend access for representatives of successful regional elites, medium-sized businesses, and public sector elites.

Acknowledgments For Natalia Akindinova, Andrey Chernyavskiy, and Nikolay Kondrashov, this chapter is the output of a research project implemented as part of the Basic Research Programme at the National Research University Higher School of Economics. For Andrei Yakovlev, this chapter has been produced in the context of a research link between the National Research University Higher School of Economics and the Research Centre for East European Studies at the University of Bremen. The German partner has received financial support from the Alexander von Humboldt Foundation. The authors are grateful to the Suntory Foundation for the support of a series of workshops in the framework of a book project, Economics of European Crises and Emerging Markets, initiated by the Institute of Economic Research (IER), Hitotsubashi University, and the Vienna Institute for International Economic Studies (wiiw). The authors would like to thank Richard Frensch, Silvana Malle, and Julian Cooper for their comments on the first draft of this chapter, as well as Tammy Bicket and Dawn Brandon for the editing of the paper. Comments provided by participants of the EACES conference in September 2016 are also appreciated.

Notes

1. This is true except for 20–25 of the most developed countries that have achieved the stage of open access order (OAO) and where a developed market economy is combined with sustainable democracy.
2. It is precisely within this context that North et al. (2009, 2013) mention the transition to open access orders, at the same time emphasizing that this process is not predetermined and linear; in many cases, the ruling elites turned out to be incapable of reconsidering rent distribution agreements, which led to the collapse of the LAO, acute sociopolitical upheavals, and the degradation of public order in those countries.

3. This process within the business environment is described in detail in the research by Volkov (1999, 2002).
4. Mikhail Khodorkovsky was one of oligarchs who supported President Yeltsin in the mid-1990s. In exchange for his support he gained control over a large oil company, Yukos, during loan-for-shares auctions. He significantly improved the performance of Yukos in the early 2000s. However, in Autumn 2003, after conflict with the government, Khodorkovsky was arrested on charges of tax evasion and was convicted to long-term imprisonment. He was released in 2013 and moved abroad.
5. This result was achieved—according to returns of the Levada Centre polls, the popularity ratings of Dmitry Medvedev and Vladimir Putin in the autumn of 2009 were the same as in June 2008.
6. *Valorization* means the revaluation of the estimated pension capital that made it possible to considerably raise the pensions of people with many years of Soviet service.
7. See the website at: https://www.gazeta.ru/comments/2009/09/10_a_3258568.shtml
8. This law, among other things, obliged officials and their family members to publish annual income and property declarations.
9. This reform, initiated by Dmitry Medvedev in 2009 and implemented in 2011, involved the adoption of the Law on Police, changes in the structure and reattestation of the senior staff of the Interior Ministry, and a 22% reduction in Interior Ministry personnel, with a simultaneous increase of salaries.
10. See the website at: http://asi.ru/eng/
11. See the website at: http://asi.ru/investclimate/
12. See the website at: http://2020strategy.ru/
13. This was not only about the negative public image of NGOs supported by foreign grants. The government shut down access to all public sources of finance for NGOs included in the register of foreign agents. Discretionary application of this law also significantly increased the cost of operations for all NGOs (due to additional reporting and regular inspections by the Ministry of Justice and the Prosecutor General's Office).
14. Russian mass media described the Izborsk Club in 2012–2013 as a think tank close to the Kremlin—see the website at: http://www.kp.ru/daily/25946/2890297/ or http://www.kommersant.ru/doc/2102396
15. See the website at: http://www.izborsk-club.ru/content/articles/1039/
16. It should be mentioned that this success was boosted by modernization and the input of new capacities in the chemical industry during the previous decade.
17. See the website at: http://www.dw.com/en/crimean-pensioners-turn-on-medvedev/a-19285822

18. See the website at: http://www.forbes.ru/forbes-woman/karera/281919-minfin-ne-sprashivali-vo-skolko-oboidetsya-reshenie-po-krymu
19. See the website at: http://www.rbc.ru/economics/24/03/2016/56f2a2639a79474acf897c86

References

Blasi, J., Kroumova, M., & Kruse, D. (1997). *Kremlin capitalism: The privatization of the Russian economy*. Ithaca: Cornell University Press.

Connolly, R. (2016). The empire strikes back: Economic statecraft and the securitization of political economy in Russia. *Europe-Asia Studies, 67*, 135–167.

Cooper, J. (2016). The military dimension of a more militant Russia. *Russian Journal of Economics, 2*, 129–145.

Doner, R. F., & Schneider, B. R. (2016). The middle-income trap: More politics than economics. *World Politics, 68*, 608–644.

Gaddy, C. G., & Ickes, B. W. (1998). Russia's virtual economy. *Foreign Affairs, 1998*, 53–67.

Hellman, J. (1998). Winners take all: The politics of partial reform in post-communist transitions. *World Politics, 50*, 203–234.

Hellman, J., Jones, G., & Kaufmann, D. (2003). Seize the state, seize the day: State capture and influence in transition economies. *Journal of Comparative Economics, 31*, 751–773.

Karaganov, S. (2007). New age of confrontation. *Russia in Global Affairs, 4*, 240–242.

Lane, D. (2008). From chaotic to state-led capitalism. *New Political Economy, 13*, 177–184.

Laruelle, M. (2015). *A nationalist kulturkampf in Russia? The Izborsky club as the anti-Valday*. Mimeograph.

Malle, S. (2012). The policy challenges of Russia's post-crisis economy. *Post-Soviet Affairs, 28*, 66–110.

Malle, S. (2013). Economic modernization and diversification in Russia: Constraints and challenges. *Journal of Eurasian Studies, 4*, 78–99.

Malle, S. (2016). Economic sovereignty: An agenda for militant Russia. *Russian Journal of Economics, 2*, 111–128.

North, D., Wallis, J., & Weingast, B. (2009). *Violence and social orders: A conceptual framework for interpreting recorded human history*. New York: Cambridge University Press.

North, D., Wallis, J. J., Webb, S., & Weingast, B. R. (Eds.). (2013). *In the shadow of violence: The problem of development in limited access societies*. New York: Cambridge University Press.

Shleifer, A., & Vishny, R. W. (1993). Corruption. *Quarterly Journal of Economics, 108*, 599–617.

Simachev, Y., Yakovlev, A., Kuznetsov, B., Gorst, M., Daniltsev, A., Kuzyk, M., & Smirnov, S. (2009). *Assessment of policy measures to support Russia's real economy* (Working Paper No. 102). Bremen: Research Centre for East European Studies.

Volkov, V. (1999). Violent entrepreneurship in post-communist Russia. *Europe-Asia Studies, 51*, 741–754.

Volkov, V. (2002). *Violent entrepreneurs: The use of force in the making of Russian capitalism*. Ithaca: Cornell University Press.

Yakovlev, A. (2006). The evolution of business–state interaction in Russia: From state capture to business capture. *Europe-Asia Studies, 58*, 1033–1056.

Yakovlev, A. (2014). Russian modernization: Between the need for new players and the fear of losing control of rent sources. *Journal of Eurasian Studies, 5*, 10–20.

Yakovlev, A. (2016). What is Russia trying to defend? *Russian Journal of Economics, 2*, 146–161.

CHAPTER 12

The Impact of Crisis on Firm Creation and Regeneration in Russia: Regional Panel Data Analysis

Ichiro Iwasaki and Mathilde Maurel

12.1 Introduction

The consequences of the global financial crisis on world economic growth and the policy implications that can be drawn from it have become widely debated. In Russia, they were dramatic, given the country's dependence on the oil sector and the fiscal turmoil that resulted. This chapter examines firm creation and regeneration in Russia, using Schumpeterian terminology: its dependence on the oil price level and volatility, which reflect the natural resource curse. Under those circumstances, the crisis surged in 2008.

In many countries, including Russia, the recovery has been unusually sluggish and has been characterized by persistently high unemployment rates and a lasting effect on long-term potential gross domestic

I. Iwasaki (✉)
Institute of Economic Research, Hitotsubashi University, Tokyo, Japan

M. Maurel
Centre d'Economie de la Sorbonne, Université Paris 1 Panthéon-Sorbonne/CNRS/Fondation pour les Etudes et Recherches sur le Développement International, Paris, France

P. Havlik, I. Iwasaki (eds.), *Economics of European Crises and Emerging Markets*, DOI 10.1007/978-981-10-5233-0_12

product (GDP). Remedies to it are numerous: the Schumpeter (1911) view insists on declining prices and wages as the prerequisites for a robust firm's destructive creation. More recent analysis disentangles the short-run and long-run perspectives and focuses on the capacity to rebound, which, in turn, depends upon a variety of factors.

In this new strand of the literature, Coricelli and Maurel (2011) focus on transition countries and show that the transitional recession is particularly deep with long-term consequences. They argue that the capacity to rebound, influenced by the depth and length of the crisis, depends foremost on the quality of the financial institutions, as measured by the Financial Reform database of the IMF's Research Department (Abiad et al. 2008), and on trade liberalization. Iwasaki et al. (2016) concluded similarly by stressing the importance of property rights and the efficient functioning of the commercial courts in the recovery of Russian firms in the recent period.

In this chapter, we pay attention to the specifics of Russia, a country heavily specialized in the oil sector, and, as such, threatened by the Dutch disease. Our analysis is structured as follows. Initially, in Sects. 12.2 and 12.3, we provide a review of the related literature and an overview of firm creation and regeneration at the federal and regional levels during the period from 2008 to 2015 based on data provided by the Russian statistical office. Next, in Sect. 12.4, we describe our empirical strategy. Then, in Sects. 12.5 and 12.6, we estimate a fixed-effects model to examine the determinants of Russian firms' creation and regeneration, focusing on the impact of the world oil price and the exchange rate adopted as proxies for the crisis shock. We also run supplementary regressions to deal with problems related to endogeneity and regional heterogeneity and perform additional robustness checks. Finally, we summarize the major empirical findings and, based on them, argue policy implications in Sect. 12.7.

Results are consistent and show in a robust way that our variables of interest, which are proxies for the dependence of the Russian economy on the oil sector, have a strong influence on firm creation and regeneration in this country. This has worrisome policy implications, as being able to fight effectively against the Dutch disease is more an exception than the rule. Distinguishing between different types of natural resources, Havranek et al. (2016) suggest that the only room for manoeuvering probably lies in improving the institutional environment, which echoes the conclusions of

Iwasaki et al. (2016). We demonstrate that oil price volatility hampers firm entry and turnover through increasing uncertainty, as well as exchange rate appreciation, which is one of the channels of transmission of Dutch disease.

12.2 Related Literature and Theoretical Underpinnings

The impact of the crisis is exacerbated in countries that are poor, institutionally underdeveloped, undergoing intermediate stages of financial development, and unable to conduct countercyclical fiscal policies; it also has dramatic acuity in resource-abundant, -dependent, and -exporting countries. Hnatkovska and Loayza (2004) reported that the negative effect of volatility on growth has become considerably larger in the past two decades, and that it is mostly due to large recessions rather than normal cyclical fluctuations. This chapter seeks to determine whether the 2008 global crisis has impacted the dynamics of Russian firms' incorporations and liquidations, with a special focus on two variables of interest, the oil price and oil price volatility.

From 2008 to 2012, the global financial shock as well as the European debt crisis revealed different adjustment strategies to crisis. The membership of the European Monetary Union (EMU) prohibited depreciation as a quick remedy for the adjustment of unit labour costs to regain international competitiveness. The loss of independent monetary policies made price and wage adjustments necessary, which magnified the recession and provoked different policy responses. Whereas Ireland (as in the Baltic countries and Bulgaria) embarked on drastic reforms in the private and public sectors, political resistance delayed reforms in Greece and paved the way for the recent political crisis. Russia faced its greatest crisis since the default of August 1998, demonstrating the enormous vulnerability of the Russian economy to fluctuations in the world markets.

This situation is reminiscent of a discussion during the world economic crisis in the 1930s. Whereas Keynes (1936) called for depreciation to provide a short-term growth impulse, Hayek (1937) stressed the need for price and wage adjustments. While the former emphasized the need for a timely anti-cyclical macroeconomic impulse, the latter believed in the self-stabilizing forces of the market. In the same vein, Mundell (1961) assumed that countries need to preserve the exchange rate as an adjustment mechanism, even more so if prices and wages are not flexible, while Hayek (1937) and Schumpeter (1911) insisted that declining prices and wages are the prerequisites for a robust recovery after a crisis. In the Russian context, addressing the country's dependence on and addiction to resource (oil and gas) rents is key and could be achieved through the diversification of Russia's economy (Gaddy and Ickes 2010). Exchange rate manipulation cannot be considered a way to solve the crisis, while the fall of the ruble is the most dramatic reflection of the fluctuations of the world markets, which have plunged Russia into unemployment and fiscal turmoil.

A clear distinction between the short and the long run was formalized in the nineties, where endogenous growth theorists show (both at the theoretical and empirical levels) that there is a relation between short-term economic instability and long-run growth. According to Aghion and Saint-Paul (1993), this relation can be positive or negative. If volatility is associated with the occurrence of recessions, and if recessions lead to higher research and development and/or the destruction of least-productive firms, then higher long-run growth can occur alongside higher volatility. This is the "creative destruction" view that dates back to Schumpeter (1939). On the other hand, a negative link between volatility and growth could occur if recessions are tied to a worsening of financial and fiscal constraints, which is more likely to occur in developing countries. In this case, recessions can lead to less human capital development and decreased learning by doing, which, in turn, induces smaller growth rates. Assuming that volatility is a proxy for flexibility, and focusing on developing countries, Damette et al. (2016), Kocenda et al. (2013), and Maurel and Schnabl (2012) argue that exchange rate flexibility can be beneficial to short-run growth but painful in the long run. In their framework, long-term growth can be achieved only via price and wage flexibility and stable exchange rates. Of course, their focus was not on oil-producing countries.

The connection between volatility and growth can also be direct if volatility is a proxy for the risk of investment projects. Countries that aim for higher average growth rates must accept correspondingly higher risks. Without risk-sharing mechanisms and the proper monitoring and enforcement of contracts, investors will not pursue risky projects that would otherwise be optimal. Volatility can also reflect economic uncertainty, whether this comes from political insecurity (Alesina et al. 1996), macroeconomic instability, or institutional weaknesses (Rodrik 1991; Iwasaki et al. 2016, for an application to the Russian case). The negative effect of uncertainty on economic growth is driven by firms' underinvestment or investment in the "wrong" projects (Bertola and Caballero 1994).

Beyond the divide of the short and long runs, the most recent literature on growth focuses on the detection of the depth and length of a crisis as well as the associated capacity to rebound. Recently, Cerra and Saxena (2008) examined a variety of country groups and found varying degrees of persistence of output loss following different financial and socioeconomic crises. They argued that most of the time, crises are not neutral regarding long-run average growth, and the return to the latter depends upon a range of institutional features. In contrast, Papell and Prodan (2012) found that most recessions associated with financial crises in advanced countries do not cause permanent reductions in potential GDP. They recognized that the situation is different for emerging countries where potential GDP was only restored in two of the six cases analysed. Coricelli and Maurel (2011) demonstrated that more flexible financial institutions diminish the length and depth of crises. They highlighted the importance of reform complementarity in emerging countries, including Russia.

The literature on the natural resource curse is old and dates back to Corden and Neary (1982), who analysed the curse in terms of exchange rate appreciation. Furthermore, Sachs and Warner (1995) showed that resource-rich countries tend to grow more slowly than resource-scarce countries. The literature investigates different transmission mechanisms, from which institutional background plays a key role. Certain natural resources, such as diamonds and precious metals, are more likely to induce a curse than others, such as oil discoveries.

In an innovative paper, Brunnschweiler and Bulte (2008) distinguished resource dependence, which refers to the necessity of exporting the natural resources, from resource abundance. They also treated institutions as endogenous. Sala-i-Martin and Subramanian (2013) documented that oil tends to cause real exchange rate appreciation and harm other export sectors of the economy, while Gylfason and Zoega (2006) suggested that natural resource richness crowds out both human and physical capital. Another stream of literature examines the impact of natural resources on variables other than economic growth: corruption, political instability and the likelihood of conflicts, and democratic institutions.

Keeping the above discussions in the extant literature in mind, in the following sections we will take a closer look at firm creation and regeneration in Russia and then empirically examine their determinants, focusing on recent world crises.

12.3 Firm Creation and Regeneration in Russia: A Statistical Overview

In this section, we overview the recent trends in firm creation and regeneration in Russia overall and its regions in the 2008–2015 period. Data are sourced from the Russian Federal State Statistics Service (ROSSTAT), which provides monthly data of newly established firms and liquidated firms over the federation, and yearly data for federal districts and constituent entities. Hereinafter, we define *firm creation rate* and *firm regeneration rate* as "the number of newly established firms per 1000 organizations" and "the excess of newly established firms over liquidated firms per 1000 organizations," respectively. The firm creation rate measures the dynamism of new business emergence, while the firm regeneration rate implies the intensity of the replacement of inefficient businesses by promising ones.

Panel (a) of Fig. 12.1 shows the dynamics of firm creation in Russia. It is said that firm creation in Russia is characterized by a low level, as compared with other emerging economies (Aidis and Adachi 2007; Estrin and Prevezer 2010). Nevertheless, after the outbreak of the global financial crisis in 2008, the country experienced a noticeable shift downwards. Actually, the seasonally adjusted firm creation rate fell sharply from 10.1 in September 2008 to 7.4 in January 2010. In February 2010 and onwards, firm creation seemed to revert to the levels of mid-2011. However, it stagnated around the 8.0 level until the end of 2015. On an annual basis, as shown in Panel (a) of Fig. 12.2, there was a significant decline in the creation of Russian firms from 115.2 firms per 1000 organizations in 2008 to 88.7 in 2009, and then remaining at practically the same level between 2010 and 2015.

Panel (b) of Fig. 12.1 illustrates the time-series changes in the firm-regeneration rate. It exhibits a much stronger decline during the same period against the background of a significant increase in firm liquidations (Iwasaki et al. 2016). In fact, the seasonally adjusted rate of firm regeneration continued to fall from 6.8 in September 2008 to 0.5 in November 2014 with weak fluctuations. During this period, the monthly rate dropped to a negative value in a total of 11 months, indicating that the exit of Russian firms could not be fully covered by the new entries. As a result, according to Panel (b) of Fig. 12.2, the annual rate of firm regeneration depicts a great degradation from 79.2 in 2008 to around 7.0 in 2012–2014. This can be attributed to the uncertainty and instability due

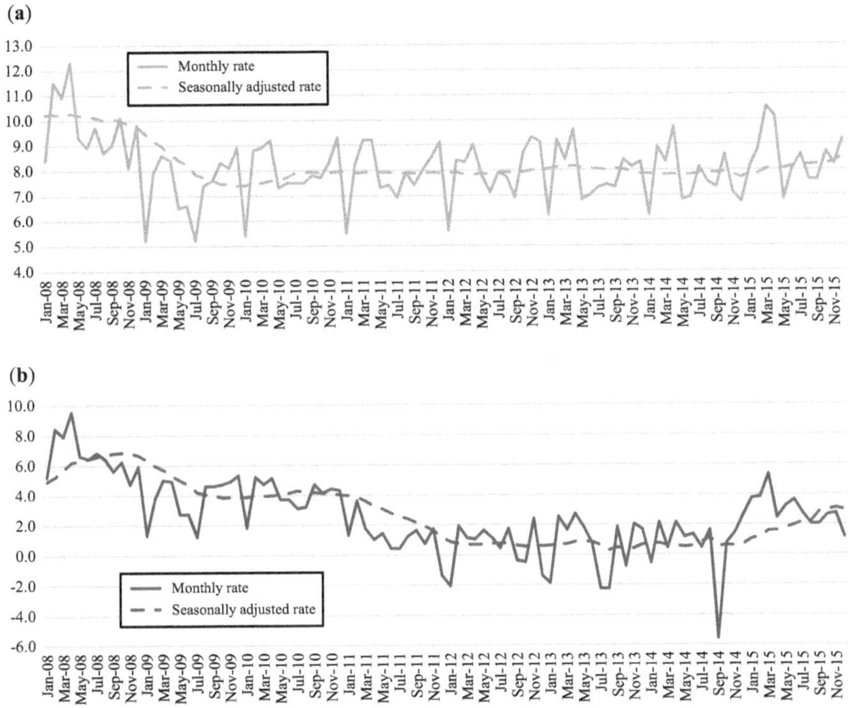

Fig. 12.1 Dynamics of firm creation and regeneration in Russia, 2008–2015. (**a**) Firm creation rate. (**b**) Firm regeneration rate
Note: The firm creation rate denotes the number of newly established firms per 1000 organizations. The firm regeneration rate denotes the excess of newly established firms over liquidated firms per 1000 organizations.
Source: Authors' illustration based on the data available at the ROSSTAT website (http://www.gks.ru/)

to erratic fluctuations in the world oil market triggered by the 2008 financial shock and subsequent crisis in Europe.

The above observations are confirmed in a vector autoregressive (VAR) setting using monthly data, where firm creation and regeneration rates are regressed on a time trend variable. Namely, the firm regeneration rate decreased monthly by 0.0155 at the 5% significance level during the period from January 2008 to December 2015, while the time trend variable is estimated with a negative sign but its statistical significance is only

(a)

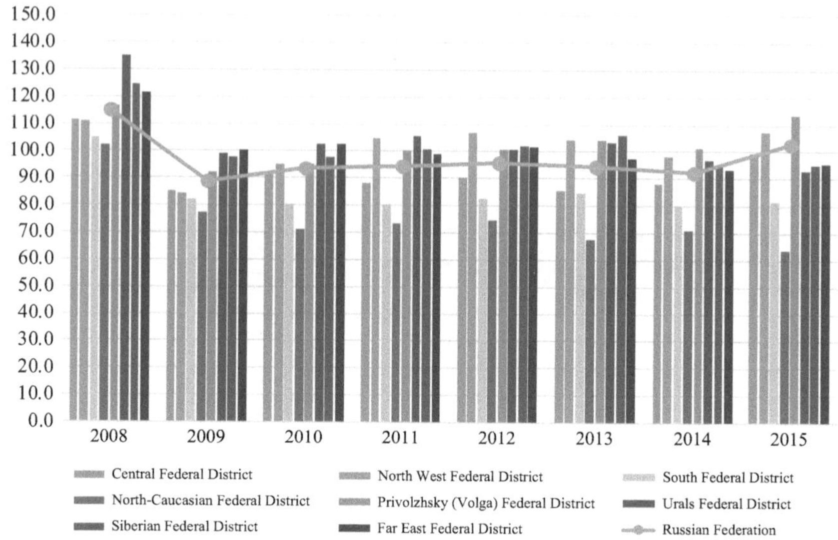

(b)

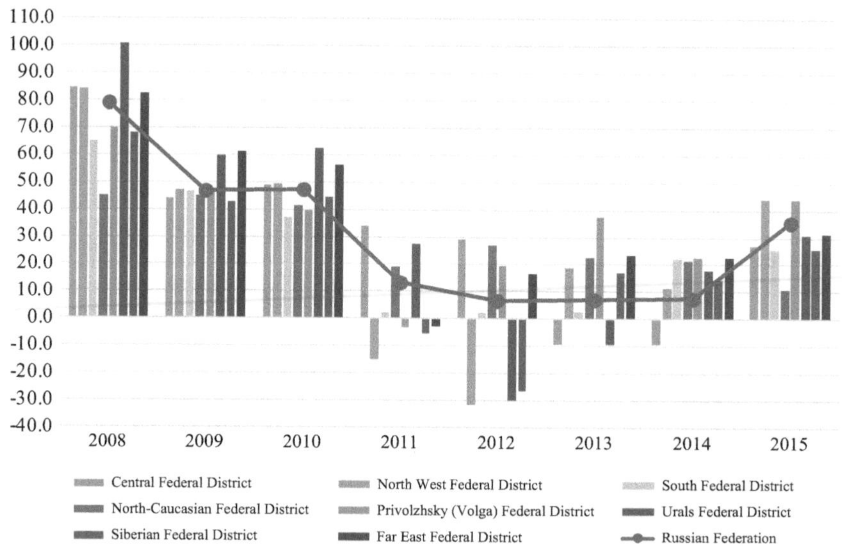

Fig. 12.2 Dynamics of firm creation and regeneration in Russian federal districts, 2008–2015. (**a**) Firm creation rate. (**b**) Firm regeneration rate

Note: The firm creation rate denotes the number of newly established firms per 1000 organizations. The firm regeneration rate denotes the excess of newly established firms over liquidated firms per 1000 organizations.

Source: Authors' illustration based on the data available at the ROSSTAT website (http://www.gks.ru/)

31% in the case of the firm creation rate.[1] These results imply that the crisis shock caused a massive and continuous liquidation of Russian businesses and resulted in the longitudinal slump in firm regeneration along with the significant downward shift of the rate of firm creation witnessed in 2009 and 2010.

Figure 12.2 also reports changes in firm creation and regeneration rates at the federal district level. Here, we can observe a weak but negative trend in firm creation, while a notable decreasing trend exists in the case of firm regeneration during the period of 2009–2014. In other words, just as with the whole federation, Russian districts have also experienced an accelerated decrease in firm turnover since the global financial crisis, due to the tremendous increase of firm shutdowns. Moreover, as shown in Panel (b) of the same figure, in the North West, Urals, and Siberian Federal Districts, a significantly negative rate of firm regeneration was recorded in 2011–2012, suggesting that the degree of crisis shock might be heterogeneous among Russian districts. In addition, Fig. 12.3 provides evidence that the volatility of the firm creation and regeneration rates was great between Russian constituent entities in recent years.

To summarize, the observations in this section suggest that both firm creation and regeneration in Russia were strongly affected by the 2008 financial shock and subsequent financial and political crises. All federal districts followed the same pattern, showing that the crisis negatively influenced Russian firms and entrepreneurs regardless of their geographical location and specialization. At the same time, however, we should note that the level and volatility of firm creation and regeneration rates were significantly varied across Russian districts and regions and, accordingly, their interrelationship changed over time. In the following sections, given the profound dependence of the Russian economy on the oil sector, we will investigate to what extent firm creation and regeneration in Russia during the crisis period can be explained by the world oil price and its volatility.

12.4 Empirical Methodology and Testable Hypotheses

In this and the following two sections, we will empirically examine the determinants of firm creation and regeneration in Russia using regional-level panel data for the period between 2008 and 2015. Inspired by the findings in the previous section, we intend to perform regression analysis, paying special attention to the recent world crisis from the 2008 global

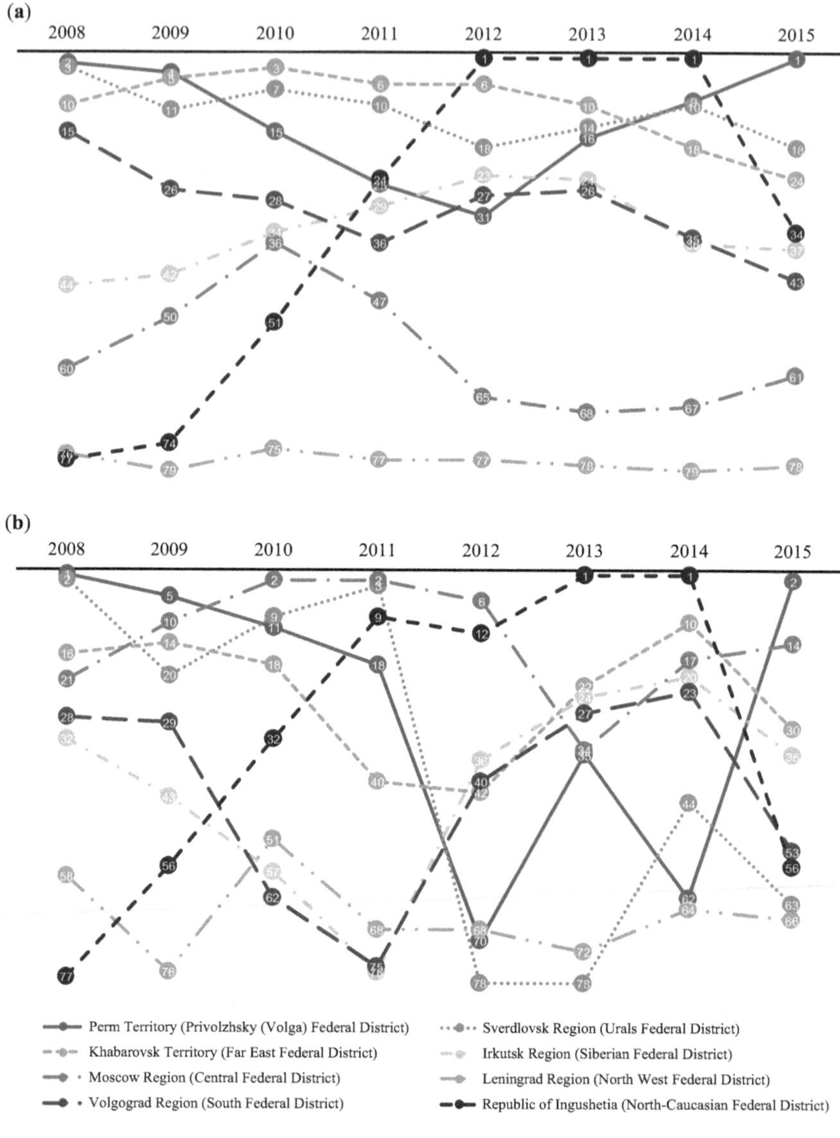

Fig. 12.3 Ranking of selected Russian regions among 80 entities in terms of firm creation and regeneration rates, 2008–2015. (**a**) Firm creation rate. (**b**) Firm regeneration rate

Note: The firm creation rate denotes the number of newly established firms per 1000 organizations. The firm regeneration rate denotes the excess of newly established firms over liquidated firms per 1000 organizations.

Source: Authors' illustration based on the data available at the ROSSTAT website (http://www.gks.ru/)

financial shock to the Russia-Ukraine conflict. More specifically, we will estimate a multivariate panel data regression equation that takes a natural logarithm of the firm creation or regeneration rate as a dependent variable and a proxy for the crisis shock to Russian firms and entrepreneurs as an independent variable, while controlling for other potentially explanatory factors.[2] In this section, we select independent variables and argue their possible association with the dependent variables, that is to say, a testable hypothesis.

To assess the impact of the world crisis on firm creation and regeneration in Russian regions, we adopted a natural logarithm of the world oil price, which is represented by the annual average of the spot prices of Dated Brent, West Texas Intermediate, and the Dubai Fateh. As argued in Kuboniwa (2014), the world oil price is extremely sensitive to a global-scale crisis, and it greatly influences the economic and business circumstances in Russia. Hence, we expect the world oil price to effectively capture the macroeconomic shocks of the recent world crises on the Russian economy, assuming that:

Hypothesis H_1 A weakening world oil price tends to hamper firm creation and regeneration in Russia, ceteris paribus.

In the empirical analysis, we also examined the possible influence of world oil price volatility measured by a coefficient of variation computed using monthly data. Jo (2012) found that an oil price uncertainty shock has immediate and persistent negative effects on world industrial production, implying that high volatility of the world oil market greatly worsens the global business climate. It is likely that this effect is especially strong in Russia, taking into consideration the heavy dependence of its national economy on the development of the oil sector. In fact, estimating the VAR model, with a time span covering from 1995:Q1 to 2009:Q3, Ito (2012) verified the strong impact of oil price volatility on the Russian economy, indicating that a 1% increase (decrease) in oil prices contributes to the 0.44% growth (decline) in real GDP in the long run. Consequently, we make the following prediction:

Hypothesis H_2 Volatility of the world oil price is negatively associated with firm creation and regeneration in Russia, ceteris paribus.

As an alternative proxy for the world crisis shock to Russian firms and entrepreneurs, we also employ the official exchange rate for the Russian ruble to the US dollar. Through their advanced time-series analysis,

Bouoiyour et al. (2015) found a close nexus of the world oil price with Russia's real exchange rate. Figure 12.4 illustrates that, in Russia, these two markets are deeply interconnected. Accordingly, we expect that the exchange rate is negatively correlated with the firm creation and regeneration rates. Hereinafter, we call a natural logarithm of the world oil price and exchange rates as well as volatilities of these market prices "crisis variables".

In the regression estimation, besides the macroeconomic shock from the world crisis, we also control for a series of factors that represent medium-term economic growth, wage levels, regional integration with the world economy, financial constraints, the quality of the social infrastructure, interfirm competition, market size and density, urbanization, public security, and natural obstacles to business.

Medium-term economic growth is expressed by the past three-year average of the real growth rate of gross regional product (GRP). It is argued that economic expansion makes room for firm creation, keeping existing firms in the market. Therefore, we expect a positive association of this

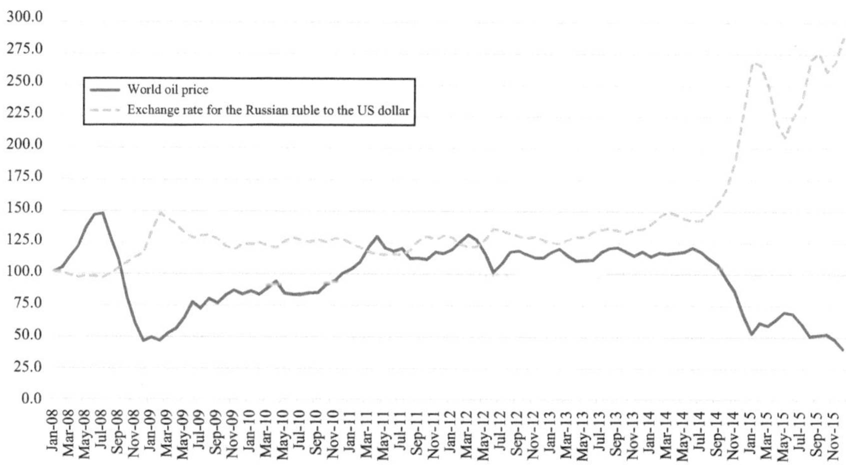

Fig. 12.4 Dynamics of the world oil price and the exchange rate in Russia, 2008–2015

Note: January 2008 = 100

Source: Authors' illustration based on the data available on the website of the IMF Commodity Price Database (http://www.imf.org/external/np/res/commod/index.aspx/) and the Bank of Russia (http://www.cbr.ru/statistics/). The world oil price is a simple average of the spot prices of Dated Brent, West Texas Intermediate, and the Dubai Fateh.

variable with the firm creation and regeneration rates. A natural logarithm of real wages is adopted to control for the costs of starting and operating a business, assuming that higher wage levels tend to restrain firm creation and regeneration. Total trade and foreign direct investment (FDI) as a percentage of GRP are used to grasp the impact of regional integration with the world economy. The international trade of goods and services is expected to have a similar effect of economic growth, while the advancement of foreign companies tends to crowd out domestic businesses.[3]

Financial constraint is measured by a natural logarithm of the number of credit organizations and their branches per 100,000 residents, which is considered to be one of the major barriers to both starting up and running businesses in Russia (Puffer and McCarthy 2001; Pissarides et al. 2003). The quality of the social infrastructure is proxied by a natural logarithm of the number of personal computers with Internet connection per 100 workers, taking into account the fact that information technology plays an important role in contemporary Russian business. A natural logarithm of firms and organizations per 10,000 residents, total population, and population density is utilized to estimate the effect of interfirm competition, market size, and density, respectively. We expect that the former factor is negatively associated with firm creation and regeneration. On the other hand, the latter two factors are likely to have a promoting effect.

Furthermore, the share of urban residents in the total population is introduced to test the positive impact of urbanization on firm creation and regeneration. A natural logarithm of the number of registered criminal cases per 100,000 residents is employed to measure the degree of public security. In a region with low public security, it is probable that, due to the high cost of opportunity, the establishment of businesses is greatly restrained and, at the same time, some existent firms are forced to exit the market, if the other conditions are the same. Finally, the average temperature in January serves as a proxy for natural obstacles to business, assuming that more severe climate conditions compel Russian firms and entrepreneurs to accept higher initial sunk costs that may restrict firm creation and regeneration.

In addition to the 12 control variables mentioned above, we also introduce a time trend variable into the right-hand side of the regression equation to grasp the longitudinal tendencies of business environments and circumstances in Russia. The definitions, descriptive statistics, and sources of the aforesaid variables are described in Table 12.1.

Table 12.1 Definitions, descriptive statistics, and sources of variables used in the empirical analysis

Variable group and name	*Additional definition*	*Descriptive statistics*			*Source*
		Mean	*S.D.*	*Median*	
Firm creation and regeneration variables					
Log of the firm creation rate	Log of the number of newly established firms per 1000 organizations	4.50	0.22	4.49	ROSSTAT (http://www.gks.ru/)
Log of the firm regeneration rate	Log of the excess of newly established firms over liquidated firms per 1000 organizations; When the firm regeneration rate (x) takes a negative value, the formula—sign (x) × log ($\|x\|$)—is used.	2.33	2.52	3.33	ROSSTAT
Crisis variables					
Log of the world oil price	Log of the simple annual average of spot prices of Dated Brent, West Texas Intermediate, and the Dubai Fateh computed using monthly data	4.44	0.26	4.57	IMF Commodity Price Database (http://www.imf.org/external/np/res/commod/index.aspx/)
Volatility of the world oil price	Coefficient of variation of the above-defined world oil price computed using monthly data	12.29	8.39	10.36	IMF Commodity Price Database
Log of the exchange rate	Log of the annual average official exchange rate for the Russian ruble to the US dollar computed using monthly data	3.52	0.25	3.45	Bank of Russia (http://www.cbr.ru/statistics/)
Volatility of the exchange rate	Coefficient of variation of the above-defined exchange rate computed using monthly data	22.17	13.35	18.28	Bank of Russia

Control variables					
GRP growth rate	Real growth rate to previous year (%); lagged 3-year moving average	3.90	3.43	3.60	ROSSTAT
Log of real wages	Wage in 2005 = 100; lagged 3-year moving average	4.67	0.04	4.66	ROSSTAT
Total trade as a % of GRP	Lagged 3-year moving average	24.19	21.75	17.53	ROSSTAT
FDI inflow as a % of GRP	Lagged 3-year moving average	3.66	5.57	2.02	ROSSTAT
Log of the number of credit organizations and their branches per 100,000 residents	Lagged 3-year moving average	0.93	0.50	0.92	ROSSTAT
Log of the number of PCs with Internet connections per 100 workers	Lagged 3-year moving average	2.56	0.53	2.64	ROSSTAT
Log of the number of firms and organizations per 10,000 residents	Lagged 3-year moving average	5.49	0.40	5.49	ROSSTAT
Log of the total population	Unit is 1000 persons; lagged 3-year moving average	7.13	0.90	7.12	ROSSTAT
Log of the population density	Per km^2; lagged 3-year moving average	2.82	1.71	3.18	ROSSTAT
Urban population rate	In % of total population; lagged 3-year moving average	69.08	13.11	70.20	ROSSTAT
Log of the number of registered criminal cases per 100,000 residents	Lagged 3-year moving average	7.50	0.44	7.57	ROSSTAT
Average temperature in January	In centigrade; lagged 3-year moving average	−12.09	7.70	−10.40	ROSSTAT
Time trend variable	2008 = 0	3.50	2.29	3.50	Authors' calculation

12.5 Estimation Results

In this section, we will first report and interpret the results of the baseline panel data estimation. Then, we will examine possible simultaneity between the crisis variables and the dependent variables, as well as the heterogeneity of the Russian regions.

Results from the baseline estimation are shown in Table 12.2. Here, as indicated in Table 12.1, a lagged three-year moving average was used not only for the GRP growth rate, but also for the other control variables to avoid possible endogeneity with the dependent variables. With respect to the crisis variables, we utilized non-lagged values to capture the direct and immediate impacts of the world crises on firm creation and regeneration under the assumption that the world crisis shock is exogenous for the overwhelming majority of Russian firms and entrepreneurs. In all cases, the fixed-effects estimation was performed according to the Breusch-Pagan test of the null hypothesis that the variance of regional individual effects is zero and the Hausman test of the random-effects assumption. Standard errors of the regression coefficients are adjusted for possible heteroscedasticity.

Panel (a) of Table 12.2 presents the estimates of the firm creation model. In Model [1], the world oil price is estimated at the 1% significance level with a positive sign corresponding with hypothesis H_1. This result suggests that the downturn in the world oil market triggered by the crisis strongly inhibited the creation of Russian firms. In Model [2], the coefficient of the exchange rate shows a negative sign with statistical significance at the 5% level, in line with our predictions, indicating that the crisis shock through the foreign exchange market also negatively affected Russian business startups.

In regard to hypothesis H_2, Model [3] provides supporting evidence: in fact, the volatility of the world oil price is negatively associated with the firm creation rate at the 1% significance level, while, at the same time, the world oil price itself shows a significant and positive estimate, as does that in Model [1]. This result enables us to maintain that the violent fluctuations in crude oil prices during recent years increased uncertainty in business operations and, consequently, excessively depressed Russian entrepreneurs who considered starting new businesses. Furthermore, the volatility of the exchange rate is also estimated with a significant and negative coefficient in Model [4]. Based on these results, we conjecture that the deeply interconnected markets of crude oil and foreign exchange have the potential to produce a negative synergy effect on firm creation in Russia.

Table 12.2 Panel data estimation of the firm creation and regeneration model in Russian regions, 2008–2015

(a) Firm creation model				
Dependent variable	*Log of the firm creation rate*			
Estimator	*Fixed-effects*			
Model	*[1]*	*[2]*	*[3]*	*[4]*
Crisis variables				
Log of the world oil price	0.1284***		0.1577***	
	(0.028)		(0.028)	
Volatility of the world oil price			−0.0026***	
			(0.001)	
Log of the exchange rate		−0.1183**		−0.1367***
		(0.046)		(0.046)
Volatility of the exchange rate				−0.0015***
				(0.000)
Control variables				
GRP growth rate	0.0060**	0.0060**	0.0063**	0.0056*
	(0.003)	(0.003)	(0.003)	(0.003)
Log of real wages	0.2314	0.0107	0.1251	−0.2159
	(0.367)	(0.360)	(0.363)	(0.381)
Total trade as a % of GRP	−0.0001	−0.0001	−0.0003	−0.0004
	(0.001)	(0.001)	(0.001)	(0.001)
FDI inflow as a % of GRP	0.0020	0.0019	0.0020	0.0020
	(0.002)	(0.002)	(0.002)	(0.002)
Log of the number of credit organizations and their branches per 100,000 residents	−0.1518*	−0.1479*	−0.1288	−0.1267
	(0.081)	(0.082)	(0.083)	(0.085)

(*continued*)

Table 12.2 (continued)

(a) Firm creation model				
Dependent variable	*Log of the firm creation rate*			
Estimator	*Fixed-effects*			
Model	*[1]*	*[2]*	*[3]*	*[4]*
Log of the number of PCs with Internet connections per 100 workers	0.0079	0.0208	0.0203	0.0263
	(0.104)	(0.104)	(0.104)	(0.107)
Log of the number of firms and organizations per 10,000 residents	–0.5833***	–0.5883***	–0.5788***	–0.5724***
	(0.148)	(0.148)	(0.145)	(0.148)
Log of the total population	0.2799	0.3050	0.1893	0.1660
	(0.676)	(0.673)	(0.669)	(0.663)
Log of the population density	0.0859	0.0431	0.0619	0.0589
	(0.242)	(0.232)	(0.241)	(0.233)
Urban population rate	–0.0178	–0.0187	–0.0183	–0.0192
	(0.019)	(0.019)	(0.019)	(0.019)
Log of the number of registered criminal cases per 100,000 residents	–0.1383	–0.1734*	–0.1346	–0.1707*
	(0.101)	(0.099)	(0.099)	(0.098)
Average temperature in January	–0.0039	–0.0048	–0.0056*	–0.0016
	(0.003)	(0.003)	(0.003)	(0.004)
Time trend variable	–0.0307	–0.0297	–0.0306	–0.0321
	(0.021)	(0.020)	(0.020)	(0.020)
Constant term	6.2342	8.4969	7.2583	10.5484**
	(5.203)	(5.124)	(5.210)	(5.151)
N	639	639	639	639
R^2	0.02	0.12	0.05	0.10
Breusch-Pagan test[a]	392.56***	369.97***	402.51***	377.04***
Hausman test[b]	85.47***	82.66***	80.15***	73.15***
F-test (χ^2)[c]	15.99***	13.91***	21.07***	16.51***

(b) Firm regeneration model				
Dependent variable	*Log of the firm regeneration rate*			
Estimator	*Fixed-effects*			
Model	*[5]*	*[6]*	*[7]*	*[8]*
Crisis variables				
Log of the world oil price	1.6440***		1.9618***	
	(0.359)		(0.355)	
Volatility of the world oil price			−0.0278**	
			(0.011)	
Log of the exchange rate		−2.3418***		−2.8309***
		(0.697)		(0.687)
Volatility of the exchange rate				−0.0379***
				(0.005)
Control variables				
GRP growth rate	0.1204**	0.1249**	0.1179**	0.1368***
	(0.049)	(0.050)	(0.050)	(0.049)
Log of real wages	5.3422	6.4824	6.4865	12.3103***
	(4.584)	(4.620)	(4.728)	(4.463)
Total trade as a % of GRP	0.0337**	0.0331**	0.0359**	0.0403***
	(0.015)	(0.015)	(0.015)	(0.015)
FDI inflow as a % of GRP	−0.0654*	−0.0652*	−0.0647*	−0.0682**
	(0.034)	(0.033)	(0.035)	(0.034)
Log of the number of credit organizations and their branches per 100,000 residents	−1.5944**	−1.5142**	−1.8431***	−2.0485***
	(0.631)	(0.641)	(0.615)	(0.593)
Log of the number of PCs with Internet connections per 100 workers	−0.0040	−0.0299	−0.1370	−0.1787
	(0.794)	(0.811)	(0.817)	(0.771)
Log of the number of firms and organizations per 10,000 residents	−2.8065	−2.7727	−2.8586	−3.2176*
	(1.791)	(1.802)	(1.791)	(1.745)

(continued)

Table 12.2 (continued)

(b) Firm regeneration model				
Dependent variable	*Log of the firm regeneration rate*			
Estimator	*Fixed-effects*			
Model	*[5]*	*[6]*	*[7]*	*[8]*
Log of the total population	−22.7083**	−23.4029**	−21.6961**	−19.6472**
	(9.545)	(9.704)	(9.730)	(9.223)
Log of the population density	19.7832***	20.0649***	20.0285***	19.5660***
	(7.371)	(7.540)	(7.498)	(6.922)
Urban population rate	−0.0929	−0.0872	−0.0873	−0.0740
	(0.132)	(0.132)	(0.134)	(0.133)
Log of the number of registered criminal cases per 100,000 residents	−0.1087	0.1226	−0.1467	0.0659
	(0.794)	(0.794)	(0.793)	(0.793)
Average temperature in January	0.1587**	0.1586**	0.1767***	0.0734
	(0.062)	(0.064)	(0.067)	(0.065)
Time trend variable	−0.1743	−0.3150	−0.1753	−0.2540
	(0.204)	(0.246)	(0.207)	(0.245)
Constant term	116.4210**	97.8880*	105.1611*	44.1102
	(57.676)	(58.496)	(58.551)	(56.436)
N	637	637	637	637
R^2	0.05	0.04	0.10	0.02
Breusch-Pagan test[a]	27.19**	15.10***	16.31***	20.10***
Hausman test[b]	15.61***	26.69**	58.68***	74.07***
F-test (χ^2)[c]	21.97***	21.60***	20.98***	22.99***

Notes:

[a]Null hypothesis: the variance of regional individual effects is zero

[b]Null hypothesis: the random-effects assumption is valid

[c]Null hypothesis: all coefficients are zero

Figures in parentheses beneath regression coefficients are robust standard errors. ***, **, and * denote statistical significance at the 1%, 5%, and 10% levels, respectively

Source: Authors' estimation. See Table 12.1 for definitions and descriptive statistics of the variables used in the estimation

As reported in Panel (b) of Table 12.2, the baseline estimation of the firm regeneration model displays similar results to those in Panel (a). In fact, all of the crisis variables in Models [5] to [8] are estimated to have statistical significance with signs consistent with hypotheses H_1 and H_2, implying that the 2008 financial shock and subsequent crises in Europe not only negatively affected startups by Russian entrepreneurs but also strongly compelled existing companies to dissolve, as witnessed by Iwasaki (2014), in the case of large and medium-sized industrial companies, and by Sprenger (2014), in the case of former socialist enterprises.

With regard to the control variables, we found that medium-term GRP growth exhibited a positive impact both on firm creation and regeneration, implying that economic expansion promotes the establishment of new firms and, at the same time, keeps existing organizations alive. Regional dependence on international trade and direct investment from abroad does not affect the decision-making of Russian entrepreneurs who intend to newly enter the market. On the other hand, the destiny of existing firms is likely to be deeply connected with the world economy; indeed, both total trade and FDI as a percentage of GRP are significantly related to the firm regeneration rate, which is in line with our predictions. The number of credit organizations and their branches per resident is negatively associated with both firm creation and regeneration rates, which is contrary to our expectation. Intensive interfirm competition, measured by the number of firms and organizations per resident, tends to strongly block newcomers to the market. Both market size and density are significantly correlated with firm regeneration. The estimated effect of market size, however, does not correspond with our prediction, leaving grounds for controversy. Public security weakly but positively affects firm startups. In regions with harsher climate conditions, firm regeneration tends to be restrained, probably due to higher initial sunk costs.

As described above, in our baseline estimation, we treated the world oil price and the exchange rate as exogenous variables. We believe that this assumption is quite reasonable for the world oil price. On the other hand, we cannot absolutely rule out the possibility that the foreign exchange rate is simultaneously determined by the firm creation and destruction rates. In addition, firm creation and regeneration might be a stochastic process that depends on its own history. To tackle these methodological issues, we attempted to estimate a dynamic panel data model that explicitly endogenizes the crisis variables using a system generalized method of moments (GMM) estimator.

Table 12.3 presents the estimation results of the system GMM model. Here, we assumed a two-year lag structure of the crisis variables. The statistically significant estimate of the lagged dependent variable in Models [1]

Table 12.3 System GMM dynamic estimation to endogenize crisis variables

Dependent variable	*Log of the firm creation rate*		*Log of the firm regeneration rate*	
Model	*[1]*	*[2]*	*[3]*	*[4]*
Lagged dependent variable	0.4340**	0.4820***	−0.0258	−0.0416
	(0.170)	(0.180)	(0.053)	(0.053)
Crisis variables (endogenous variable)				
Log of the world oil price	0.1704***		1.6318***	
	(0.028)		(0.351)	
Log of the exchange rate		−0.2926***		−1.1873*
		(0.059)		(0.666)
Control variables				
GRP growth rate	0.0047	0.0056*	−0.0046	0.0168
	(0.003)	(0.003)	(0.052)	(0.050)
Log of real wages	0.3916	0.5229	5.7279	9.4428**
	(0.388)	(0.333)	(4.808)	(4.788)
Total trade as a % of GRP	−0.0016*	−0.0017**	0.0419**	0.0450**
	(0.001)	(0.001)	(0.018)	(0.019)
FDI inflow as a % of GRP	0.0001	0.0001	−0.0529	−0.0560
	(0.003)	(0.003)	(0.048)	(0.048)
Log of the number of credit organizations	−0.1971***	−0.1625**	−1.6243*	−1.8248*
and their branches per 100,000 residents	(0.072)	(0.073)	(0.901)	(0.970)
Log of the number of PCs with Internet	0.0349	0.0374	−2.3855**	−2.3403**
connections per 100 workers	(0.081)	(0.081)	(1.039)	(1.048)
Log of the number of firms and	−0.0357	0.0162	−7.5903***	−7.6433***
organizations per 10,000 residents	(0.216)	(0.209)	(2.733)	(2.749)
Log of the total population	−0.3359	−0.6094	−13.0114	−12.7748
	(0.738)	(0.746)	(9.835)	(10.041)

Log of the population density	0.3261	0.4426	14.7990**	15.5340**
	(0.334)	(0.296)	(6.360)	(6.393)
Urban population rate	−0.0268	−0.0242	−0.1431	−0.1002
	(0.018)	(0.017)	(0.239)	(0.243)
Log of the number of registered criminal cases per 100,000 residents	−0.1005	−0.1031	−1.6981	−1.8680
	(0.097)	(0.092)	(1.443)	(1.438)
Average temperature in January	−0.0002	0.0043	−0.0051	0.0077
	(0.004)	(0.004)	(0.076)	(0.072)
Time trend variable	0.0033	−0.0451**	−0.2396	0.2281
	(0.022)	(0.023)	(0.277)	(0.328)
Constant term	6.1525	2.0515	85.8687	97.8597
	(5.458)	(6.332)	(70.404)	(68.348)
N	559	559	553	553
Arellano-Bond test[a]	1.65*	2.20**	2.87***	−3.00***
Sargan test[b]	207.12***	189.77***	102.98***	109.99***
Wald test (χ^2)[c]	606.77***	616.36***	288.62***	276.65***

Notes:

[a]Autocorrelation test for AR(2). Null hypothesis: no autocorrelation

[b]Test results that use estimates with normal standard errors. Null hypothesis: overidentifying restrictions are valid

[c]Null hypothesis: all coefficients are zero

Figures in parentheses beneath regression coefficients are robust standard errors. ***, **, and * denote statistical significance at the 1%, 5%, and 10% levels, respectively

Source: Authors' estimation. See Table 12.1 for definitions and descriptive statistics of the variables used in the estimation

and [2] indicates that firm creation is likely to be a path-dependent process in the Russian regions. The result, that all of the crisis variables are significantly estimated with a sign corresponding to hypothesis H_1 as those in the baseline estimation, suggests that the linkage between the world crises and the creation and regeneration of Russian firms is robust, even under the assumption of their endogenous relationship. We also found that the control variables are rather sensitive to the choice of estimator used: in fact, the combination of statistically significant control variables is quite different from that in the baseline estimation.[4]

Finally, we address the issue of the heterogeneity of the Russian regions. Russia is a huge country; hence, it is argued that there is great variation among regions in the socio-economic systems as well as in the market/industrial structure. To examine the possible influence of regional heterogeneity, we re-estimated Models [1] and [5] in Table 12.2 by dividing observations into four subsample groups, taking into account historical and geographical similarities of the federal districts.

Table 12.4 shows the results. The signs and statistical significances of the control variables differ remarkably between the subsamples, suggesting that the systems of firm creation and regeneration are indeed manifold across the Russian regions. Nevertheless, the world oil price exhibits a significant and positive coefficient in seven of the eight models. This surprisingly robust estimate of the world oil price implies that every Russian region may be extremely vulnerable to a global crisis, thus, explaining why the creation and regeneration of Russian firms were greatly obstructed by the crisis shock of recent years.

12.6 Robustness Check

In the previous section, we mainly utilized a fixed-effects model to obtain estimates of crisis variables and examined their possible simultaneity with the dependent variables by estimating a system GMM dynamic model. As an additional robustness check, we also performed the estimation using a population-average estimator, a between-effects estimator, a random-effects estimator, a different GMM estimator and a multilevel mixed-effects estimator, and found no remarkable differences from the estimation results reported in Tables 12.2 and 12.3.

We also conducted a supplementary estimation, in which various sample restrictions were placed on the regression models, which confirmed that these limitations do not substantially change our major empirical

Table 12.4 Examination of heterogeneity among Russian regions, 2008–2015

(a) Firm creation model				
Dependent variable	*Log of the firm creation rate*			
Estimator	*Pooling OLS*	*Random-effects*	*Fixed-effects*	*Random-effects*
Target regions	*North Caucasus and Southern districts*	*Central and North West districts*	*Volga and Urals districts*	*Siberian and Far East districts*
Model	*[1]*	*[2]*	*[3]*	*[4]*
Crisis variables				
Log of the world oil price	0.3700***	0.1469***	0.1331***	0.0952***
	(0.115)	(0.033)	(0.040)	(0.033)
Control variables				
GRP growth rate	0.0072	0.0039	0.0036	0.0037
	(0.011)	(0.004)	(0.008)	(0.003)
Log of real wages	2.6797***	0.3282	−0.4306	−0.4884
	(1.008)	(0.375)	(0.758)	(0.487)
Total trade as a % of GRP	−0.0024	−0.0015	0.0130**	0.0000
	(0.002)	(0.001)	(0.005)	(0.001)
FDI inflow as a % of GRP	−0.0123	0.0034	0.0009	0.0021
	(0.014)	(0.006)	(0.012)	(0.002)
Log of the number of credit organizations	−0.1112**	−0.0245	−0.1776	−0.1013
and their branches per 100,000 residents	(0.050)	(0.100)	(0.163)	(0.074)
Log of the number of PCs with Internet	−0.0381	−0.2977***	−0.4670**	−0.0551
connections per 100 workers	(0.132)	(0.104)	(0.206)	(0.069)
Log of the number of firms and	−0.2150*	−0.2634	−0.8244**	0.0533
organizations per 10,000 residents	(0.111)	(0.165)	(0.326)	(0.085)

(*continued*)

Table 12.4 (continued)

(a) Firm creation model				
Dependent variable	*Log of the firm creation rate*			
Estimator	*Pooling OLS*	*Random-effects*	*Fixed-effects*	*Random-effects*
Target regions	*North Caucasus and Southern districts*	*Central and North West districts*	*Volga and Urals districts*	*Siberian and Far East districts*
Model	*[1]*	*[2]*	*[3]*	*[4]*
Log of the total population	−0.0435	−0.0378	−5.5335**	0.1313***
	(0.033)	(0.084)	(2.228)	(0.029)
Log of the population density	0.1532**	0.0848***	6.4698*	0.0291
	(0.066)	(0.029)	(3.229)	(0.025)
Urban population rate	0.0067	0.0139***	−0.0319*	−0.0017
	(0.005)	(0.005)	(0.016)	(0.001)
Log of the number of registered criminal cases per 100,000 residents	−0.0789	0.0503	0.0297	−0.1389*
	(0.123)	(0.132)	(0.195)	(0.080)
Average temperature in January	−0.0279	0.0101*	−0.0039	−0.0054
	(0.020)	(0.006)	(0.004)	(0.004)
Time trend variable	0.0091	0.0478**	0.0892**	−0.0415***
	(0.037)	(0.024)	(0.040)	(0.015)
Constant term	−8.5274	3.1380	34.3673***	6.7246***
	(5.410)	(2.144)	(10.829)	(2.405)
Control for region-level fixed effects	Yes	Yes	No	Yes
N	103	224	144	168
R^2	0.53	0.20	0.12	0.70
Breusch-Pagan test[a]	0.00	198.92***	32.63***	9.61***
Hausman test[b]	2.53	17.33	23.52*	15.96
F-test/Wald test (χ^2)[c]	6.66***	352.14***	749.88***	1618.69***

(b) Firm regeneration model				
Dependent variable	*Log of the firm regeneration rate*			
Estimator	*Pooling OLS*	*Random-effects*	*Pooling OLS*	*Pooling OLS*
Target regions	*North Caucasus and Southern districts*	*Central and North West districts*	*Volga and Urals districts*	*Siberian and Far East districts*
Model	*[5]*	*[6]*	*[7]*	*[8]*
Crisis variables				
Log of the world oil price	0.6926	1.6716***	1.1928**	2.5653***
	(1.084)	(0.536)	(0.577)	(0.676)
Control variables				
GRP growth rate	0.0875	0.1131	−0.0348	0.0828
	(0.071)	(0.072)	(0.090)	(0.062)
Log of real wages	10.3115	9.9270	13.8452*	10.3621
	(10.645)	(9.449)	(7.687)	(7.917)
Total trade as a % of GRP	0.0233	−0.0092	0.1082***	0.0167**
	(0.031)	(0.009)	(0.036)	(0.008)
FDI inflow as a % of GRP	0.0805	0.0020	0.0225	−0.0435**
	(0.222)	(0.079)	(0.102)	(0.020)
Log of the number of credit organizations and their branches per 100,000 residents	0.8902*	0.2717	−1.7283*	−2.6171***
	(0.511)	(0.904)	(0.878)	(1.006)
Log of the number of PCs with Internet connections per 100 workers	−2.3061*	0.4971	0.6408	3.0480***
	(1.265)	(1.317)	(1.278)	(0.862)
Log of the number of firms and organizations per 10,000 residents	−3.5423***	−0.6607	−5.2150***	−1.6457*
	(1.266)	(1.345)	(1.969)	(0.978)
Log of the total population	0.5321	0.3644	−1.5678**	0.5782*
	(0.321)	(0.543)	(0.711)	(0.317)
Log of the population density	0.5423	−0.4114*	0.1763	−0.4401
	(0.568)	(0.218)	(0.358)	(0.287)

(*continued*)

Table 12.4 (continued)

(b) Firm regeneration model				
Dependent variable	*Log of the firm regeneration rate*			
Estimator	*Pooling OLS*	*Random-effects*	*Pooling OLS*	*Pooling OLS*
Target regions	*North Caucasus and Southern districts*	*Central and North West districts*	*Volga and Urals districts*	*Siberian and Far East districts*
Model	*[5]*	*[6]*	*[7]*	*[8]*
Urban population rate	−0.0270	0.0398	0.1425***	0.0271
	(0.071)	(0.034)	(0.046)	(0.017)
Log of the number of registered criminal cases per 100,000 residents	2.6081*	0.3989	1.5310*	−1.9706*
	(1.523)	(0.973)	(0.818)	(1.133)
Average temperature in January	0.1347	0.2787***	0.0876	0.0524
	(0.194)	(0.059)	(0.071)	(0.050)
Time trend variable	0.5143	−0.0223	−0.0059	−1.0697***
	(0.356)	(0.327)	(0.267)	(0.232)
Constant term	-44.8032	−39.5090	−39.0897	−15.8521
	(54.828)	(42.145)	(38.347)	(40.448)
Control for region-level fixed effects	Yes	Yes	Yes	Yes
N	103	224	144	166
R^2	0.42	0.24	0.32	0.46
Breusch-Pagan test[a]	0.00	2.17*	0.00	0.06
Hausman test[b]	15.59	19.74	5.91	18.11
F-test/Wald test (χ^2)[c]	7.37***	480.35***	3.71***	11.00***

Notes:
[a]Null hypothesis: the variance of regional individual effects is zero
[b]Null hypothesis: the random-effects assumption is valid
[c]Null hypothesis: all coefficients are zero
Figures in parentheses beneath regression coefficients are robust standard errors. ***, **, and * denote statistical significance at the 1%, 5%, and 10% levels, respectively

Source: Authors' estimation. See Table 12.1 for definitions and descriptive statistics of the variables used in the estimation

findings. More specifically, supplementary regressions were conducted in the following six settings: (1) excluding Moscow and St. Petersburg, which are under the direct control of the federal government (i.e., federal cities), from observations; (2) excluding so-called "resource-rich" regions from observations; (3) dividing observations into those for the years 2008–2011 and those for the years 2012–2015; (4) dividing observations into two subsamples by the median of GRP per capita in 2008; (5) limiting regions to those with FDI as a percentage of GRP within the mean ±1 standard deviation; (6) limiting regions to those with total trade as a percentage of GRP within the mean ±1 standard deviation.

The above results of the robustness check led us to the judgement that the estimation results reported in this chapter are fairly robust across the various specifications, apart from the regional heterogeneity examined in Table 12.4.

12.7 Conclusions

This chapter is based on a rich and unpublished panel dataset of regional-level data for the period 2008–2015. Our regression analysis gave special attention to three overlapping aspects: the recent downturns that characterized the period of investigation, the associated decrease in the oil price and increase in oil price volatility, and the natural resource curse. More specifically, we took the firm creation or regeneration rate as the dependent variable and examined two assumptions: first, that the weakening of the world oil price tends to hamper the creation and regeneration of Russian firms; and second, that the volatility of the world oil price is negatively associated with firm creation and regeneration. We used the exchange rate for the Russian ruble to the US dollar as the independent variable in addition to the world oil price as an alternative proxy for the crisis shock. Moreover, as potentially explanatory factors of firm creation and regeneration in the Russian regions, we simultaneously controlled for GRP growth rate, real wage level, total trade volume and FDI inflow as a percent of GRP, the number of credit organizations and branches per 100,000 residents, the number of PCs with Internet connections per 100 workers, the number of firms and organizations per 10,000 residents, the population size and density, the urban population rate, the number of registered criminal cases per 100,000 residents, and the average temperature in January.

Our assumptions are validated. First, the decline of oil prices and the appreciation in the exchange rate during the crisis period strongly inhibited the creation and regeneration of Russian firms. Second, violent fluctuations in crude oil prices and the exchange rate increased the uncertainty in business startups and operations and, accordingly, greatly depressed Russian entrepreneurs who were considering launching new businesses; many companies were forced to liquidate. On top of these findings, we obtained supporting evidence that economic growth strongly encourages firm creation and regeneration, and that integration with the world economy is significantly related to firm regeneration. We also found that intensive interfirm competition blocks newcomers to the market. Population density also plays a key role in firm turnover. Public security has a weak but positive effect on firm creation. In regions with harsh climate conditions, firm regeneration becomes weak, which may reflect high initial sunk costs.

The above empirical results are reproducible under a series of robustness checks. First, we treated the endogeneity of the crisis variables and dependent variables by using the system GMM estimator. Second, we examined the influence of regional heterogeneity. Third, we performed supplemental regressions using various estimators in addition to the fixed-effects and system GMM models. Finally, we imposed many kinds of sample restrictions to ensure that our results were not due to the presence of outliers.

Our findings have two policy implications, namely that the oil curse is a blessing in Russia. Appreciation of the exchange rate impedes the development of other sectors, which could employ entrepreneurs and workers. The Russian economy, based essentially on oil- and gas-related activities, is insufficiently diversified to cope with the negative impact of falling prices of Russian natural resources. The second important external factor is related to the vulnerability of the economy to world crises. Although the degree of the integration of the Russian economy into the global economy is relatively low, recent economic and political crises and the increase in oil price volatility have depressed the creation and regeneration of Russian businesses.

To conclude, the recent global crises hardly discouraged firm entries and turnovers in Russia, as it was common to all countries. The problem is that the dominating presence of the oil sector in the Russian economy and the high value of the Russian ruble due to the Dutch disease deter companies seeking to perform in other manufacturing sectors.

Acknowledgments This chapter is an updated and substantially revised version of Iwasaki et al. (2016). We gratefully acknowledge financial support from the Japan Securities Scholarship Foundation, the Nomura Foundation, and the Joint Usage and Research Centre of the Institute of Economic Research, Hitotsubashi University, in addition to the Suntory Foundation—the main sponsor of the project. We also wish to thank Vasily Astrov, Jan Hanousek, Mario Holzner, and Andrei A. Yakovlev for their valuable comments and suggestions, and Tammy Bicket for her editorial assistance. Needless to say, all remaining errors are solely our responsibility.

Notes

1. The estimation results are as follows:

$$\textit{Firm creation rate} = \underset{(0.946)}{4.321^{***}} - \underset{(0.004)}{0.0040} \times \textit{Trend} \qquad N = 80,\ R^2 = 0.275$$

$$\textit{Firm regeneration rate} = \underset{(0.607)}{1.403^{**}} - \underset{(0.007)}{0.0155^{**}} \times \textit{Trend} \qquad N = 80,\ R^2 = 0.635$$

   Figures in parentheses beneath regression coefficients are standard errors. *** and ** denote statistical significance at the 1% and 5% levels, respectively. Estimates of the lagged dependent variables are omitted for brevity.
2. If the firm regeneration rate took a negative value, we used a natural logarithm of its absolute value multiplied by minus one to fit the regression estimation. Empirical results, however, are not greatly different, even if a non-log-transformed variable is utilized.
3. See Iwasaki and Suganuma (2015a, b) for recent developments in international trade and FDI in Russia.
4. As reported in Table 12.3, the Arellano-Bond test for AR(2) rejects the null hypothesis of no autocorrelation in Models [1] to [4]. The Sargan test also rejects the null hypothesis that overidentifying restrictions are valid in all cases. The estimation results of the dynamic model, therefore, have some room for improvement in model specification.

References

Abiad, A., Detragiache, E., & Tressel, T. (2008). *A new database of financial reforms* (Working Paper No. 08/266). Washington, DC: International Monetary Fund.

Aghion, P., & Saint-Paul, G. (1993). *Uncovering some causal relationships between productivity growth and the structure of economic fluctuations: A tentative survey* (Working Paper No. 4603). Cambridge, MA: National Bureau of Economic Research.

Aidis, R., & Adachi, Y. (2007). Russia: Firm entry and survival barriers. *Economic Systems, 3*, 391–411.

Alesina, A., Ozler, S., Roubini, N., & Swagel, P. (1996). Political instability and economic growth. *Journal of Economic Growth, 2*, 189–213.

Bertola, G., & Caballero, R. J. (1994). Irreversibility and aggregate investment. *Review of Economic Studies, 61*, 223–246.

Bouoiyour, J., Selmi, R., Tiwari, A. K., & Shahbaz, M. (2015). The nexus between oil price and Russia's real exchange rate: Better paths via unconditional vs conditional analysis. *Energy Economics, 51*, 54–66.

Brunnschweiler, C. N., & Bulte, E. H. (2008). The resource curse revisited and revised: A tale of paradoxes and red herrings. *Journal of Environmental Economics and Management, 55*, 248–264.

Cerra, V., & Saxena, S. C. (2008). Growth dynamics: The myth of economic recovery. *American Economic Review, 98*, 439–457.

Corden, W. M., & Neary, J. P. (1982). Booming sector and de-industrialisation in a small open economy. *Economic Journal, 92*, 825–848.

Coricelli, F., & Maurel, M. (2011). Growth and crisis in transition: A comparative perspective. *Review of International Economics, 19*, 49–64.

Damette, O., Maurel, M., & Stemmer, M. (2016). *What does it take to grow out of recession? An error-correction approach towards growth convergence of European and transition countries* (Working Paper No. 2016.41). Paris: Centre d'Economie de la Sorbonne, Université Paris 1 Panthéon-Sorbonne.

Estrin, S., & Prevezer, M. (2010). A survey on institutions and new firm entry: How and why do entry rates differ in emerging markets? *Economic Systems, 34*, 289–308.

Gaddy, C. G., & Ickes, B. W. (2010). Russia after the global financial crisis. *Eurasian Geography and Economics, 51*, 281–311.

Gylfason, T., & Zoega, G. (2006). Natural resources and economic growth: The role of investment. *The World Economy, 29*, 1091–1115.

Havranek, T., Horvath, R., & Zeynalov, A. (2016). Natural resources and economic growth: A meta-analysis. *World Development, 88*, 134–151.

Hayek, F. V. (1937). *Monetary Nationalism and International Stability*. London: Longmans.

Hnatkovska, V., & Loayza, N. (2004). *Volatility and growth* (Policy Research Working Paper No. 3184). Washington, DC: World Bank.

Ito, K. (2012). The impact of oil price volatility on the macroeconomy in Russia. *Annals of Regional Science, 48*, 695–702.

Iwasaki, I. (2014). Global financial crisis, corporate governance, and firm survival: The Russian experience. *Journal of Comparative Economics, 42*, 178–211.

Iwasaki, I., & Suganuma, K. (2015a). The impact of FDI and socio-cultural similarity on international trade: Poisson pseudo-maximum likelihood estimation of a Russian trade model. *Economics Bulletin, 35*, 1020–1033.

Iwasaki, I., & Suganuma, K. (2015b). Foreign direct investment and regional economic development in Russia: An econometric assessment. *Economic Change and Restructuring, 48*, 209–255.

Iwasaki, I., Maurel, M., & Meunier, B. (2016). Firm entry and exit during a crisis period: Evidence from Russian regions. *Russian Journal of Economics, 2*, 162–191.

Jo, S. (2012). *The effects of oil price uncertainty on the macroeconomy* (Working Paper No. 2012–40). Ottawa: Bank of Canada.

Keynes, J. M. (1936). *The General Theory of Employment, Interest, and Money.* London: Macmillan.

Kocenda, E., Maurel, M., & Schnabl, G. (2013). Short- and long-term growth effects of exchange rate adjustment. *Review of International Economics, 21*, 137–150.

Kuboniwa, M. (2014). A comparative analysis of the impact of oil prices on oil-rich emerging economies in the Pacific Rim. *Journal of Comparative Economics, 42*, 328–339.

Maurel, M., & Schnabl, G. (2012). Keynesian and Austrian perspectives on crisis, shock adjustment, exchange rate regime and (long-term) growth. *Open Economies Review, 23*, 847–868.

Mundell, R. (1961). A theory of optimum currency areas. *American Economic Review, 51*, 657–665.

Papell, D. H., & Prodan, R. (2012). The statistical behavior of GDP after financial crises and severe recessions. *B. E. Journal of Macroeconomics, 12*, 1–31.

Pissarides, F., Singer, M., & Svejnar, J. (2003). Objectives and constraints of entrepreneurs: Evidence from small and medium size enterprises in Russia and Bulgaria. *Journal of Comparative Economics, 31*, 503–531.

Puffer, S. M., & McCarthy, D. J. (2001). Navigating the hostile maze: A framework for Russian entrepreneurship. *Academy of Management Executive, 15*, 24–36.

Rodrik, D. (1991). Policy uncertainty and private investment in developing countries. *Journal of Development Economics, 36*, 229–242.

Sachs, J. D., & Warner, A. M. (1995). *Natural resource abundance and economic growth* (Working Paper No. 5398). Cambridge, MA: National Bureau of Economic Research.

Sala-i-Martin, X., & Subramanian, A. (2013). Addressing the natural resource curse: An illustration from Nigeria. *Journal of African Economies, 22*, 570–615.

Schumpeter, J. (1911). *Theorie der wirtschaftlichen Entwicklung: Eine Untersuchung ueber Unternehmergewinn, Kapital, Kredit, Zins und den Konjunkturzyklus (The theory of economic development: An inquiry into profits, capital, credit, interest, and the business cycle)*. Berlin: Duncker and Humblot Gmbh. (in Germany).

Schumpeter, J. A. (1939). *Business cycles: A theoretical, historical, and statistical analysis of the capitalist process* (First ed.). New York/London: McGraw-Hill.

Sprenger, C. (2014). Privatization and survival: Evidence from a Russian firm survey. *Economic Annals, 59*, 43–60.

CHAPTER 13

Conclusions: The Crisis Left Deep Scars on European Emerging Markets

Peter Havlik and Ichiro Iwasaki

Nearly a decade after the outbreak of the global financial crisis, Europe and the European emerging markets are still struggling with the consequences. In the meantime, extensive academic literature has been devoted to exploring the origins of the crisis; its impacts on individual countries and regions; and macroeconomic, sectoral, social, and political consequences. The present European disarray over migration and Brexit, the East-West conflict over Ukraine, and the Transatlantic rift that has opened with the Trump presidency are among the broader consequences indirectly (and sometimes even directly) related to the global financial crisis of 2008–2009. The present volume explores selected impacts of this crisis on emerging markets in Central, Eastern, and Southeastern Europe (CESEE). It deals with both cross-country impact analyses on the region as a whole and selected country-specific issues, focusing on the Czech Republic, Hungary, Poland, and Russia.

P. Havlik (✉)
Vienna Institute for International Economic Studies, Vienna, Austria

I. Iwasaki
Institute of Economic Research, Hitotsubashi University, Tokyo, Japan

P. Havlik, I. Iwasaki (eds.), *Economics of European Crises and Emerging Markets*, DOI 10.1007/978-981-10-5233-0_13

Chapter 2 describes economic growth and convergence patterns in the CESEE region over the past two decades, focusing on the real economy. It underlines the diverging growth experiences of individual countries, including different impacts and responses to the crisis. While the economic convergence and catching-up had been generally impressive before the crisis, especially in the Baltic States and in Poland—the latter being the only country that avoided negative growth in 2009—in other countries, particularly Hungary, the catching-up process has stalled. The crisis not only interrupted the catching-up process but pushed it back several years. Diverse growth performance has been accompanied by uneven structural changes. Emerging markets in Central Europe that have been closely integrated in the German-CEE manufacturing value-chain perform better and have been more resilient to the crisis. These experiences, as well as disappointments with the pre-crisis growth model, suggest a need for economic policy adjustments. The latest economic developments and forecasts indicate a resumption of economic convergence, albeit at a slower pace than during the pre-crisis period, despite elevated geopolitical uncertainties. Chapter 3 investigates financial impacts of the crisis on the CESEE region, effects of deleveraging, and current account developments. It underlines the important distinction between FDI flows in export-oriented manufacturing (prevalent in Central Europe) and domestically oriented import-intensive flows in banking, trade, and real estate activities that may lead to unsustainable imbalances. Chapter 4 empirically investigates effects of FDI inflows on different groups of emerging economies using panel data: both EU members and other East European economies.

Chapter 5 analyses long-term labour market developments in the Czech Republic and discovers that less-educated men were hit hardest by the crisis, as jobs requiring only medium or low skills were cut. Chapter 6 illustrates how ownership form and firm size affected reactions to the crisis in the Czech Republic. Within a broader sample of countries, the labour market performance during the crisis and various firm characteristics are also investigated in Chap. 10. From a different angle, impacts of the crisis on the firm creation rate in Russia are analysed in Chap. 12. The authors confirm that oil prices and related exchange rate fluctuations strongly affected firms in that country. As mentioned above, the crisis undermined trust in the traditional economic model. Subsequent economic policy changes have, so far, been most pronounced in Hungary and Poland: either in a covert protectionism (Chap. 7) or by a shift to an increased local commitment to subsidiaries by global companies (Chap. 8). The impact of the Ukraine-Russian conflict on

Polish trade is econometrically simulated using the CGE model in Chap. 9. Last, but not least, Chap. 11 discusses not only economic impacts of the crisis on Russia, but also explores (failed) attempts to change the Russian economic development model and the key associated political constraints.

The whole volume, thus, provides various insights and evidence-based analysis of multiple effects of the crisis on Eastern European emerging markets in the areas of economic and financial developments, labour markets, and firm creation and destruction, as well as on far-reaching economic policy changes and even affected global political developments. The selected country case studies underline the editors' argument for differentiated impacts of the crisis, going far beyond purely economic factors. These conclusions are sobering enough, yet the implication is that impacts of the crisis are continuing and may even manifest themselves in new or broader forms in the future, not just in the emerging markets covered by this volume. Further efforts are required to explore these new aspects of the crisis.

Index

P. Havlik, I. Iwasaki (eds.), *Economics of European Crises and Emerging Markets*, DOI 10.1007/978-981-10-5233-0

V

W

X

Y

Kolibri 360 GmbH
Ferdinand-Jühlke-Straße 7
99095 Erfurt, Deutschland
produktsicherheit@kolibri360.de